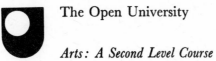

The Open University

Arts: A Second Level Course

The Early Roman Empire and the Rise of Christianity   Units 13–16

THE RISE OF CHRISTIANITY

Prepared for the Course Team by Francis Clark

The Open University Press

The Open University Press,
Walton Hall, Milton Keynes, Bucks.

First published 1974.

Designed by the Media Development Group of the Open University.

Printed in Great Britain by
Martin Cadbury, a specialized division of Santype International,
Worcester and London.

ISBN 0 335 00616 7

This text forms part of the correspondence element of an Open University Second Level Course. The complete list of units in the course is given at the end of this text.

For general availability of supporting material referred to in the text, please write to the Director of Marketing, The Open University, P.O. Box 81, Walton Hall, Milton Keynes, MK 7 6AT.

Further information on Open University courses may be obtained from the Admissions Office, The Open University, P.O. Box 48, Walton Hall, Milton Keynes, MK 7 6AB.

CONTENTS

Section		*Page*
1.0–1.1	**INTRODUCTION**	7
1.2–1.4	Reading	7
1.5–1.8	Exercises: a word of encouragement	8
1.9–1.10	Some textual points	10
1.11–1.12	Radio and television programmes	10

PART ONE: ORIGINS

	(A) WHAT HISTORICAL EVIDENCE IS AVAILABLE?	12
2.0–2.4	Roman history and Christian history	12
2.5–2.14	Independent testimonies	13
2.15–2.17	Scantiness of the evidence	16
2.18–2.27	The sources for early Christian history	18
2.28–2.31	Archaeological evidence?	20

3.0–3.2	(B) THE POLITICAL SETTING IN WHICH CHRISTIANITY AROSE	22
3.2–3.5	(i) The Maccabean movement	23
3.6–3.7	(ii) Roman influence in the Levant	24
3.8–3.9	Rome and the New Testament: a supplementary exercise	26
3.10	(iii) The desert frontier	28
3.11	(iv) Herodian rule in Palestine	28
3.12–3.22	Six Herodian princes: an exercise	29

4.0–4.4	(C) THE RELIGIOUS AND CULTURAL SETTING IN WHICH CHRISTIANITY AROSE	31
4.5–4.18	Sects and movements in Judaism: (a) The Pharisees; (b) The Sadducees; (c) The Herodians and the 'Hellenists'; (d) The Essenes; (e) The Qumran Sect; (f) The Zealots; (g) John the Baptist and his disciples; (h) The Messianic expectation; (i) The 'sheep without a shepherd'; (j) The Church as a Jewish sect	33
4.19–4.24	The non-Jewish world	36
4.25–4.32	Syncretism, Gnosticism and Christian doctrine	39

5.0	(D) JESUS OF NAZARETH	43
5.1–5.2	Can we know facts about 'the Jesus of history'?	43
5.3–5.6	Form criticism of the Gospels	44
5.7–5.10	The 'gospel before the Gospels'	47

5.11–5.15	Myth and authenticity	48
5.16–5.19	The ministry of Jesus	50
5.20–5.22	The teaching of Jesus	51
5.23–5.31	(1) on 'personal' religion	52
5.32–5.38	(2) on 'community' religion	53
5.39–5.40	The climax of the Gospels	55

PART TWO: PAUL AND THE PAULINE CHURCHES

6.0–6.4	(A)	HERALDS OF THE RESURRECTION	58
6.5–6.7		The early chapters of *Acts*: an exercise	59
7.0	(B)	THE STUDY OF PAULINE CHRISTIANITY	60
7.1–7.4		The sources	61
7.5–7.7		The biographical pattern	62
8.0–8.1	(C)	PAUL'S LIFE AND MISSIONARY ACTIVITY	63
8.2–8.4		Early life and 'conversion'	64
8.5–8.10		Reorientation and first mission	66
8.11–8.14		Macedonia and Greece	68
8.15–8.18		The Ephesus phase	69
8.19–8.25		The climax: Jerusalem, Caesarea and Rome	70
9.0–9.5	(D)	PAUL'S KEY IDEAS AND THEIR PRACTICAL APPLICATION	73
9.6–9.8	(a)	The sovereignty of God	75
9.9–9.10	(b)	The inner predicament: man's sin and its consequences	75
9.11–9.13	(c)	The outer predicament: the menace of demonic powers	76
9.14–9.16	(d)	The divine solution: man liberated from all evil and reconciled to God through Jesus Christ	77
9.17–9.18	(e)	The transcendent status of the Lord Jesus	78
9.19–9.23	(f)	Justification by faith: the complete gratuitousness of grace	78
9.24–9.27	(g)	The Church as the body of Christ and the new Israel	80
9.28–9.30	(h)	Life in Christ and in the Spirit	81
9.31–9.34	(i)	Paul's sacramentalism	82
9.35–9.37	(j)	The eschatological perspective	83
9.38–9.42	(k)	The new law of liberty	84
9.43–9.46	(l)	The place of Israel in God's plan	86
10.0–10.5	(E)	THE PLACE OF PAUL IN THE EARLY CHURCH	87

PART THREE: THE DEVELOPING CHURCH

11.0–11.2	(A) OTHER FOUNDATIONS	92
11.3–11.16	Non-Pauline missionary activities	92
12.0–12.3	(B) THE FORMATION OF THE NEW TESTAMENT	96
13.0–13.3	(C) THE BELIEF OF THE EARLY CHURCH CONCERNING THE DIVINITY OF JESUS CHRIST	97
13.4–13.9	Christology: an exercise	99
13.10–13.11	Investigation of the New Testament data	101
13.12–13.17	(i) Data from *Acts*, reflecting the Christology of the early Palestinian church	103
13.18–13.33	(ii) Data from the Synoptic Gospels	103
13.34–13.44	(iii) Data from the Pauline letters	108
13.45–13.52	(iv) Data from the Fourth Gospel	111
13.53–13.55	(v) Data from other books of the New Testament	113
13.56–13.64	Christology and monotheism	115
14.0–14.2	(D) THE HOLY SPIRIT AND THE TRINITY	118
	(E) CHRISTIAN LITERATURE OF THE SUB-APOSTOLIC AGE	119
15.0–15.2	In the footsteps of the Apostles	119
15.3–15.18	Survey of the post-apostolic writings: (a) *1 Clement;* (b) The *Didache;* (c) the letters of Ignatius of Antioch; (d) *The Epistle of Polycarp*; (e) *The Epistle of Barnabas*; (f) The Apologists; (g) *The Shepherd of Hermas*; (h) *The Martyrdom of Polycarp*; (i) Papias; (j) anti-Gnostic writings	120
15.19–15.24	Two representative testimonies	124
	(F) THE GEOGRAPHICAL EXPANSION OF THE CHURCH	127
16.0–16.2	Bridgeheads and the first advance	127
16.3–16.10	Casting light backwards	128
16.11	Case-studies in church development	131
16.12–16.18	(a) Ephesus	131
16.19–16.39	(b) Rome	134
	(G) STRUCTURES, TRADITION AND SCRIPTURES	140
17.0–17.3	Threats to the Church's survival	140
17.4–17.5	The Church meets the challenge	141
17.6–17.9	(a) Structures of ministry and ecclesiastical government	142

17.10	(b)	Apostolic succession and tradition	143
17.11	(c)	The 'rule of faith' in the baptismal creed	143
17.12–17.13	(d)	The New Testament canon	143
17.14	(e)	Inter-church communication	144
17.15–17.18	(f)	Unity in worship	144

18.0–18.9   **APPENDIX:** The excavations under St Peter's, Rome, and the television programme on 'The Shrine of St Peter'   146

19.0   **BIBLIOGRAPHY**   151

INDEX TO UNITS 13–16   154

SCRIPTURE REFERENCES   163

MAPS

Map A: The earliest Christian churches   11
Map B: The Church in the second century   57
Map C: Christian writers of the second century   91
Back cover map: Palestine in the time of Jesus

1.0 INTRODUCTION

The last four units of this course are devoted to the study of the rise of Christianity. This study is divided into three parts. Part One, entitled 'Origins', deals with the historical and religious situation out of which Christianity arose, and with the life and teaching of Jesus of Nazareth. Part Two is entitled 'Paul and the Pauline Churches'. Part Three, 'The Developing Church', follows the story of the early Church up to the second half of the second century. The Introduction and Part One together are equivalent to about one and a half units in length; Part Two is equivalent to about one unit, and Part Three is equivalent to about one and a half units. This unit division is not marked in the text, but you can bear it in mind when you are planning how to fit the material into your available study time. I gratefully acknowledge many helpful comments and suggestions which I received while writing successive drafts of these units, especially from John Ferguson, Terry Thomas, Prudence Smith, Colin Russell, Whitfield Foy, Arthur Jones and Maurice Bévenot. I remain solely responsible for all shortcomings and for any questionable judgements in these pages.

1.1 In these few weeks we cannot hope to do more than indicate the main outlines of the history of early Christianity. No subject has been studied more intensively. No literature has been so assiduously read, learned and commented on, all through the centuries, than the Scriptures. During the past hundred years or so biblical scholarship and the study of early Church history have become highly specialized. Books and learned journals devoted to these subjects fill whole libraries, and every year more and more of them pour from the press. Understanding of the Scriptures and of Christian origins is all the time being deepened, corrected and refined. University chairs, lectureships and very considerable financial resources are devoted to the furtherance of this study. Throughout the world the Christian Churches maintain numerous colleges and research institutions in which the subject is constantly being explored and developed. There are also independent scholars working in the field, and there is no lack of critical studies of early Christianity by authors who are uncommitted to any Christian belief, or who are opposed to it.

1.2 Reading

This intensely specialized study, and the range and richness of available books, can be daunting and confusing for the ordinary student who is approaching the subject with comparatively little preliminary knowledge. In this course you cannot be expected to study the material in great depth. Your aim here is not to become a biblical exegete or a specialist in Church history. On every point mentioned in these pages it would be possible to overwhelm you with a massive bibliography of books, monographs and articles, some of them focusing on one minor detail of the story, or even on a single word in a text. I want to help you to keep your head above water, and so I will indicate only a relatively few books for wider reading out of the countless works of scholarship which are available. Your main reading during these weeks will be from the New Testament itself, in the *New English Bible* translation, and from your set book by Floyd V. Filson, *A New Testament History*.[1] Probably you have

---

[1] I shall also refer to relevant passages in three other set books used earlier in this course: N. Lewis and M. Reinhold, *Roman Civilization: Sourcebook*, vol. II; E. T. Salmon, *A History of the Roman World 30 BC to AD 138*; and Tacitus, *The Annals of Imperial Rome*.

already read at least parts of the New Testament at some time of your life, but it may well be that your recollection of particular books and texts is hazy. I recommend you to find time now to read at least one of the first three Gospels and also the *Acts of the Apostles*. St Mark's Gospel may be fresher in your mind if you took the first Arts Foundation Course, A100, in which the double unit *What is a Gospel?* was devoted to a special study of *Mark*. Now I suggest that you familiarize yourself with the longer Gospel text of *Matthew* or *Luke*. Later in the course you will be encouraged to make use of other books of the New Testament.

1.3 Filson's book is written from the standpoint of a believing Christian, and he says himself that in writing it he had in mind the needs of ministers, theological students, lay teachers and 'the serious general reader' (pp. vii and ix). One reviewer remarks that Professor Filson has made a name for himself 'for sane, reverent scholarship'. Those of you who are not Christian believers may find this 'reverence' irritating, and you may find Filson's approach to certain questions unacceptable to you because of his religious presuppositions. Those of you who are Christian believers may still find that you do not agree with his standpoint on some questions. Perhaps you will consider his attitude to the Scriptures too conservative, and would prefer a more radical criticism of them. Others again may object that the author implicitly assumes the Protestant position on controversial points of interpretation. Most of you will probably agree that the planning and order of the book could be improved, and you may observe that the author tends to repeat himself. Nevertheless, we have chosen this work as the set book for this part of the course, despite its short-comings, because it gives a fairly inclusive and not too specialized introduction to the whole period we wish to cover. It includes in one volume a survey of the pre-Christian background, of the first beginnings of Christianity, and of its spread in the later first and second centuries. (There are few comparable text-books which do that.) It gives plentiful references to the standard works, so that students who wish to go more deeply into the subject have signposts to show them where to go. While Filson's religious reverence and conservatism colour his way of writing, I don't think they distort his broader historical judgement to any significant extent. You should easily be able to recognize his 'theological' assumptions and to distinguish them from the purely historical content.

1.4 Another book which gives a good survey of first-century Christianity and its environment is *New Testament History* by F. F. Bruce (Oliphants, revised edition 1971). It is more detached than Filson's book, is written at a more advanced level, and covers a narrower time-span. A wider ranging study is Hans Lietzmann's *History of the Early Church* (English trans., Lutterworth Press 1967 reprint). Although it is somewhat dated now (it was written about forty years ago) and contains many speculative interpretations which need to be critically examined, it is still a useful and very readable summary of a vast field. Another informative survey of the first two centuries is P. Carrington's *The Early Christian Church* (Cambridge University Press, 2 vols., 1957.) Several other titles are recommended in the bibliography at the end of these units.

1.5 **Exercises:** a word of encouragement

In your study of these last four units of the course there is opportunity for you to make two kinds of response. First there are the main self-test exercises, of which there are sixteen in all. I must tell you squarely before you come to them that these exercises are very demanding, both in time and effort. For each of them you are asked to study and assimilate quite a large amount of material and to make your own summary and commentary on it. If you completed all these sixteen exercises, in all their parts, with the full supporting reading and reference to relevant texts, they would undoubtedly take up far more than the allotted study time for these weeks. Some of them (especially the exercise proposed in §§ 9.4–5 and the very long exercise proposed in §§ 13.4–5) may well dishearten you, and you may feel that they require a level of knowledge and scholarly judgement higher than can reasonably be expected of you. So I want to reassure you at the start.

1.6 These exercises are meant to help you, not to daunt you. **Do not feel you have to tackle them all, or that you have to do each of them fully.** No doubt some of you, who are already familiar with this field of study and who perhaps have a special interest in the New Testament, may want to write full answers. But for most of you it will be enough if you take the exercises as marking out areas for study, and jot down in your notebook what you think the main lines of an answer would be, and how you would support it with evidence and arguments. When I come to give my 'specimen answers' to the exercises I will do so in much more detail than I expect you to give. Although I shall invite you to look for material for these exercises in your set book by Filson, in my own answers I shall give many particulars which are not to be found in Filson. I hope that these extended answers of mine will even by themselves provide you with a fairly adequate guide to the principal questions we are to study together. Even if you have had time to give only brief consideration to the data and aims of an exercise, I think you will find that this preliminary reflection will help you to profit from the 'specimen answers', and to fit new facts and ideas into the framework of knowledge you already have. So while encouraging you not to be put off by these rather long and demanding exercises, I do not apologize for setting them. I find that Open University students prefer, as one housewife-student expressed it, 'to be challenged rather than patronized'. The starting-point for each of these main exercises is marked by a 'student-stopper' like this:

A LONG PAUSE HERE
Do not read on until you have worked on the exercise

1.7 **All the same, I do want to stress that these long exercises are optional, and you must not be worried if you do not have time to complete them.** In addition to the sixteen main exercises, you will find that at intervals throughout these pages you are asked to give a brief immediate response—a few sentences will do—to a number of incidental questions. I will not dignify these snap questions with the name of 'exercises'; they are just meant to give you a mental prod now and then! These moments for a short response are marked in the printed text by a row of crosses, like this:

✝ ✝

1.8 You may also find you have a problem with the technical terms of Christian theology. I will explain the more rarefied of these terms, such as 'eschatology', 'antinomian' and 'Christology', when we come to them. Almost all of you will have some acquaintance with other terms (such as sin, salvation, incarnation, redemption, atonement, predestination, resurrection) which have become part of English literary usage, even though their meaning, and the original metaphors on which they were based, have faded with the passage of time. I will assume that if need be you can get a fuller definition of these terms from reference books at your local library.

1.9 Some textual points

You may want a word of explanation about the method of giving references to texts of Scripture. The method adopted in these units is the same as that used by Filson in the set book. For example, '*2 Cor.* 3:4–11' means Chapter 3, verses 4 to 11 of Paul's *Second Epistle to the Corinthians*. '*Matt.* 5:28, 32; 6:6' means that you refer to *The Gospel according to Matthew*, first to Chapter 5, verse 28 and then verse 32, and then to Chapter 6, verse 6. That is, a colon separates chapter number from verse numbers, and a semi-colon separates distinct references from one another. The common abbreviations for the titles of the scriptural books can be found at the beginning of most editions of the Bible. In these units the title is spelt out in full when it first occurs, and short titles like *Mark* and *Luke* are not abbreviated.

1.10 You may note that sometimes I spell church with a small c, sometimes Church with a capital C. This is to make a distinction between the individual 'churches' or local congregations of Christians in a town or territory, and the wider 'Church' or all-embracing fellowship of Christians everywhere to which the local 'churches' were conscious of belonging. So too the term 'Gospel' with a capital G here refers to one of the first four books of the New Testament, while 'the gospel' is used as a wider term to indicate the Christian message in general.

1.11 Radio and television programmes

Accompanying these four units on the Rise of Christianity are two television programmes and four radio programmes. In the first of the two television programmes John Ferguson shows how he sees Christianity in the context of the other religions of the Roman empire. The second television programme is devoted to the excavations under St Peter's Basilica in Rome, which take us back to the time when early Christianity was beginning to penetrate the Roman world. Before seeing it, read the Appendix of these units, §§ 18.0–9 below. In Radio Programme 13 there is a discussion of the Gospels as historical documents, by Dennis Nineham, Warden of Keble College, Oxford. You can prepare for this talk by reading through §§ 5.1–5.15 of this course material. For Radio Programme 14 I take as my title, *Pagan Mysteries and Christian Passover*. Before listening to it, read over §§ 4.23–4 of these units. In Radio Programme 15 Terry Thomas discusses the writing of the Pauline epistles with wider reference to what we know about letter-writing in the ancient world. The last radio programme is a talk on *Creed and Community in the Second Century*, by Maurice Wiles, Regius Professor of Divinity in the University of Oxford. You should find this programme particularly helpful for your final revision of these four units, and especially of Part Three, for its summarizes clearly and concisely all the main themes of our study of Church development in the second century AD.

1.12 Do not expect to find that all these contributors take just the same views as those expressed in the printed course material. It is well to realize that there are many points both of fact and of interpretation on which different scholars hold different opinions. Discussion of these controversies furthers the progress of scholarship. For example, you should find it illuminating to compare what Dr Nineham says in the thirteenth radio programme about the formation of the Gospels with what I say in these pages. You may well think that my treatment of the question is too conservative, and that his more radical approach is also more penetrating. You are welcome to disagree with what you read in these units, provided you can give a reasoned argument for your variant views. In the study of religion, and especially of the Christian Scriptures, there is bound to be scope for such disagreement.

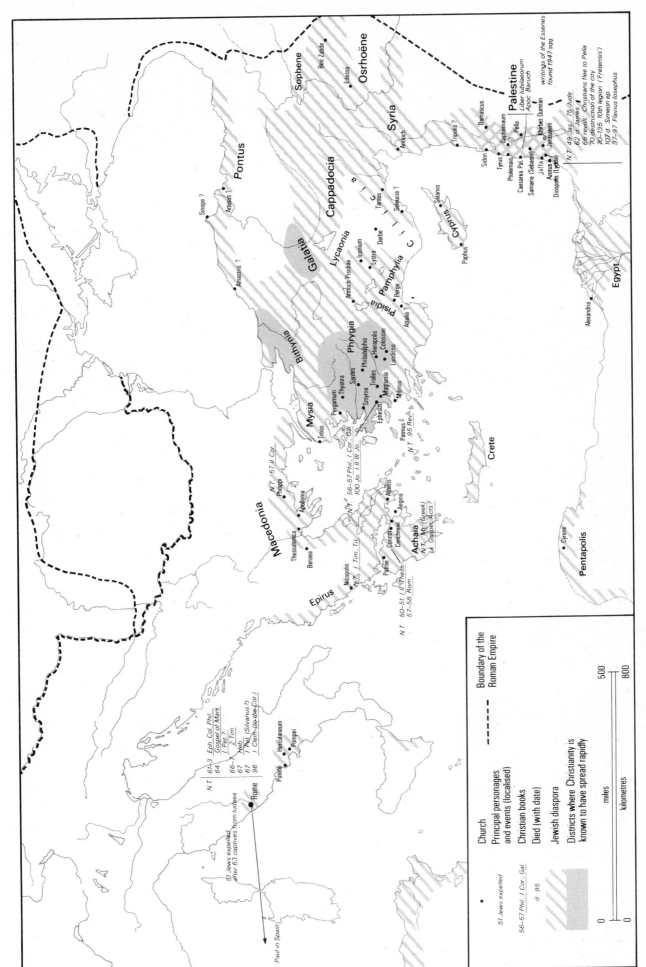

MAP A: THE EARLIEST CHRISTIAN CHURCHES
Recorded congregations of the first century. (After the map in Nelson's Atlas of the Early. Christian World.)

PART ONE: ORIGINS

(A) WHAT HISTORICAL EVIDENCE IS AVAILABLE?

2.0 Roman history and Christian history

Christians, of course, regard the origin of Christianity as the supremely important thing that happened in the era of the early Roman empire—indeed, as the most important happening in all human history. The very way that the years of history are now divided reflects the traditional Christian outlook on this point. Augustus Caesar was the founder of the Roman empire; nevertheless it is not from the Emperor Augustus but from a Jewish carpenter born during his reign, Jesus of Nazareth, that all previous and subsequent history is now dated—BC and AD. It is understandable if some of those who have inherited this traditional outlook should unreflectingly suppose that the origin of Christianity must have made a profound stir in the world of that time, and that the events described in the New Testament must have dominated the history of the time. Even in textbooks of Church history the record of Roman imperial history is seen as a kind of sketchy outline in which the history of the New Testament can be set in bold relief.

2 On the other hand, those whose scholarly concern is primarily with the story of the Roman empire may point out that, from the point of view of independent 'secular' history, there is only the scantiest documentary evidence about the origins of Christianity. That is, if one leaves out of account the specifically Christian writings of the New Testament—the provenance and interpretation of which are matters of keen controversy—there is only the barest mention of Jesus Christ in the source documents relating to the first century of what we now call the Christian era. Some radical critics have even questioned whether Jesus Christ was a historical personage at all.[1] Were it not for the great development of the Christian movement in later centuries, the few passing references to it in the non-biblical records of the period would hardly be thought worth a mention by the historian of the early Roman empire. Judged by ordinary historical criteria, Christianity during the first century was an almost imperceptible ripple in the main current of imperial history, too insignificant to affect the course of recorded events or to influence the social or cultural patterns of life in the empire.

2.2 So it comes about that historians of the early Roman empire tend to leave discussion of Christian origins to divines and Church historians, and Church historians tend to regard the history of the contemporary Roman empire as mere 'background' to what they see as the really important history—the rise of Christianity. In these units of our course we shall be studying the evidence from the viewpoint of the historian of religion rather than from that of the theologian or exegete. However, we want you to study the history of ideas as well as of events, so that you may appreciate the religious dynamism of the early Christian movement. Among the students taking this course, as well as Christian believers, there are members of other faiths and also non-believers.

---

[1] Ideological prejudices play some part here. A 52-volume Soviet encyclopaedia of universal knowledge devotes a two-line entry to Jesus Christ, laconically describing him as 'the mythological founder of Christianity'. Even a man as eminent in his own field as the philosopher Bertrand Russell could write: 'Historically it is quite doubtful whether Christ existed at all' (*Whom do Men say that I am?*, edited by H. Osborne, Faber and Faber 1932, p. 268).

We do not here presuppose a divine origin or guarantee for Christianity; on the other hand we do not presuppose a purely materialistic view of history. We want to help you to study the evidence relating to the rise of Christianity objectively, but also with the 'empathy' that gives insight into the thought-world of others.

2.3 It is true that if one ignores the New Testament writings there is only a little that can be said about the history of earliest Christianity. But it is also clear that these writings, although not historical narratives in the ordinary sense, are historical documents of the first importance. It will be necessary to give critical attention to questions of their origin, their interpretation, and their reliability as historical sources. But it would be unscholarly to dismiss them on the grounds that they are expressions of religious belief rather than statements of historical fact.

2.4 However earnestly we may seek after historical objectivity, it is almost inevitable that discussion of the Christian religion and of its founder will to some extent be coloured by presuppositions we may hold for or against that religion. So at the outset it is fair for me to 'declare an interest' as a believing member of the Christian Church. I leave it to you to judge whether this factor affects my handling of the historical issues.

Figure 1   The Citadel at Jerusalem. The mediaeval fortifications incorporate some masonry going back to ancient times. The tower on the right is called 'The Tower of David'. This was the site of the Palace of Herod, and was probably the official residence of the Roman governor when he was in Jerusalem. (Matson Photo Service, California.)

2.5 Independent testimonies

In point of fact, no scholar who has seriously studied the period doubts that Jesus Christ was a historical person and that the religious movement named after him arose during the first century AD. But how can we be sure that this movement has any firm 'anchor in history'? (The phrase is taken from your set book by Filson.) Let's put the objection this way. Most people, including scholars, would agree that there was once a personage whom we now call King Arthur, that he lived in the island of Britain during the fifth or sixth century AD, that he was a warrior chief, a leader of Romano-British resistance to the Anglo-Saxon invaders, and that he had a considerable following. But when one tries to pin this Arthur down into a framework of historical fact, to relate him with contemporaries in recorded history, to establish any firm dates, places or events with which he was certainly associated, he proves to be remarkably elusive. The story of Arthur and his knights is shrouded in a mist of folklore and romance. If there ever was an 'anchor in history' for the Arthurian saga, it has been lost in the quicksands of legend. Now isn't there a similar difficulty in finding firm historical bedrock for the early Christian movement? In the hundred or so years after the lifetime of Jesus Christ is Christianity anything more than a vague rumour in the corridors of history? If it was an important movement, why is recorded history so strangely silent about it in that age? Where are the links of established facts—links with known persons, dates, places and events—which justify us in placing the history of the early Christian Church on the same objective footing as the history of the early Roman empire that we have been studying so far in this course?

2.6 These may sound like rhetorical questions, and the Christian believer who sees the New Testament narrative as 'Gospel truth' may well be impatient with them, but they deserve a serious answer. Here is a preliminary exercise to enable you to consider an appropriate answer. In our study of early Christianity we shall be discussing evidence drawn largely from Christian sources, and we have said that the status of those sources as historical documents will have to be critically examined. But before we study the Christian sources themselves, let us ask ourselves **what independent evidence there is which confirms the existence of, and gives some information about, the Christian movement during the period from the reign of Tiberius to that of Hadrian.** *Is* it true that non-Christian historical sources relating to that period are silent about Christianity? From the earlier units of this course and from your set books (especially Filson, pages 66–8, Salmon, Part IV, Chapter IV, and Lewis and Reinhold, §§ 55, 172), you should be able to refer to several items of evidence which have a bearing on this question. Now write down as many of them as you can remember, or can find by using the index in your set books. If you are familiar with the New Testament, see if you can also indicate areas in which the scriptural records of early Christianity are confirmed by independent historical evidence.

A LONG PAUSE HERE
Do not read on until you have worked on the exercise

2.7 **Specimen answers and discussion**

(a) **Tacitus,** in his *Annals* XV. 44, written early in the second century, expressly mentions Christ, his execution under Pontius Pilate in Judaea in the reign of Tiberius, and the cruel persecution of 'great numbers' of Christians in Rome under Nero after the great fire in the summer of 64. (Text in your set book edition of the *Annals*, pp. 365–6; also in your set book of source texts edited by Lewis and Reinhold, pp. 224–7.)

2.8 (b) **Suetonius,** in his *Lives of the Caesars*, refers to Nero's punishment of the Christians, 'a set of men adhering to a novel and mischievous superstition' (*Life of Nero*, XVI). Suetonius also relates that at an earlier date Claudius had banished the Jews from Rome, since they were 'continually causing disturbances at the instigation of Chrestus' (*Life of Claudius*, XXV, 4). This may be linked with *Acts* 18:2.

2.9 (c) **The younger Pliny,** while governor of Bithynia in Asia Minor, wrote to the Emperor Trajan about the year 112, asking what to do about the problems posed by the remarkable spread of Christianity in the province. (Recall what you read about Pliny's governorship in Unit 3, § 1. 16, and locate Bithynia on the maps.) The number of those accused of being Christians was very great. The 'superstition' had spread like a plague, not only in the cities, but throughout the countryside. Before Pliny's punitive measures began to take effect, the temples had been almost deserted and the hitherto customary sacrifices and rites neglected. Pliny referred to evidence from interrogations which showed that there had been Christians in Bithynia for many years—even as many as twenty-five years previously, which takes us back to about the year 87, in the reign of Domitian. The Emperor replied with instructions about observing the due process of law in dealing with the Christians (Pliny, *Letters*, X, 96, 97; Lewis and Reinhold, pp. 582–4). A similar rescript was sent by Hadrian to Gaius Minucius Fundanus, proconsul of Asia. A Greek translation of it was quoted by early Christian writers, and the Latin original was reproduced in a fourth-century work by a Tyrannius Rufinus. (Cf. H. Bettenson, *Documents of the Christian Church*, Oxford University Press 1967, p. 7.)

2.10 (d) **Josephus,** the Jewish historian, who completed his *Antiquities of the Jews* in Rome during the reign of Domitian, twice mentions Jesus. In the first text (XX. 9. 1) he refers to the stoning of James, 'the brother of Jesus the so-called Christ', in AD 62. There is a longer passage in the same work (XVIII. 3. 3), which mentions Jesus, who 'drew to himself many Jews and many of the Greek race. . . . Pilate at the instance of the foremost men among us sentenced him to be crucified, . . . and even now the tribe of Christians named after him is not extinct'. This longer passage in Josephus, however, includes laudatory phrases about Jesus which seem to be interpolations by a later Christian scribe, quite possibly substituted for hostile phrases in the original. (Cf. Filson, pp. 67–8.)

2.11 (e) In your answer did you refer to what Dr Balsdon wrote in Unit 2, § 1.7, when discussing the surviving literary sources for the history of the Roman empire in the first century: 'The *Gospels* and the *Acts of the Apostles* are full of information about life in the eastern empire and about the Roman administration seen from the subject's point of view'? This is putting the boot on the other foot. Instead of calling into question the historicity of the New Testament writings, here is a historian calling on those writings as documentary evidence to throw light on the history of the Roman empire. You may also have recalled the two radio talks by A. N. Sherwin-White earlier in this course, in which he showed how the accounts of the trials of Jesus and Paul, in the Gospels and in the *Acts*, concord impressively with the historical evidence about legal procedure in the Roman empire. (For further study of these matters there is Dr Sherwin-White's book, *Roman Society and Roman Law in the New Testament*, Oxford University Press, 1963.)

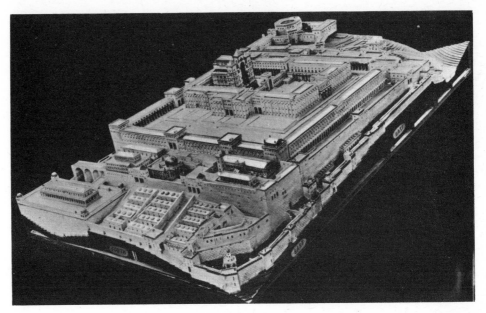

Figure 2   Model of the Temple of Herod, as it would probably have appeared in the time of Jesus. (Radio Times Hulton Picture Library.)

2.12 In the heyday of nineteenth-century criticism aimed at discrediting the New Testament, it was the fashion to dismiss *Acts* as a fictional work of the late second century, in which the author tried to make a historical reconstruction of the past but blundered. Since then, however, sound scholarship and archaeology have vindicated the accuracy of *Acts* on many substantial points of historical fact, relating to places, customs and institutions not only in Palestine and Syria, but also in Asia Minor and Greece, as well as in other parts of the Mediterranean world. This is not to deny that the author of *Acts*, like the authors of the Gospels, had a theological purpose in writing; that he puts stylized speeches into the mouths of the persons he mentions (as do other ancient writers); or that he includes in his book reports and traditions that evidently do not belong to the ordinary *genre* of historical narrative. Leaving aside for the present the question of the historicity of his narrative of events within the Christian communities themselves (we shall return to it in §§ 6.0–7.7), there is no doubt that the incidental references of the author of *Acts* to the political, social and geographical background of those events tally to an impressive extent with what we know from other historical sources. Indeed, he rounds out our knowledge gained from those sources.

2.13 He knows, for example, that the magistrates of Thessalonica were called 'politarchs'—a title unknown elsewhere in ancient literature, but discovered on inscriptions. He knows that the magistrates of Philippi were called *strategoi*, a courtesy title which has been likewise confirmed by inscriptions to the discomfiture of doubting critics. He knows that the chief municipal officer of the city of Ephesus, who had to give an account of the transactions of the city government to the Roman provincial authorities, was called the *grammateus*; that principal citizens of Ephesus, custodians of the imperial cult, were called Asiarchs; that the governor of Cyprus was a proconsul, and that the governor of Malta had the title of 'The First'. He knows that the boundary of Lycaonia lay between Iconium and Lystra; in this he contradicts another ancient source, and some critics therefore assumed that he was wrong—but once again local inscriptions have proved him right. He has accurate knowledge of many details of Roman law and administration, and his account of the disdainful attitude of Gallio, proconsul of Achaia, when the Jews brought Paul before his tribunal at Corinth (*Acts* 18:12–17), has in it the ring of truth. (Gallio was a brother of the philosopher Seneca, and a dated inscription bearing his name enables us to date Paul's stay at Corinth to the years AD 51–52 or 52–53.)

2.14 Examined by this test of historical coherence and authenticity of background, the *Gospels* and *Acts* must be acknowledged to be set convincingly in the Jewish and Roman world of the first century AD. The same must be said of the letters of Paul, which, as we shall see, corroborate the narrative of *Acts* on several points, and which also fit authentically into their social context. A classic study here is Sir William Ramsay's *St Paul the Traveller and Roman Citizen* (1897; reprinted 1960.)

2.15 Scantiness of the evidence

Nevertheless we must be cautious in our conclusions. One may still object that, even though the evidence is enough to provide a reasonable 'anchor in history' for the primitive Church, the direct references to Christ and Christians in non-Christian sources are very scanty. If it is true that there were Christians 'in great numbers' in Rome as well as in the provinces, even in the first century, how is it that there is no record of any person known to us from independent historical sources becoming a Christian in the period we are considering? And if Jesus made so great an impact on the Jewish community of his time, how is it that the rabbinical sources are so strangely lacking in any original data concerning him? Questions like these are useful to set us thinking about the problems of early Christian history. We should be able to give them a fuller answer as we go along. Can you give any comments on them at this stage?

✠ ✠

2.16 *My comments:* For one thing, recall (from Unit 2, §§ 1.1–1.8) how relatively few historical writings have survived from the period under discussion. Many important events or facts of contemporary Roman history are known to us only from a single passage in either Tacitus or Suetonius. The testimony of Tacitus about the execution of Christ by Pontius Pilate and the persecution of the Christians in Rome in the reign of Nero is as solid a piece of evidence as one could expect. It is no matter for surprise that during the early years of its growth the Christian Church, an 'underground' movement of eastern Mediterranean origin drawing its members mainly from immigrants belonging to the lower orders, should have made few converts in the ranks of the Roman 'establishment' and left few traces in its records. There is a similar lack of evidence about individual converts to the other Eastern cults which were also popular in the Roman world at that time. One cannot say confidently that there were *no* Christian converts in the higher ranks of Roman society in the early period. Indeed, we shall see later (in § 16.25) that it is probable that even a niece of the Emperor Domitian became a Christian before AD 95, and there is other evidence to show that membership of the Church was not confined to the underprivileged and those of lowly estate—although its message was especially appropriate for them.

Figure 3 Greek inscription from Herod's Temple forbidding 'strangers' (i.e. non-Jews) to enter the Temple Court under pain of death. (Israel Department of Antiquities and Museums.)

2.17 The reticence of the Jewish rabbinical sources about Jesus is harder to explain. Here, surely, we should expect to gain some fresh light and independent information about the career of a Jew who, the Gospels relate, caused so great a stir in the life of his own people. We must realize that first-century Palestinian Judaism relied on oral, not written, transmission of what it thought worth preserving. The rabbinical traditions were not written down until towards the end of the second century, to be eventually codified in the *Mishnah*. By that time the breach between Church and Synagogue had long been complete, and Jewish Christians were regarded by the rabbis as apostates to be blotted out of remembrance. The rabbinical sources do contain some allusions to disputes between the rabbis and Christians. On page 68 Filson summarizes the few direct references to Jesus in these sources, as found in developed form in the fifth-century redaction of the Babylonian *Talmud*. He regards these references as original and independent evidence about details of the life and death of Jesus, but I am not so convinced. Most if not all of them may well be polemical taunts based on particulars taken from the Christian Gospels.

2.18   The sources for early Christian history

The few pieces of historical evidence about early Christianity which are provided by non-Christian sources have a special value. But for our study of early Christianity we must, for the most part, turn to the Christian writings themselves, and to the Jewish religious writings which the Christians knew and used. These documents must naturally be interpreted in the light of what we know about contemporary Jewish and Roman society. **What are the main sources available for this study?** Before I give my list, jot down your own answer. I don't mean you to give the names of all the relevant books and documents, but try to indicate the chief categories of such sources, drawing on your general knowledge and on the information given by Filson, pages 65–71, 158–62, and in his Chronology, pages 397–400. In this exercise try to include the main Christian sources, or Jewish writings used by Christians, which bear on the history of early Christianity up to the last quarter of the second century AD.

A LONG PAUSE HERE
Do not read on until you have worked on the exercise

2.19   **Specimen answers and discussion**

(a)   In the first place there are **the twenty-seven books of the New Testament.** The four Gospels tell of the life and teaching of Jesus Christ. The first three Gospels, *Matthew*, *Mark* and *Luke*, are evidently closely related; the fourth, the *Gospel according to John*, has notably different characteristics. The book of the New Testament which most resembles a historical narrative in the ordinary sense is the *Acts of the Apostles*. The letters of Paul are of first importance for understanding the growth and beliefs of the early Christian communities. Later we shall be saying more about the establishment of the 'canon' of the New Testament—that is, the process by which those twenty-seven books and no others were accepted in the Church as authentic Scripture.

2.20   (b)   There are also **the thirty-nine books of the Hebrew Scriptures** (called the 'Old Testament' by Christians). Some knowledge of the content of those books, and of their place in Jewish life in the time of Jesus and of Paul, is essential in order to understand the teaching of the New Testament writers and the thought-world of the early Christians. We assume that you either have a text of the whole Bible, or at least can easily have access to one.

2.21   (c)   In addition to the thirty-nine books of the Hebrew Scriptures, which were accorded special religious authority by the Jews of Palestine, there were a number of other Jewish religious writings which originated in the last few centuries of the pre-Christian era. Fifteen of these books, or parts of books, were regarded by other Jews (especially in Egypt) as possessing religious authority, and were included in the Greek Septuagint translation of the Scriptures, made by Greek-speaking Jews in Alexandria in the third century BC. (See the note on the meaning and origin of this term on p. 38 of Filson's book.) These writings are usually called **'the Apocrypha'**—the word in Greek means 'hidden matters', but in English usage 'apocryphal' has come to mean 'unauthentic'. Protestant Christians do not include them in the canon of Scripture, that is, in the list of authentic books of holy writ. The Church of

England accords them a kind of intermediate status. They are often printed as an appendix to editions of the Bible. However, twelve of the fifteen writings *are* included in the canon of Scripture accepted by the Roman Catholic Church, and are thus printed as integral parts of the Bible in Catholic editions. These twelve texts are: *Tobit*; *Judith*; an additional part of *Esther*; *The Wisdom of Solomon*; *Ecclesiasticus*; *Baruch* (which has two parts); three additional parts of *Daniel*; *1 Maccabees*; *2 Maccabees*. Catholic scholars usually call these writings 'deutero-canonical' (i.e. 'belonging to the second canon') rather than 'apocryphal', and they reserve this latter term for other writings, discussed in the next paragraph and in paragraph (f) below.

2.22   (d)   In addition, there are several other Jewish religious writings (sometimes called **'inter-testamentary books'**) dating from the period before or just after the rise of Christianity, which are not accepted by either Jews or Christians as inspired Scripture, but which are relevant to a study of the *milieu* in which Christianity arose. These include books with titles such as the *Book of Enoch*, the *Assumption of Moses*, the *Testaments of the Twelve Patriarchs*, the *Book of Jubilees*, the Jewish *Sybilline Oracles*, the *Psalms of Solomon* and the *Ascension of Isaiah*. Most of them are called **'pseudepigrapha'**; that is, writings put out under a false name. Some of them are of Judaeo-Christian origin— a term which means that they arose in early Christian communities made up of Jews who had accepted Christianity, and who still followed, to a large extent, the Jewish way of life and thought. There is an English translation of most of these writings by R. H. Charles, *The Apocrypha and Pseudepigrapha of the Old Testament* (two vols., Oxford University Press 1913). The same author gives a useful summary of the writings in the context of their period in his *Religious Development Between the Old and New Testaments* (Williams and Norgate 1914).

2.23   (e)   Of specifically Christian sources, I have so far mentioned only the New Testament. But in addition there are a number of other early Christian writings, dating from before the last quarter of the second century, which amplify the historical picture we have of the rise of Christianity. In Part Three, Section (E), 'Christian Literature of the Sub-Apostolic Age', I shall be saying more about these writings. Among them, special importance is accorded to the writings of authors known as **'The Apostolic Fathers'**, some of which date from the end of the first century or the early years of the second. There is no hard-and-fast rule to determine which authors should be included in this category. These writings are important for our understanding of the way Christianity was developing from the close of the first century onwards. Especially noteworthy are the letter to the Corinthians attributed to Clement of Rome, and the letters of Ignatius of Antioch.

2.24   (f)   Although some of the writings included under (d) were of Judaeo-Christian origin, they are usually classified, rather arbitrarily, under the title 'apocrypha and pseudepigrapha of the *Old* Testament' because of their attribution to pre-Christian authors. There were also many other writings, originating in Judaeo-Christian or Gentile Christian circles, which are called **'apocrypha and pseudepigrapha of the New Testament'**. They bear such names as: the *Gospel of Peter*, the *Gospel of the Nazaraeans*, the *Acts of John*, the *Acts of Paul*, the *Gospel of the Egyptians*, the *Gospel of Thomas*, the *Revelation of Peter*, the *Acts of Pilate*, the *Pseudo-Clementine Epistles*. These apocrypha are mainly of a legendary and bizarre character, and are often tinged with Gnostic notions (cf. §§ 4.25–32 below). They made up a very considerable body of literature, though much of it survives only in fragmentary form. They can be studied in a monumental work of scholarship, *New Testament Apocrypha* by Hennecke-Schneemelcher (English translation, edited by R. McL. Wilson, 2 vols., Lutterworth 1965). There is an earlier English translation by M. R. James, *The Apocryphal*

New Testament, Oxford University Press 1924; second edition 1955). Many of these writings originated at a date later than the period we are studying, but even these may incorporate earlier material, and can throw light on earlier developments. Again, classification of the various documents can be artificial. Some of those usually included under (e), such as the *Didache* or *Teaching of the Twelve Apostles*, or the *Epistle of Barnabas*, could logically be included in the category of 'apocrypha and pseudepigrapha'.

2.25 (g) I said earlier that the Christian documents must be interpreted in the light of the other sources relating to contemporary Jewish and Roman society. These sources, even if they do not refer directly to Christian origins, provide a framework within which to situate and evaluate the history of Christianity as it grew from its first beginnings to emerge as an already powerful movement by the end of the second century. You have already been introduced to sources for the contemporary Roman history in Unit 2 of this course and in Appendix II of Salmon. Among Jewish sources, especially important are: the **Talmud**, the vast collection of Jewish traditions, codified some centuries later but containing much information relevant to first-century Judaism; the writings of **Josephus**—the *Antiquities of the Jewish People* (written about AD 93) and the *History of the Jewish War against the Romans* (written about AD 77); and the writings of **Philo** of Alexandria. In a special category is the Qumran literature, the **'Dead Sea Scrolls'** discovered in the mid-twentieth century in sites associated with an ascetic Jewish sect that lived near the north-west shore of the Dead Sea (cf. Filson pp. 53–5, and §§ 4.11–13 below).

2.26 (h) In addition to these documentary sources, we cannot exclude the possibility that there was authentic but unwritten information about the earliest period of Christianity, handed down by **oral tradition** and recorded in writing only after a considerable lapse of time. There were indeed traditions for which this claim was later made, but the historian must judge them critically. It does not appear that any significant amount of original information about the beginnings of Christianity was preserved by such unwritten traditions. A very few 'agrapha', or sayings of Jesus not written in the Gospels, can probably be accepted as authentic, out of a much greater quantity which cannot. They are sifted by J. Jeremias, in *Unknown Sayings of Jesus* (English trans. S.P.C.K. 1964), who discusses critically the various sayings which have been found in early Egyptian papyri, in the writings of Church Fathers, in apocryphal works, and in later Jewish and Moslem sources.

2.27 I should remark that although I have listed the various documentary sources in different categories, according to their subject-matter and origin, we must not presuppose here that these categories mark off different degrees of historical value. In a course of this nature, which does not rely on any credal presuppositions, we cannot assume that because a document is included in the Christian Bible its historical accuracy is guaranteed, or that it is necessarily superior as a documentary source to other writings not included in the Bible. Each document must be judged on its merits as a historical source and on the evidence of its contents. Later we shall be saying more about the critical study of the New Testament writings in particular.

2.28 Archaeological evidence?

You may ask: Is there no direct archaeological or other non-literary evidence relating to the earliest period of Christianity? Well, it is certainly true that archaeology, and the study of surviving monuments, art, inscriptions and coins, have given us plenty of information relating to the persons, cities, sites, routes, institutions and artefacts mentioned in the New Testament, and this provides a check on the accuracy of the New Testament accounts. (A useful reference work here is J. Finegan's *The Archeology of the New Testament*, Princeton University Press 1969.) But of buildings, gravestones, monuments, inscriptions, papyri, art, utensils, etc., no unmistakably Christian object has yet been discovered which can be dated with certainty to the first century AD. Perhaps the earliest surviving such object so far known is a fragment of papyrus in the John Rylands Library, Manchester, brought to light in 1935, which is no less than a piece of the eighteenth chapter of the *Gospel of John*. It is pronounced by experts to have been copied in Egypt not later than the middle of the second century, and quite possibly as early as 120–130. (See Figure 18.)

Figure 4 Aerial view of the Jordan Valley, looking north towards the Sea of Galilee. (Matson Photo Service, California.)

2.29 One of the most fascinating areas of archaeological interest is undoubtedly the space lying beneath the dome of St Peter's, Rome. It is arguable that the evidence provided by recent excavations there takes us back to a very early period in the history of Christianity in Rome. We shall be saying more about this later in the course.

2.30 Someone may object that among the archaeological discoveries I have not mentioned the famous acrostic-palindrome word-square made up of five Latin words:

```
R O T A S
O P E R A
T E N E T
A R E P O
S A T O R
```

This word-square has been found in many different parts of the Roman empire, including Corinium (Cirencester) in Britain and in the ruins of Pompeii. A rough literal meaning could be: 'Arepo the sower holds the wheels by his work'. Several cryptic allusions are supposed to be contained in this word-square, which, it is argued, show that it is of Christian origin. By rearranging the letters in the five words they can be made to spell PATER NOSTER twice. True, there is only one N, but by writing the twofold PATERNOSTER in the form of a Greek cross, the single N can be made to do duty twice at the point of intersection. This leaves two A's and two O's left over, but these are explained as Alpha and Omega repeated—the first and last letters of the *Greek* alphabet, given a special Christian significance in *Revelation* 22:13. The letter T, which occurs in the centre of each outside line, is seen as the shape of Christ's cross. This 'tau' cross, of course, has to be a different shape from the four-armed cross made by the twofold PATERNOSTER. The word ROTAS ('wheels') spelt backwards or forwards four times round the four sides of the acrostic, is taken as an allusion to a passage in the Old Testament, the vision of the prophet Ezekiel, who saw four mysterious wheels 'which went on their four sides without turning as they went' (*Ezek.* 1:17).

2.31 Since this word-square has been found at Pompeii, it has been argued that it proves the presence of Christianity there before AD 79, when the city was destroyed. Now say what *you* think about this piece of 'archaeological evidence' for early Christianity, and the arguments based on it. Are they convincing?

✚ ✚

My answer: That there were Christians in Pompeii is quite possible—*Acts* 28:14 mentions that Paul found fellow-Christians at nearby Puteoli. But for several reasons I think the ingenious attempts to claim this word-square as a Christian cryptogram are unconvincing. It is the (almost) double anagram of the term PATER NOSTER ('Our Father' in Latin) that seems to impress people most. This phrase is, of course, one of the commonest of everyday phrases in all languages. Although the two Latin words became a hallowed formula and the usual Latin name for the Lord's Prayer in later centuries, they would hardly have been a distinctive Christian formula before the year 79. The recently-written Gospels, containing the words of the Lord's Prayer, were in Greek; there is no trace of any Latin formularies of prayer or worship at that early date, or indeed during the first hundred years and more of the Church's existence. (Greek remained the language of Christian prayer and worship even in Rome itself until well into the third century.) *Revelation*, in which the 'Alpha and Omega' formula is given a mystic significance, was not written until several years after the destruction of Pompeii. It is intriguing to note all the different allusions and arguments that have been wrung out of this magic word-square to attest its Christian origins, but they do not add up to a cogent proof. I recommend a reading of Ronald Knox's *Essays in Satire* as an amusing demonstration of the fascinating discoveries of hidden meaning that can be made by shuffling letters about in almost any chosen text or inscription.

(B) THE POLITICAL SETTING IN WHICH CHRISTIANITY AROSE

3.0 The earlier political background to New Testament history is discussed by Filson in his first chapter. It is a rather confused story, and you need not spend much time studying all the details which Filson gives about Jewish political history in the last two centuries BC—the ups and downs of guerrilla warfare, the frequent foreign invasions, the rivalries of princes and powers, the palace intrigues and the constant sequence of bloody deeds. Just run briskly through that chapter, and then answer the questions that I suggest in the following exercise.

3.1 On page 34 of your set book Filson writes:

For the study of New Testament history, it is essential to know the political background. The earlier Maccabean movement in Seleucid times, the Roman rule of the Mediterranean area, the Roman and Herodian rule in Palestine, the Nabatean activity to the immediate east and south, and the

Parthian threat on the east and northeast give the setting for the rise and westward spread of the Christian faith.

Taking the chief points mentioned in that paragraph, I want you to write brief notes to explain them, saying why the following factors 'give the setting for the rise and westward spread of the Christian faith': (i) **The Maccabean movement**; (ii) **Roman influence in the Levant**; (iii) **The desert frontier to the east** ; (iv) **Herodian rule in Palestine**. (I use the term 'Levant' here as a convenient abbreviation to refer to the whole area of the eastern Mediterranean seaboard and the neighbouring countries.)

A LONG PAUSE HERE
Do not read on until you have worked on the exercise

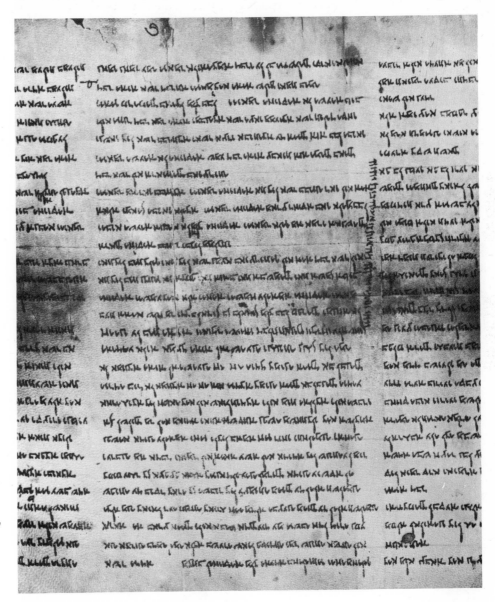

Figure 5   A text from the Dead Sea Scrolls, found near Qumran. This is the Isaiah Scroll, open to show the passage which is now numbered Chapter 38:8–40:2. (Israel Department of Antiquities and Museums.)

Specimen answers and discussion

3.2   (i)   The Maccabean movement

When Alexander the Great died his generals divided his empire between them and founded dynasties. The Ptolemaic dynasty was based in Egypt, the Seleucid dynasty in Syria. The Ptolemies ruled Palestine until about 198 BC., when the area fell under the control of the Seleucids. It is perhaps not clear from Filson's account that 'Judaea' was then a pocket state, consisting only of the area of Jerusalem and a few miles around it. The Jewish High Priest headed the administration of this miniature state, which was allowed internal autonomy to run its own affairs in accordance with traditional Jewish law and custom. The Jews of Palestine outside the little hierocratic enclave looked to the Temple as the centre of their religion, but did not live under the peculiar political régime of Jerusalem.

3.3 The foreign rulers and their local government promoted the spread of Hellenistic culture, and this brought increasing conflict with the traditional Jewish way of life. The conflict reached a climax in 167 BC when the Seleucid king Antiochus Epiphanes tried to hellenize the citadel of traditional Judaism. He installed the worship of Olympian Zeus in the Temple consecrated to Yahweh,[1] the God of Israel—this was the 'abomination of desolation' (cf. *1 Maccabees* 1:54). The Jews were to be forced to renounce their holy Law and to profane all they held sacred. Pagan worship, including the sacrifice of swine, was ordered to be observed in towns throughout Palestine.

3.4 The fierce Maccabean revolt which broke out as a consequence secured the restoration of Jewish Temple worship in 164 BC (an event still commemorated by the Jews in the annual feast of *Hanukkah*). A confused guerrilla struggle continued until a precarious national independence was eventually won, under the Maccabean or Hasmonean dynasty. This dynasty ruled an expanded Jewish state for over seventy years, until the Roman conquest. By their excesses the later Hasmonean leaders alienated the most observant Jews and provoked them to separatism and extremism.

3.5 The Maccabean movement was important for future developments because it sharpened and channelled Jewish nationalism; it shaped the course of Jewish religious politics in later years; it provided a heroic folk-saga to which the Jewish people could look back for inspiration, and a precedent for their disastrous revolt against Rome 233 years later; and it produced *The Book of Daniel*, one of the most powerful writings in the Bible.[2] *Daniel* was a forerunner of similar apocalyptic works, and, as we shall see, one of the visions it describes has a bearing on the interpretation of the mission of Jesus in early Christianity.

3.6 (ii) Roman influence in the Levant

Rome first began to take an interest in Jewish affairs at the time of the Maccabean wars. Judas Maccabaeus secured a treaty of friendship with Rome, though this did not have much effect at that time. The Romans were steadily extending their influence eastwards, in Asia Minor, Syria and Egypt. When Pompey conquered Judaea in 63 BC it was the end of Jewish national independence. A considerable measure of autonomy was still conceded to princes like Herod who could be relied upon to be loyal to Rome. For 130 years more the Jews attempted to preserve their national identity under the foreign domination. Finally the fierce spirit of resistance flared up into open revolt. The Roman legions crushed the turbulent nation in a full-scale war and destroyed Jerusalem and its Temple in AD 70. (Cf. Salmon, pp. 194–7, and Lewis and Reinhold pp. 91–2.)

---

[1] *Yahweh* is the correct transliteration of the Hebrew name. The form *Jehovah* was based on a misunderstanding of the later Hebrew vocalization.

[2] 'Daniel is the first to have comprehended all earthly history as a great unity which moves towards a final goal according to a divine plan, and his understanding determined the thought and action of mankind for two millennia. The visions which he saw and described originate in Persian mythology, but the explanation owed its origin to the spirit of Jewish religion.' (H. Lietzmann, *op. cit.*, p. 25). It would be very interesting to discuss this far-reaching claim about the subsequent influence of *Daniel*.

Figure 6   Present-day Samaritans at their annual Passover service on Mount Garizim. The elders are praying before a stone altar. The lambs are for the Passover sacrifice. This small ethnic group has worshipped here for some 2,500 years. (Israel Government Tourist Office.)

3.7   The Roman overlordship meant that Judaea was drawn into a wider world of international relations, of communications and trade, and of cultural influences. The Jews became very numerous throughout the Roman world—amounting, it has been variously estimated, to between four and seven millions, perhaps as many as seven per cent of the total population of the empire. Jewish communities were to be found in all the chief cities and trading ports of the Mediterranean. They were especially numerous in Alexandria and in Rome.

Figure 7   The Wailing Wall at Jerusalem. The lower part of the wall, built of massive blocks, is a remaining section of Herod's Temple complex. (Israel Government Tourist Office.)

These expatriate Jews, making up what was called the 'Diaspora' or 'dispersion', were more than eight times as numerous as the Jews in Palestine. Attached to most of the Jewish communities were Gentile 'proselytes' or converts, and also groups of 'God-fearers' who acknowledged the truth of the Jewish religion and contributed to its support, but did not take the decisive step of binding themselves to the full observance of the Mosaic Law. The Jewish religion had a privileged position in the empire. These factors, as we shall see, were to be of great importance for the future spread of Christianity. (Cf. Unit 1, § 1.14.)

3.8 Rome and the New Testament: a supplementary exercise

Although the progress of Roman imperial history in the first century was not perceptibly affected by the rise of Christianity, it is nevertheless true that the rise of Christianity can only be properly understood in the context of Roman imperial history. Here is a supplementary exercise to bring this point home. In their subject-matter the New Testament writings span the period of the first century of our era; from your general knowledge of them and from what you have read elsewhere, **note some of the references in the New Testament to Roman rule and institutions.**

A LONG PAUSE HERE
Do not read on until you have worked on the exercise

3.9 Specimen answers and discussion

Here are some points—by no means all—which you could have mentioned in your answer, to show how the emergence of Christianity was conditioned by the fact of Roman rule throughout the whole Mediterranean area:

(a) Luke's Gospel, relating the circumstances of the birth of Jesus Christ, links it with an imperial decree and with the rule of a Roman provincial governor: 'In those days a decree was issued by the Emperor Augustus for a general registration throughout the Roman world. This was the first registration of its kind; it took place when Quirinius was governor of Syria' (*Luke* 2:1–2).

(b) The overriding power of Rome and the subordination of the Jewish nation to its alien control are alluded to in many parts of the Gospel narrative. The 'publicans' or tax-gatherers appear in the Gospels as a detested class, not simply for their dishonesty and rapacity but because they are political collaborators, tools of the Roman masters. People in a crowd around Jesus bring up the question of the Galileans whose blood Pontius Pilate, the Roman prefect or procurator of Judaea, had shed while they were offering victims in sacrifice at the Temple (*Luke* 13:1). The enemies of Jesus try to ensnare him into seditious statements that would bring him into conflict with Roman authority: 'Are we or are we not permitted to pay taxes to the Roman Emperor?' (*Matthew* 22:17). Jesus takes in his hand the silver coin bearing the image and title of Tiberius, and answers with a forthright distinction between what is due to Caesar and what is due to God. The Gospels also relate a prediction by Jesus of the destruction of the Temple in Jerusalem (*Matt.* 24:1–2); it was in AD 70 that the Roman army under Titus stormed Jerusalem and the Temple was destroyed.

(c) All four Gospels relate how, after the arrest of Jesus, he was brought before the same Roman magistrate, Pilate, and questioned by him. He was scourged by Roman soldiers, sentenced to death by Roman authority and executed in the Roman manner by crucifixion. A squad of Roman soldiers under a centurion was set to keep watch at his tomb.

(d) Among the early converts to Christianity a specially significant place was accorded to the Roman centurion Cornelius, from Italy, whose baptism by Peter pointed the way to the extension of the Christian mission to the non-Jewish world (*Acts* 10).

(e)   The *Acts of Apostles*, as we have seen, are full of allusions to the institutions, administration and social customs of the Roman empire. Refer again to the examples I gave in § 2.13. You may recall others mentioned in earlier units of this course.

(f)   Paul of Tarsus, a Jew who proclaimed his Roman citizenship with insistence (*Acts* 16:37–9; 22:25–9), became the chief herald of Christianity throughout the Roman provinces of Asia Minor and Greece. Arrested by the Romans in Jerusalem, he appealed directly to be tried at the imperial tribunal in Rome, and the last clear record we have of him in the New Testament shows him preaching Christianity in the city of Rome itself, during a two-year stay there (*Acts* 28:30–1). Paul's letters contain many indirect allusions to the contemporary setting of Graeco-Roman society. In his letter to the Philippians, he relates how his trials have led to the advance of the gospel, so that it has become known 'throughout the whole praetorian headquarters' (1:12–13), and in conclusion he sends greetings from 'the saints . . . especially those of Caesar's household' (4:22; the *New English Bible* translates, less literally, 'those who belong to the imperial establishment').

(g)   The time would come when official suspicion and popular prejudice would bring conflict between Roman society and the growing communities of Christians, which at least in some places had to face a 'fiery ordeal' (*1 Peter* 4:12–19). Towards the end of the first century, probably in Domitian's reign, about the year 95, *Revelation* alluded in symbolic language to the Roman emperor and state wielding universal and oppressive power, and raging with bloody fury against Christ's own (Chapter 17). The doom of Rome, the 'mighty city of Babylon', is graphically foretold in Chapter 18.

Figure 8   The spring of Ain Feshka, in the region near Qumran, to the north-west of the Dead Sea. (Israel Government Tourist Office.)

3.10   (iii)   The desert frontier to the east

Filson mentions the occasional invasions and interventions in Judaean politics from powers to the east. These events are not of major concern in our present study. Still, the Parthian empire to the east of the Euphrates and the desert kingdoms to the south and east of Judaea do have an indirect importance in our story. Because the Parthians and the desert princelings were outside the main Roman world, and because that desert region reaching away to Mesopotamia was a political and cultural frontier which Rome had constantly to defend, the main lines of communication ran northwards and westwards, not eastwards. Political realities, trade interests and cultural influences linked the Levant with the Mediterranean world rather than with the land mass to the east. The incorporation of Judaea into the Roman world in the first century BC meant that the Roman empire was to be the terrain in which the new religion of Christianity would develop. Although that religion was Semitic in its origin its development was to proceed mainly through the medium of Hellenistic and Roman cultural forms.

3.11 Because the mother tongue of Jesus and of his first disciples was Aramaic (a form of the Syriac language which was spoken—with variant dialects—over a wide area, including not only Palestine and Syria but also in the territories to the east and north-east), one might suppose that, when the Church expanded, its main thrust would be into those regions. When in the first and second centuries Christianity began to spread outwards from Palestine and Syria, there was some missionary initiative towards the east, by way of eastern Asia Minor and 'the fertile crescent' of territory linking north Syria with Mesopotamia. This was the work of Aramaic-speaking missionaries from west Syria. Greek, however, was the main language of the developing Church, and the medium of the New Testament writings; this language factor also served to channel the Church's expansion into the provinces of the Roman empire.

3.12 **(iv) Herodian rule in Palestine**

The Herodian family originated in the desert to the south of Judaea, but their ambition and opportunities brought them into the mainstream of politics in the Hellenistic and Roman world. For well over a hundred years members of the dynasty founded by Herod the Great played a prominent role in the history of Palestine. Herod's own reign was the golden age of the family's influence, but right up to the time of the destruction of Jerusalem in AD 70 members of the family continued to be given some measure of authority and autonomy by Rome, as a means of keeping order and obtaining due tribute from a region notoriously difficult to govern.

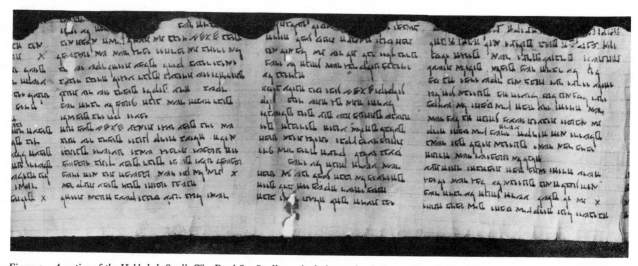

Figure 9   A section of the Habbakuk Scroll. The Dead Sea Scrolls survived nineteen hundred years through being preserved in pottery jars and hidden in inaccessible caves in the cliffs near Qumran. (Israel Department of Antiquities and Museums.)

3.13 Herod the Great rose to power in the upheavals of the Roman civil wars and their aftermath. Shrewd, energetic and farsighted, he was also wily, cruel and arbitrary. He ruled the Jews for nearly forty years, and his reign shaped the political and religious pattern of the land in which Jesus of Nazareth was born. During his long reign Herod's constant policy was to retain the favour and support of those who held power at Rome, whoever they might be, and he often fought as an ally of the Roman armies. He was rewarded, especially by Augustus, with rule over a kingdom of ever-widening extent. He rebuilt the

Temple at Jerusalem on a magnificent scale in an attempt to win the favour of the Jewish people. Although disliked by patriotic Jews—for the Herodian family had dispossessed and liquidated the last members of the Hasmonean dynasty—Herod's rule was regarded as preferable to direct domination by the pagan Romans. In the main he respected the religious sensibilities of his Jewish subjects, and presented himself as the protector of their religion—while doing the same for other religions within his domains, and taking special care to build temples dedicated to Rome and Augustus. By his control of the appointment of the High Priests he exercised an indirect but effective sway over the community life of his Jewish subjects.

3.14 Six Herodian princes: an exercise

Herodian rulers and members of their families are mentioned several times in the New Testament. Their relationships are somewhat confusing, and you may not find it easy to get a clear idea of who was who. The confusion is not lessened by the practice of New Testament writers of calling three of them 'King Herod' without differentiation. In an appendix on page 401 Filson gives some useful notes about the more prominent members of the family, and references (not complete) to places in the New Testament where they are mentioned. Using these references and the fuller information in Filson's chapters, do the following supplementary exercise, which may help you to sort out the various 'Herods' of the New Testament narrative, and to realize more clearly how the rule of these native princes fitted in with the overall Roman control of Palestine and the surrounding regions.

3.15   Six of the princes named on page 401 of Filson's book were territorial rulers mentioned in the New Testament. **Say who those six were, and how they fit into the New Testament story.**

A LONG PAUSE HERE
Do not read on until you have worked on the exercise

3.16 Specimen answers and discussion

(i)   **Herod the Great** was king of Judaea and neighbouring territories at the time of the birth of Christ. *Matt.* 2:1–18 testifies to Herod's notoriety for callous cruelty, and to his obsessive fear of any threat to his position.

3.17   (ii)   **Archelaus,** a son of Herod the Great by Malthace of Samaria (one of his ten wives), was named in his father's will to succeed him as king, but when Augustus confirmed his succession it was only with the title of 'ethnarch' over Judaea, Samaria and Idumaea. *Matt.* 2:22 also testifies to the ill-repute in which Archelaus was held: Joseph was afraid to go into Judaea, but decided to withdraw to Galilee. So inept and tyrannical was Archelaus as a ruler that in AD 6 Augustus deposed him. From that time until AD 41 Judaea was under direct Roman rule, administered by a prefect or procurator, who was subordinate to the legate of Syria. So it came about that when the climax of the ministry of Jesus of Nazareth led him to the final confrontation in Jerusalem, it was a Roman magistrate and not a Herodian prince who wielded power there and who sentenced him to death.

3.18   (iii)   **Philip,** son of Herod the Great by Cleopatra of Jerusalem, is mentioned in *Luke* 3:1 as 'prince (tetrarch) of Ituraea and Trachonitis', to the north-east of the Sea of Galilee. (See the map on the back cover of these units.) As a ruler he had a better reputation than others of his family. *Matt.* 16:13–20 mentions a journey of Jesus into the territory of Philip, to Caesarea Philippi, a city which the tetrarch had rebuilt and renamed in honour of Caesar Augustus.

3.19 (iv) **Herod Antipas,** another son of Herod the Great by Malthace, was, like his brother Archelaus, thoroughly hated. After his father's death he was accorded the title of tetrarch, with rule over Galilee and Peraea, the district along the bank of the Jordan north-east of the Dead Sea. Antipas is called simply 'Herod' in the Gospels, and he is the most prominent Herod in the New Testament story. It was in his trans-Jordanian territory that John the Baptist carried out his ministry, and it was this Herod who put John to death (*Mark* 6:14–29). Superstitious, he feared that Jesus was John the Baptist restored to life. Jesus warned his followers against 'the leaven of Herod' (*Mark* 8:15). Told that Herod was seeking to kill him too, Jesus referred to Antipas as 'that fox' (*Luke* 13:31–2). Herod Antipas figures also in the story of the trial of Jesus. Pilate, hearing that the prisoner was of Nazareth and therefore belonging to the Galilean jurisdiction, sent him to Herod for the tetrarch to take cognizance of the case (*Luke* 23:6–12). Antipas had assiduously sought and obtained the favour of Tiberius, but in AD 39 Caligula deposed him and banished him to Gaul.

3.20 (v) **Herod Agrippa I** was a grandson of Herod the Great. He grew up in Rome, in close friendship with members of the Roman imperial family. In AD 37 Caligula made him ruler of the territories which had been ruled by Philip, recently dead, and other territories besides, with the title of 'king'. Two years later the emperor bestowed the tetrarchy of the deposed Antipas on Agrippa as well. Shortly afterwards the new emperor Claudius decided to revert to indirect rule over turbulent Judaea through a native prince, and added Judaea and Samaria to Agrippa's kingdom. With all these acquisitions Agrippa eventually ruled domains as extensive as those of Herod the Great. He was religiously acceptable to the Jews, as his grandfather had not been, for he was descended from the Hasmonean line of Jewish patriot kings, and cultivated a name for piety and respect for the Jewish law. He features in the *Acts of the Apostles* (12:1–91) as the 'King Herod' who initiated a persecution of the newly formed Christian community in Jerusalem. He beheaded James, the brother of John, and seeing that such measures were popular then imprisoned Peter, intending to deal with him likewise. Peter, however, escaped. *Acts* 12:20–23 describes the dramatic death of this Herod, which occurred in AD 44. The account of the event by the Jewish historian Josephus differs in details but agrees substantially with that of *Acts*.

3.21 (vi) **Herod Agrippa II,** son of the Agrippa just referred to, is also mentioned in *Acts*. Aged 17, he was considered by the emperor to be too young to succeed to his father's extensive kingdom, and in AD 44 a Roman procurator once more took over direct rule of Palestine, including Judaea and Galilee. The younger Agrippa was, from AD 48 onwards, given the title of king by Claudius, together with successive gifts of territory to go with it. To this kingdom Nero added Galilee and Peraea. Herod Agrippa II has a lengthy mention in *Acts* (25:13–26:32). Paul testified that the king was 'expert in all Jewish matters, both our customs and our disputes' (26:2). In AD 62, as Josephus relates, Agrippa intervened after the stoning to death of James, 'the brother of Jesus, the so-called Christ', to remove the High Priest Annas from office. He was watchful, as the Herods always were, to avert any wrathful reaction from the Roman overlords which might be provoked by infringement of their prerogatives. When the great Jewish revolt broke out in AD 66 Agrippa tried vainly to pacify the Jews, and then fought by the side of Vespasian against the insurgents. (See the words attributed to him by Josephus, in Lewis and Reinhold, p. 412.)

3.22 None of those Herodian princes corresponded to the Jewish hope of a duly anointed king who would embody the national cause, a king to bring back the golden age of David and Solomon and usher in the new Messianic era.

Yet through the troubled years of early Christianity in Judaea and in the neighbouring territories, they were the only kings the people knew. They are a significant part of the political background to the Gospel narrative. Herodian influence is also relevant to the religious setting in which Christianity arose, and this brings us to the next subject for discussion.

4.0 (C) THE RELIGIOUS AND CULTURAL SETTING IN WHICH CHRISTIANITY AROSE

The Jews were only a minority of the population of Palestine—probably not much more than half a million out of a total population of between one and a half and two million. They were more numerous in the southern highlands, the district called Judaea. They lived in close proximity to the non-Jewish majority of the population, especially in the northern and eastern regions of Palestine, but this led·them to develop even more strongly their sense of religious separatism from their Gentile neighbours. (There were, of course, individuals—like Simeon in Luke's Gospel—with a wider vision and a sense of Israel's religious mission to the Gentiles.)

Figure 10   The excavated ruins of Khirbet Qumran, where the quasi-monastic community, probably of Essenes, had their headquarters. In the hills beyond are the entrances to some of the caves in which the Dead Sea Scrolls were found. (Israel Government Tourist Office.)

4.1 By the lifetime of Jesus of Nazareth, Jewish religious nationalism had developed and sharpened through centuries of challenge, reacting energetically against the many alien influences which threatened all the time to erode it. In its strictest form, it reacted against the Hellenistic culture which was dominant throughout the eastern Mediterranean lands; it reacted against the ritual impurity incurred by any contact with the foreign pagans; it reacted against the dilution of faith and observance among those Jews who lived closely intermingled with the Gentile inhabitants of the land, especially in the northern region called 'Galilee of the Gentiles'; it reacted against the Samaritans, who, though also tracing their religion back to the Hebrew patriarchs, were regarded by the Jews as beyond the pale; it reacted against the humiliating presence of the Roman power; it reacted against the compromising politics of the Herodian client-princes, who, while they paid lip-service to Jewish religious aspirations, were regarded as tools of the pagan conquerors; it even reacted against the High Priests and the Temple hierocrats themselves when these were seen to put the interests of their caste before the sacred interests of Israel.

4.2 In that fierce zeal for national separatism and legal purity there was an element of class antagonism. The Jewish 'establishment'—the aristocratic families, landowners, local authorities and Temple caste—tended to come to terms with the outsiders on whom ultimately the survival of their position and fortunes depended. Nationalist intransigence drew its chief strength from the less privileged ranks of society. It was this unyielding religious loyalty, this conviction of God's covenant with Israel, this collective consciousness of a divinely guided history and special destiny, this dedication and meticulous observance of their *Torah* or 'Law', that set the Jews apart from all other nations. It was because of all this that the Jewish people had a unique character and preserved their separate identity through the vicissitudes of centuries; and it was this that brought them to the disastrous confrontation with Rome in the war of AD 66–73.

Figure 11   Bethlehem today: view from the south-west. (Matson Photo Service, California.)

4.3 The Hebrew Scriptures, translated and paraphrased into the everyday speech of the people (Aramaic for most of the Jews of Palestine), together with the 'oral *Torah*' handed on by authorized teachers, were the basis of all religious observance and belief. Read what Filson says (on pages 37–48) about the place of Scripture in everyday life, and also about the other institutions and practices which shaped the religious life of Jews—the Temple worship, the synagogue services, the annual festivals, and, most intimately, the devout practices and prayers of the family at home. Jewish religion was not individualistic but collective, and the piety of the home built up this sense of the solidarity of God's people. (For the advanced student, a useful work of reference is G. F. Moore's *Judaism in the First Centuries of the Christian Era*; three volumes, Harvard University Press, 11th impression 1970. It gives a detailed account of the beliefs, practices and piety of Jews in the period that concerns us here. The chapters on the Synagogue and the Schools in Judaism are especially noteworthy. Another valuable work is J. Bonsirven's *Palestinian Judaism in the Time of Jesus Christ*, English trans., Holt, Rinehart and Winston, New York 1973.)

4.4 Why is it necessary to have a knowledge of Jewish religion and Jewish national aspirations in order to understand the origins of Christianity?

✠ ✠

Answer: Because Jesus of Nazareth was one of this remarkable race, and so were all his chosen Apostles. His life, teaching and actions were conditioned by the intense religious and national concerns of his people. The religion of the New Testament was grafted on to the religion of the Old Testament.

4.5   Sects and movements in Judaism

Judaism in the time of Jesus was not monochrome; it was a whole spectrum of differing parties and opinions. The aim of the next exercise is to make you aware of this diversity of parties within the overall national unity. Drawing on Filson's second chapter and on your reading of the New Testament, **list and briefly describe the various parties, sects and movements within Judaism** about the time of the ministry of Jesus—that is, in the first half of the first century. Where you can, refer to a New Testament text in which each of the various groups is mentioned. You need not follow the order given by Filson. If you have been able to read more widely you may find that other authors differ from him in their description of the different sects, and in the relative importance they attribute to them.

A LONG PAUSE HERE
Do not read on until you have worked on the exercise

4.6   **Specimen answers and discussion**

(a)   **The Pharisees,** according to Josephus, numbered over 6,000 in the time of Herod the Great. Their teachings and attitudes were shared by a far greater number. They were descended, it seems, from the '*Hasidim*', the 'godly ones' who stood out against religious and political compromise in the era of the Maccabees and the Hasmonean rulers. The name 'Pharisees' probably meant 'separated', and they can indeed be regarded as the puritan party in Judaism, standing for scrupulous correctness of observance and aloofness from any contact with the ungodly multitude who 'knew not the Law' (cf. *John* 7:49). They gave a large place to authoritative tradition as well as to the Hebrew Scriptures, and they admitted doctrines—such as belief in the immortality of the soul as well as the resurrection of the body, belief in other-worldly rewards and punishments, and detailed beliefs about angels and devils—which their opponents, the Sadducees, rejected as unscriptural and alleged to be imported from alien sources. Most of the 'scribes' or 'lawyers', the professional teachers and interpreters of the Mosaic law, belonged to the party of the Pharisees.

4.7   The Pharisees are presented in a very unfavourable light in the Gospels, as self-righteous hypocrites, harsh legalists and implacable enemies of Jesus (e.g. *Matt.* 23:1–36; *Luke* 37–53; and *passim* in *John*). Jewish sources, however, present the zeal and devotion of the Pharisees much more favourably. It was as a 'Pharisee born and bred' that Paul had been trained up in the strictest piety and zeal for the Law (*Acts* 22:3; 23:6–9; *Galatians* 1:13–14). It was the Pharisees who restored the Jewish sense of nationhood and purpose after the disaster of AD 70, and from that date onwards they became the predominant religious movement in Judaism.

4.8   (b)   **The Sadducees** were the 'establishment' party, drawn from a relatively few wealthy and priestly families. The High Priests were chosen from among these families, which dominated the Sanhedrin, or national religious council. They were conservative in doctrinal matters, sophisticated and cynical in manipulating their power and influence for worldly ends. The preference of the people was firmly against them and in favour of the Pharisees, and the Sadducean leaders found it politic to take heed of popular sentiment and of the programme of the Pharisees in their conduct of affairs. *Acts* 23:6–9 refers to the doctrinal antagonism between Sadducees and Pharisees.

4.9 (c) **The Herodians,** referred to more than once in the Gospels as enemies of Jesus (*Mark* 3:6; 12:13), were not a sect. They were the supporters of Herodian rule, and especially of Herod Antipas, and thus, by implication, of the Roman authority that maintained the Herodian princes in office. With them may be mentioned the **'Hellenists'** (cf. *Acts* 6:1), the numerous Greek-speaking Jews, whose cultural outlook was usually more liberal than that of the strict 'Hebrews'. The great majority of all Jews were, of course, 'Hellenists' in this sense, since Greek was spoken everywhere by the Jews of the Diaspora. Alexandria was the principal centre of Jewish culture expressed in the Greek language. Although Aramaic and Hebrew-speaking Jews looked askance at their hellenized co-religionists, the latter were often intensely loyal to the Law and the Temple. Recent scholarship has shown that Hellenist influence even in Palestinian Judaism was greater than was hitherto supposed, and that hard-and-fast boundaries cannot be drawn here. Hellenist Jews were to provide most of the first converts in the primitive Church and to make possible its missionary expansion.

4.10 (d) **The Essenes** were one of the puritan groups who, in the tradition of the *Hasidim*, withdrew into strict separation—stricter even than that of the Pharisees—to avoid all contact with the ungodly. They are not mentioned by name in the New Testament, but we know a fair amount about them from Josephus, Philo and Pliny. Their adherents are said to have numbered about 4,000. There were enclosed communities of Essenes who led an ascetic and almost monastic life. Their way of life was much respected, even by those who did not follow it.

4.11 (e) **The Qumran Sect:** In the years from 1947 onwards fascinating discoveries were made at Ain Feshka and Qumran, among the desert cliffs near the north-west shores of the Dead Sea. A considerable quantity of manuscript literature, known as 'The Dead Sea Scrolls', was brought to light, and the remains of a complex of buildings, which had been the headquarters of a religious sect in the second and first centuries BC and the first century AD, were excavated. It was an archaeological discovery of the first magnitude, and for years the learned world resounded with reports and reactions. At times the discussions were heated. There were spirited controversies as scholars put forward rival theories, claims and counter-claims. Some authors even asserted that the Qumran discoveries had changed the whole picture of the origins of Christianity.

4.12 Chief interest centred on the enigmatic 'Teacher of Righteousness', on his role as founder-hero of the Qumran sect and on the place of the sect in contemporary Judaism. Evidently it was not a central place. Its members were ultra-separatists fanatically exclusive in their zeal for legal purity. They repudiated the authority of the official priesthood and would have nothing to do with the Temple ritual which was the focal point of Jewish religious observance. In their fastness in the desert hills, away from the haunts of the ungodly, they observed their own cenobitical discipline and rites, with a regular rhythm of prayer, work and study of the holy Law. Nevertheless, for all their apartness, they shared the nationalist expectations of their fellow-countrymen to an intense degree. They looked forward to a final apocalyptic conflict in which the faithful Jews, God's elect, would wreak his vengeance on the children of darkness. It appears that the Qumran community shared in the national ruin of the war of AD 66–73. The settlement was destroyed and its members either slain or dispersed.

4.13 After some twenty-five years of intensive study and discussion of the Qumran documents and sites, we can stand back from the controversies and survey the positive gains. It is now generally agreed that the Qumran Sect had strong affinities with the Essenes, and it seems very probable that the complex known as Khirbet Qumran was in fact the main Essene centre mentioned by Pliny as sited in that very locality. On pages 53–6 of his book Filson gives a brief résumé of the main facts about the Qumran community, and discusses similarities and dissimilarities with the early Christian movement. The Qumran discoveries have in many ways been of great importance and interest for scholarship, clarifying and adding many details to what was previously known about Jewish religious movements and ideas in the 'inter-testamentary' period. They have also posed several problems which still require further study. However, now that the first excitement and the dust of controversy has subsided, it cannot be seriously maintained that they have given us a significantly different picture of the origins of Christianity.

4.14 (f) **The Zealots** were men who turned to violence in pursuit of their ideals. The Pharisees, the Essenes and the Qumran sectaries, and indeed all observant Jews, deplored the pollution that came from contact with the Gentile world, and especially the rule of ungodly foreigners over Israel. But the opposition of the Zealots took the form of militant resistance to any compromise. They were ready to resort to the sword or dagger in pursuit of their objectives, and they looked back to the successful Maccabean revolt two centuries earlier for their model. Between AD 6, the date of the first direct take-over of power in Judaea by the Romans, with its accompanying census (cf. *Acts* 5:37), and AD 66, when the great rebellion against Rome broke out, bands of Zealots, in fact if not in name, were constantly demonstrating their fanatical readiness to fight and die for the honour of their God and Law and for the independence of his people. They can hardly be regarded as an organized party during all those years, but their spirit of righteous ruthlessness, ever ready to strike down enemies and traitors to the national cause, was much respected by the common people, and is a constant feature of Jewish history throughout the period we are considering. One of Jesus's chosen Apostles was named Simon the Zealot (*Luke* 6:15). There were many, both admirers and enemies, who thought that Jesus might prove to be a national resistance leader who could rally the people to an armed uprising against foreign rule.

4.15 (g) **John the Baptist and his disciples** were a religious group who made a considerable impact on Jewish society and even farther afield. John was a revivalist preacher of repentance and spiritual purification who made a great stir in the years from about AD 26 to 28. Some of his ascetic practices were akin to those of the Essenes, and the scene of his ministry was not far from the Qumran locality. However, his lone mission to the multitudes was quite unlike the aloof communal discipline of the Qumran sect. His influence, and the alarmed reaction of Herod Antipas, is attested by Josephus as well as in the Gospels, where an important role is ascribed to John as the 'forerunner' of Jesus. Some of those who heard the Baptist's message became followers of Jesus. We see from *Acts* (18:24–6; 19:1–7) that many years later there were still disciples, even in Asia Minor, who honoured the memory of the austere prophet and practised 'the baptism of John'.

4.16 (h) **The Messianic expectation** should be mentioned as a generalized movement throughout the Jewish world, not confined to any of the various sects, parties or groups so far mentioned. Jews everywhere were borne up by the hope of the speedy coming of the Messiah, the Davidic king and national leader promised for so long (e.g. *Samuel* 7:8–16; *Isaiah* 9:2–7; *Jeremiah* 33:14–16; *Psalms* 89:19–37, *Daniel* 9:25–7; etc.), who would usher in 'the Day of the Lord', a new golden age in which all Israel's ills would be set to rights. The followers of Jesus would acclaim him as this eagerly awaited Messiah. The sense of expectant excitement was heightened by the apocalyptic prophecies which were circulating about this time. Although there was this general expectation of the

Messiah, there was no clear picture of what he would be like or how he would appear on the scene. Some fringe groups even looked for the descent of a celestial figure who was visualized as a kind of chamberlain at the throne of God. I shall be saying more about this concept later, in §§ 13.22–23. Although the Messianic expectation centred mainly on the concept of a nationalist and military Messiah, there were also some inklings, based on scriptural texts like the Isaian Servant Songs (especially *Isaiah* 52:13–53:12), of a suffering and atoning Messiah, who would have a more universal and spiritual mission.

4.17 (i) **The 'sheep without a shepherd'**: We must remember that the majority of Jews in that period were folk of poor estate, whom Jesus would liken to 'sheep without a shepherd' (*Matt.* 9:36), and who did not belong to any organized sect or party. For some, the religious traditions of their race had ceased to seem important, and these did not scruple to rub shoulders with their unbelieving neighbours or to adopt some of their ways of acting and thinking. Most, however, clung to their ancestral faith and customs, honouring the name of Yahweh, though unskilled in the niceties of the Law and having little contact with the religious leaders, scribes and lawyers, who despised them. It was to be a bitter reproach levelled against Jesus by his puritan critics that he mixed with this ritually unclean rabble (*Mark* 7:1–5).

4.18 (j) **The Church as a Jewish sect:** The primitive Christian Church was for a time regarded as a Jewish sect—'the sect of the Nazarenes' (*Acts* 24:5). In this course our primary concern is to trace the rise and early growth of the Christian movement, so we shall not be saying much about the further progress of the parties and movements within Judaism after the Christian communities had formed a separate Church. As a consequence of the fall of Jerusalem in AD 70 Pharisaism became dominant over all other sects, and a new chapter opened in the history of Judaism. It can be argued that these later developments did affect the progress of the growing Christian Church. Can you suggest how?

✠ ✠

An answer: If the disastrous war of AD 66–73 had not occurred it is possible that the latitude allowed by the existing sectarian pluralism within Judaism would have enabled the Judaeo-Christian church to continue as a kind of heterodox Jewish sect. At the same time the Christian community of Jerusalem would have retained the primacy it undoubtedly possessed in the apostolic Church. In such circumstances the development of the Church's mission could well have followed a different course. In all probability there would have been a further increase in the tension that already existed between the Jerusalem leadership and Gentile Christianity, ending perhaps in open schism. Even as it was, the Judaeo-Christian groups drew apart from the Gentile churches, but since the former no longer possessed a primacy, the development of the main Church was little affected by the estrangement.

4.19 The non-Jewish world

The seed-ground in which Christianity sprang up was the Jewish religious culture, but it was also conditioned in its growth by religious and cultural factors in the wider non-Jewish environment. This is especially true of the second phase of development, when 'the sect of the Nazarenes' began to spread its influence farther afield, and from the original nucleus of believers in Palestine missionaries went out to found Christian communities in Syria, Asia Minor, Greece and in Rome itself. In Units 10–11 John Ferguson discussed

Figure 12   The Church of the Nativity at Bethlehem. (Matson Photo Service, California.)

the religions of the contemporary Roman empire, and in Units 4–5 he described the main philosophical schools of the age. What was the reaction of Christianity to the existing religions and systems of thought with which it came into contact? In the main, it was one of firm insistence on its own uniqueness, and an attitude of spiritual aloofness from all pagan cults, as befitted the 'new Israel' and the people of the 'New Covenant'. But when one probes more deeply one finds that the barriers between the new faith and what we are accustomed to call 'Graeco-Roman paganism' were by no means impenetrable. A study of the documents of the early Church, especially as it grew more remote from its Jewish origins, shows that it did assimilate something from the philosophies and religious outlooks it encountered in the Graeco-Roman world. Indeed, it was impossible for the emerging Christian Church not to be affected to some extent by the environment in which it was taking shape, from which it had to make its converts in order to survive and expand, and the language of which it had to use to express its beliefs and its way of life.

Figure 13   A scene from the Andrews diptych which depicts miracles of Christ. This panel shows the miracle at Cana. Jesus changes water into wine. The Andrews diptych is in ivory. Experts dispute whether the diptych is of the fifth century or the ninth. (Victoria and Albert Museum.)

4.20   Here is a simple test to illustrate the point that even the apostolic Church could not avoid contact with pagan beliefs and theories, however alien it considered them to the truth of God revealed in Christ. Review Chapters 14, 17 and 19 of the *Acts of the Apostles*, and point out: (a) texts which explicitly mention the encounter of the Apostle Paul with some of the pagan religions referred to in Units 10–11; and (b) a text which refers to an encounter of Paul with members of the philosophical schools mentioned by John Ferguson in Units 4–5.

✠ ✠

4.21   *Answer:* (a)   *Acts* 14:11–18 describes how at Lystra in Lycaonia the people acclaimed Paul and Barnabas as gods of Olympus come down in human form. They identified Barnabas as Zeus (Jupiter) and Paul as Hermes (Mercury), because he had the gift of eloquence. (Sir William Ramsay found a dedicatory inscription at Lystra which shows that Zeus and Hermes were linked in the local cult there.) Again, in *Acts* 19:23–41 there is an account of the serious riot at Ephesus when it appeared that Paul's preaching was a threat to the cult of the goddess Artemis (Diana).

4.22   (b)   In *Acts* 17:16–34 the author once more describes Paul's hostility to the worship of pagan gods and idols, this time at Athens, and also how he joined issue with 'some of the Epicurean and Stoic philosophers' (verse 18). He then preached a sermon in words chosen to appeal to his sophisticated audience, and even made allusions to religious sentiments expressed by two classical authors (Epimenides and Aratus).

4.23   The question whether Christian theology and cult were affected by ideas and practices drawn from the religions of the Hellenistic world, particularly from **the mystery cults**, is one that is much discussed. These mystery religions promised salvation and immortality to their devotees. (cf. Units 10–11, § 5.8.) It can be inferred, from some suggestive scraps of evidence, that the 'mysteries' (*mysteria*) were usually the cultic re-enactment of the ordeal and triumph of a saviour god, which enabled the initiates to share in his vivifying influence. In these mystery cults there were also sacred meals: there is mention of them, for example, in the mysteries of Eleusis, of Attis and Cybele, of Dionysus, of Serapis, of Mithras. Some writers have supposed that the Christian Eucharist belonged to this type of cultic meal.

4.24   It is important to realize, however, how very scanty, late and conjectural is our information about what actually went on in the mystery cults, and what their myths signified. There is no proof that it was Christianity that did the borrowing—at least during the period in which the New Testament was being formed. The *Gospel of John*, where we should most expect to find it, has none of the technical terminology associated with the initiation-rites of the mystery religions. Paul often uses the word 'mystery' (*mysterion*), but I think he plainly took it, like so much of his religious vocabulary, from the Greek Septuaguint translation of the Jewish Bible, where it signifies 'a secret', often in the sense of 'a hidden matter revealed by divine aid' (e.g. *Dan.* 2.47). I do not say that it is impossible that New Testament sacramentalism could have been influenced by notions taken from the pagan mystery cults: only that it is not proven. There is a useful corrective to facile assertions on this point in A. D. Nock's *Early Gentile Christianity and its Hellenistic Background* (Harper Torchbooks 1964).

If early Christianity is to be classed among the mystery religions, it had this distinctive difference from all the others—that it was based on a historical person, Jesus of Nazareth, who had lived and died only a short time previously. In the fourteenth radio programme I speak about the theory that the Eucharist was a rite of the mystery-cult type. I argue that when looking for antecedents and parallels to the Eucharistic Supper more light can be gained by consideration of the contemporary Jewish Passover rite (cf. § 9.33–4 below). You may also compare my remarks with what John Ferguson said on the subject in Units 10–11, § 5.8. Is there a contradiction between what is said there and here?

✠✠✠✠✠✠✠✠✠✠✠✠✠✠✠✠✠✠✠✠✠✠✠✠✠

My answer: Not necessarily. There is obviously a difference of opinion about the implications of Paul's use of a term like *mysterion*. Although in that section John Ferguson points to a parallel between Christianity and the eastern mystery religions, he does not assert that there was a substantial borrowing by Christianity from those mystery religions.

Figure 14 Inscription recently found near Nazareth, mentioning the name of Pontius Pilate in the second line. This is the first epigraphical reference to Pilate ever discovered. (Israel Department of Antiquities and Museums.)

4.25   Syncretism, Gnosticism and Christian doctrines

While on this subject I must say something more about what is called **religious syncretism**, which means the tendency to bring together elements from different religions and cultures to form a more comprehensive and more flexible system of religious thought and practice. For an understanding of the survival and development of Christianity in its second phase, in the later part of the first century and during the second century, some knowledge is required of the great current of religious syncretism which was agitating the Hellenistic and near-eastern world about the time that Christianity was beginning to take root. Traditionally, Church historians represent Christianity as the only vital religious movement in a world which had become morally and spiritually bankrupt. Whatever one may hold about the uniqueness of the Christian religion, however, the view that the world surrounding it was sunk in spiritual despair and religious stagnation must be revised. It is becoming more clearly realized that the period we are considering was one of general religious vitality and creativeness, even though the forms which this movement took were richly diverse and often very strange. From your reading so far in this course, from the texts given in Lewis and Reinhold, pages 568–80, and from your general knowledge, can you mention some of the elements which went into that religious melting-pot of ideas and practices?

✠✠✠✠✠✠✠✠✠✠✠✠✠✠✠✠✠✠✠✠✠✠✠✠✠

4.26 *Answer:* There was a current of **dualistic religion**, derived originally from Iran, holding the existence of two opposing ultimate principles, one of good and one of evil; there were the **mystery cults** I have just referred to, with their salvation myths, their rites of initiation and their assurance of life after death in other-worldly bliss; there was veneration of the **tutelary spirits** of the home and fields, of the woods and waters, such as those described in Units 10–11, §§ 5.2–3 and 5.5, and in Units 12, § 3.5.3, III(d); there were the traditional **temple shrines**, almost everywhere still in vigorous activity as centres of popular devotion,[1] although among the more sophisticated the trend was to allegorize the old religion of the gods of Olympus; there was a widely prevalent trust in **astrology**, the occult wisdom of Babylonia; there was avid recourse to fortune-telling, superstition and **magic**; there was an influence from Jewish religious ideas, in particular from the **apocalyptic writings** of fringe groups in Judaism, and also a powerful undercurrent of anti-Jewish religious feeling; there was the world-denying mysticism of later **Platonism**, and the secret lore of the **Neo-Pythagoreans**; there were echoes of **the wisdom of India** and the yearning for Nirvana; and there was the religious outlook of the **Stoic philosophers,** with their stress on the universal brotherhood of man, their lofty moral code, and their elitist programme of perfection through self-mastery.

Figure 15 Jesus heals a blind man. A scene from the Andrews diptych (Victoria and Albert Museum.)

4.27 When Christianity began to be spoken of as a powerful new divine revelation, with its secret wisdom and rites, it attracted interest and imitation far beyond the circle of the relatively small and scattered communities of believers whom we speak of as 'the early Church'. In that wider sphere of religious syncretism the doctrines, practices and writings of Christianity were taken up, modified into bizarre forms, and fused with the other diverse elements I have mentioned to form a new blend of religion. Out of that sea of swirling currents of thought there arose a new wave of religious enthusiasm, which was to present a threat to the Christian Church in the second century more serious than any outward persecution—the movement called Gnosticism (from the Greek word *gnosis*, or 'knowledge'; see Filson, pp. 350–4). Gnosticism promised salvation by imparting to its initiates a divine wisdom and the secret of self-knowledge which, combined with astrological and magical techniques, would enable them to escape from their material predicament, to defeat the adverse cosmic powers, and to reach spiritual enlightenment and bliss.

[1] See Illustrations 65–83 in your set book, *Roman Art and Architecture*, by Mortimer Wheeler.

40

4.28 There may well have been a Jewish Gnosticism and a pagan Gnosticism, but what concerns us here is what is called Christian Gnosticism, about which we are quite well informed from ancient sources. These Gnostics claimed to possess special revelations from Jesus Christ and from his Apostles. Their cosmogony, borrowing from the speculations of later Platonism, included a doctrine of *aeons* or spiritual emanations from the supreme principle of good. The creator of the material world was, according to some, an independent principle of evil; according to others, he was the God of the Old Testament, a Demiurge who was distinct from the loving and merciful Father God of the New Testament.

Jesus Christ featured prominently in these Gnostic systems. He was portrayed as a kind of demigod emanating from the supreme God, as a heavenly redeemer descending to rescue the sparks of spiritual reality imprisoned in the darkness of the material world. Since they held matter to be evil, the Gnostics played down or denied the reality of Christ's incarnation. Those called 'Docetists' held that Christ only *appeared* to have an ordinary material body; that he was a celestial being who was not truly born of Mary, did not truly suffer the vicissitudes of bodily life, and did not truly die the death of crucifixion. In the New Testament, in particular in the Johannine writings, reaction against Docetism is already expressed. (e.g. *John* 1:14; 4:6; 19:28, 30, 34; *1 John* 4:2–3; *2 John* 7.) Docetic notions are also vehemently condemned in the letters of Ignatius of Antioch at the beginning of the second century. Some Gnostics distinguished between a mere man, Jesus, and a supernal being, Christ, who dwelt in him.

Figure 16 The Sea of Galilee today, with Tiberias in the foreground. (J. Allan Cash.)

4.29 **When did Gnosticism originate?** Was Gnosticism a syncretistic adaptation of New Testament Christianity, or was New Testament Christianity perhaps an adaptation of Gnosticism? At the time that Christianity was beginning to spread from its Palestinian homeland, some ideas akin to those of later Gnosticism were already 'in the air', as we can see from remarks in Paul's letters to the Corinthians and Colossians. We do not, however, find evidence of an organized Gnostic religion, system or sect at that time. When we come to discuss the emergence of early Christianity we must indeed consider the possibility that what we call Gnosticism may have provided the mythological framework in which Paul and other New Testament writers expressed their understanding of the Christian revelation. This in fact is the thesis of Rudolf Bultmann (e.g. in *The Theology of the New Testament*, Vol. I, pp. 164–83; English trans., S.C.M. Press 1952). He and his school assert this thesis mainly on the basis of similarities between some New Testament concepts and what we know of Gnosticism in the later second century. They provide little actual evidence to prove that Gnostic theological categories were in fact already available in the second half of the first century to express the distinctive New Testament doctrines which they think were cast in a mythological mould. (Except, perhaps, in their appeal to the notion of a celestial 'Son of Man'. Whether this can rightly be called 'a Gnostic myth' or not, it was admittedly already present in Jewish apocalyptic thought. See §§ 13.21–27 below.)

4.30 Bultmann's work has created a profound stir in the world of biblical scholarship during the past thirty-five years or so. He holds that in the Christian religion there is an authentic divine message, of timeless and absolute value for human existence, but its permanent relevance can only be grasped when it is liberated from its fortuitous wrappings of myth. Evidently when this programme of 'demythologizing' the New Testament is pursued with logical rigour, it must make a radical difference not only to Christians' intellectual understanding of their faith, but also to their ways of prayer and piety.

Figure 17 Another scene from the Andrews diptych. Jesus heals the paralytic and bids him to take up his bed and walk. (Victoria and Albert Museum.)

4.31 If evidence is lacking to prove that early Christianity borrowed its distinctive beliefs from Gnosticism, there is evidence in plenty (especially since the discovery of an extensive Gnostic library at Nag Hammadi in Egypt in 1945–6) that later Gnostic sects borrowed boldly from New Testament Christianity, and were eager to claim the authority of Christ's Apostles for their own fanciful conceptions and apocryphal writings. By the end of the period we are considering in this course, Gnosticism was infiltrating the Christian communities, presenting a radically different creed under the guise of Christianity. Its main areas of origin were Syria and Egypt, but it spread throughout the empire. This, of course, is looking ahead. It is a development we shall have to bear in mind while we are studying the history of the early Church. We shall see that reaction against the Gnostic threat was a principal factor in bringing the Church of mainstream Christianity to define its credentials and to consolidate its structures and institutions (cf. §§ 17.3, 17.10–13 below).

4.32 At the same time we must recognize that in this later confrontation of the Church with Gnosticism the traffic in ideas, terminology and ritual practices was not all in one direction. There were Gnostic thinkers of great metaphysical subtlety, and there were Gnostic devotional practices that appealed to the religious sensibilities of the people. The Gnostic system did possess a certain creative genius and a religious dynamic; it could not be dismissed by a merely negative polemic. Its challenge had to be met in an intellectual encounter. When, from the end of the second century onwards, Christian speculative theology began to develop, especially in Alexandria, Christian thinkers were not uninfluenced by the writings and spiritual outlook of their Gnostic adversaries. It is becoming clearer that some elements of Gnostic thought and practice were adapted subsequently and absorbed into the theology and devotional observances of the main Christian Church. But since these developments took place after the period we are studying in this course, we cannot pursue them in these pages.

5.0 (D) JESUS OF NAZARETH

What we have done so far is to survey the environment in which Christianity arose. It is evident that at the centre of our study must stand the enigmatic figure of Jesus of Nazareth. In the early Church men did not speak of the abstract term 'Christianity', but they spoke much about 'The Lord Jesus Christ'. They were not concerned with semantic problems of religious language, nor with discussions about the history of religions, nor with theories of social reform. They concentrated with single-minded devotion on the person of Jesus. They thought of him not only as a great and good man who had been unjustly put to death (though they did indeed place great stress on the fact and consequences of his death); not only as a teacher of noble ideals; not only as the founder of their movement who had given it the initial impetus and fired others with enthusiasm to continue it; but as **the Risen Lord,** the one who was now permanently and mysteriously alive and in whom they found a new kind of life for themselves, uniting them with him and with one another. It was not a dead victim but the living Christ, the source of Spirit, life, love and power, whom they proclaimed. It was this Christ-centred conviction that gave dynamism to the new movement, and that marked out its converts wherever it spread.

5.1 Can we know facts about 'the Jesus of history'?

What did those early converts know about Jesus of Nazareth as a historical personage? Indeed what can *we* know with certainty about 'the Jesus of history' (a phrase which is often used in contradistinction to 'the Christ of faith')? Traditionally, Christians look to the four Gospels as the documentary sources for their knowledge of what Jesus did, taught, suffered and achieved. The word 'gospel' is the English translation of the Greek *euangelion*, which means 'good news'. Many Christians, scholars as well as simple believers, would argue that the figure of the historical Jesus, and the salient facts about his ministry, stand out with unmistakable clarity from the pages of the Gospels. They would put the case as follows:

From those writings, it must surely be admitted, there emerges the picture of a character of extraordinary nobility and energy. The four evangelists narrate the sayings and doings of Jesus in language which is concise and restrained, yet powerful and evocative. They show him as a Jew whose life and thought was set authentically in the world of Jewish traditions and aspirations. They give concordant emphasis to the account of his trial, sufferings, death and resurrection. Those who come to read the Gospel story of Jesus of Nazareth with a fresh and open mind rarely fail to be impressed and moved by what they read. The Gospels bring their central character vividly before the reader, or at least convey to the reader something of the vivid impression he made on the crowds who flocked round him and on his closest associates. Despite the evangelists' differences in style and expression, and despite the variety of strands woven together to make up their narratives, the character of Jesus as shown in the Gospels remains distinctive, integrated, coherent and unique. The scriptural record of his life and death, so it is urged, resounds with the very ring of truth. Is not this the fountain-head of Christian history, explaining all that followed? Surely the Gospels can be accepted as proof of Christianity's claim to be rooted in historical events?

5.2 The Gospels certainly purport to tell us about the life and teaching of Jesus, what happened, and with what consequences. On an uncritical reading of them, one might assume that they are straightforward historical records. But on closer study, the matter of 'Gospel truth' is found to be not so simple. Can you give some reasons why scholars are cautious about accepting the Gospels as historical records in the ordinary sense?

✠ ✠

Some points for an answer: Our written Gospels do not date from the actual lifetime of Jesus Christ, and they present many puzzling features. The earliest of them was probably not compiled until about thirty years after his death. They were·not written in Aramaic (the language of Jesus and his disciples) but in Greek. There are obvious similarities between the first three, *Matthew*, *Mark* and *Luke*, which are called the 'Synoptic Gospels'. (This name means that they give their narrative 'from the same viewpoint'; the 'Synoptics' are thus distinguished from the Fourth Gospel, *John*, which was written later and has its own distinctive perspective.) But as well as a large measure of verbatim agreement between the first three Gospels, there are also intriguing dissimilarities and sometimes discrepancies between them. There are many relatively minor but sometimes significant differences of wording in the way they narrate the same episode; one or other of the Gospels contain passages that the others do not; and their order, arrangement and editing of the material differ quite considerably. So an intricate literary problem arises about which Gospel depends on which, and to what extent. It is complicated by their evident dependence on other sources which have not survived. Moreover, although the Gospels purport to relate what Christ did and said, they are found to have implicit allusions to the needs and controversies of the growing Christian communities at a somewhat later time. Doctrinal preoccupations govern the evangelists' use of their material. Finally, there is a more fundamental reason why some critics call into question the historicity of the Gospels: namely, because they contain accounts of miraculous happenings, and of divine or supernatural intervention in the course of events, which seem to those critics to belong to the realm of mythology rather than history.

5.3 Form Criticism of the Gospels

Whatever one may think about the historical possibility or impossibility of miracles or of divine intervention in human affairs, it is at least now evident that the process of the formation of the Gospels was not nearly so simple as Christians have traditionally supposed until quite recent times. During the past fifty years a refined technique of biblical study known as **'Form Criticism'** has been developed, which has brought about considerable advances in the understanding of this process of Gospel formation. This technique seeks to

identify the various component elements of the Gospels and to classify them in various categories. Different authors use different terminology, but there is now fairly common agreement in classifying the Gospel materials in five main categories: 'pronouncement stories', 'miracle stories', 'sayings and parables', 'stories about Jesus', and the long concluding 'Passion narrative' (cf. the first Arts Foundation Course, A100, Units 19–20, §§ 3.3–3.3.4).

Figure 18 The earliest known fragment of New Testament manuscript. This piece of papyrus, dating from the first half of the second century, contains words from the Gospel of John. *(John Rylands Library, Manchester.)*

The Form Critics aimed to explain the origin and purpose of each textual item, or at least the reason for its preservation, by getting back to its *Sitz im Leben*, or the 'life situation' in the community in which it was used. Some of them supposed that the Gospel writers found to hand only a motley array of disconnected items, and then linked them into a consecutive narrative—a rather artificial supposition. **'Redaction Criticism'** improves on the earlier methods of Form Criticism by paying special attention to the editorial purpose and method of each individual evangelist. Such editorial factors can explain why a text or pericope is cast in a certain form, and how the connected narrative took shape.

5.4　There have been, needless to say, heated controversies in this field of scholarship and not all the findings of Form and Redaction Criticism have proved equally useful. The more radical exponents of these methods have argued that the Gospels tell us nothing certain about the historical Jesus, but reveal simply the faith of the developing Christian communities and the early Church's reflection on its own spiritual experience and needs. Many other scholars, however, reject this view as arbitrary and one-sided. Filson puts forward some pertinent considerations on this question on pages 75–82, which may help you to gain a fuller perspective. While Form Criticism has produced valuable results and has given us a new understanding of the make-up of the Gospels, it has also provided the occasion for much unsubstantiated conjecture. At times it has degenerated into a mere guessing game, with authors vying with one another to produce ingenious hypotheses and reconstructions. When you come across some of this kind of writing, use your critical faculty to distinguish what is well-founded analysis from what is merely a clever but unproved hunch.

5.5　A less radical and, to my mind, more common-sense explanation of the origin of the Synoptic Gospels can be stated as follows. Following the normal practice among the Jews, the first disciples of Jesus committed to memory the teachings of their master and also facts about him which they considered important to recall. These oral traditions were passed on in fairly standardized forms, but

45

naturally with many individual variations. Jesus and his first followers doubt-less preached only in Aramaic (though some at least of them may well have known Greek, for that language was widely used in Palestine, especially in Galilee). At a fairly early date, the first Aramaic preaching material would have been rendered into Greek, for the sake both of the Jewish-Christian 'Hellen-ists' and of the Gentile converts. Various elements in this tradition were modi-fied, adapted and added to, according to the situation and requirements of groups of Christians during the first few decades of the Church's existence. During this period before the Synoptic Gospels were written, it is not unlikely that written materials were already being used by teachers to aid them in their proclamation of the main elements of the Christian message. These elements evidently included collections of pithy sayings of Jesus, summaries of his parables, anthologies of 'proof-texts' from the Old Testament to show how in Christ the scriptural predictions were fulfilled, and also a continuous narrative of the closing period of his ministry.

Figure 19 Jesus heals a leper: scene from the Andrews diptych. (Victoria and Albert Museum.)

So well developed was the art of memory among the Jews, that it is not essen-tial to postulate the existence of *written* aids in the earliest period of Christianity. But at least when the new faith spread farther afield, oral transmission of the message would no longer be sufficient for Greek-speaking teachers and their disciples, accustomed to having things in writing. So eventually the Christian 'good news', as it had been received from the apostolic preaching and moulded in the usage of the local communities, was cast into the form that we call Gos-pels, some time during the second half of the first century.

5.6 It is clear enough that the evangelists did have an overriding theological purpose, that they did edit the materials they incorporated in their accounts, and that the appearance of chronological sequence in their narrative is often a literary or mnemonic device to link together disparate items of the tradition. Yet it is also clear that they did not start merely with disconnected items, and that they did not originate the process of forming a connected narrative. What is the chief passage in the Gospels which could be cited in justification of this last assertion? (I have already mentioned it more than once.)

✠✠✠✠✠✠✠✠✠✠✠✠✠✠✠✠✠✠✠✠✠✠✠✠

Answer: All three synoptic evangelists reproduce in substantially the same order the 'Passion narrative', which had evidently been handed on in a standardized sequence from the earliest period. This fairly lengthy account describes the climax of Christ's life and ministry—the events in Jerusalem, his Last Supper, arrest, trials, crucifixion and resurrection. The first Christians evidently considered this account to be of great importance, and we see from Paul's letters and from *Acts* that it formed the core of their 'good news'.

5.7 The 'gospel before the Gospels'

It is now usually agreed that the author of *Mark* was the pioneer in the process of formulating the earlier tradition in a written Gospel, and that the authors of *Matthew* and *Luke* used Mark's first summary as the main basis of their longer and more literary works, supplementing it from other sources. However, there are too many unresolved questions in the fascinating puzzle known as 'the Synoptic problem' to say that any of the theories so far proposed about the interrelationships between the Greek texts of the first three Gospels is completely satisfactory. While there are persuasive reasons, based on textual comparison and criticism, for inferring that there is a literary dependence of *Matthew* and *Luke* on *Mark*, there are also a few awkward instances in which it appears much more probable that *Matthew* or *Luke* have preserved a more primitive and authentic form of a phrase or a pericope than *Mark*. It is at least clear that lying behind the three Synoptic Gospels, and providing material for them all, were earlier accounts which must have been already current in a fairly standardized form of expression, whether in writing or in oral recitation.

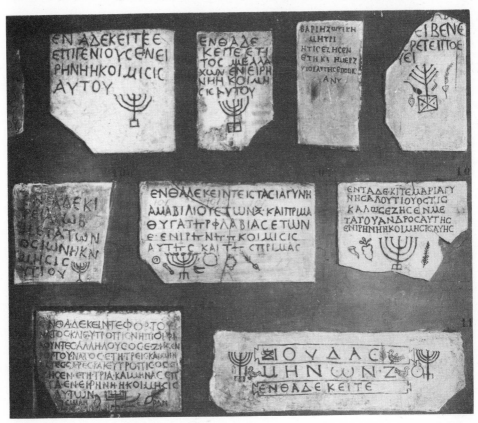

Figure 20 Inscriptions in Greek from the Jewish catacombs of Monteverde, Rome. Note the design of the Menorah, or seven-branched candlestick. This catacomb was in use in the first century AD. (Pontifical Archaeological Commission.)

5.8 This 'gospel before the Gospels' was being preached as the vital message in the first Christian communities in the formative period of Christianity before there was any New Testament to read. Remember that of the writings later included in the canon of the New Testament the earliest in date were the letters of Paul, which belong to a period from the late forties to the early sixties of the first century. In those letters Paul makes a number of references to matters which we find also spoken of in the Gospels, and what he says concords with what the Gospels say about Christ. He quotes directly a narrative of Christ's Last Supper which corresponds closely to the accounts later written down by the authors of the Synoptic Gospels. Evidently this particular passage had become crystallized in liturgical usage, and Paul himself testifies that the Lord's Supper was being regularly celebrated in the communities of his time. Apart from this stylized repetition of Christ's words at the Last Supper, however, we can find in Paul's writings hardly any other verbatim parallels to the text of the Gospels. This is not a proof that the tradition was not yet standardized at the time he was writing. There is a similar absence of Gospel quotations in the *Acts of the Apostles*, which contain several reports of Paul's preaching about Jesus Christ; yet the author of *Acts* was certainly familiar with the Gospel story and its traditional formulation, for he was himself the author of the *Gospel according to Luke*.

5.9 Paul insistently distinguishes between his own instructions or interpretations of Christian teaching and what he expressly calls 'not mine, but the Lord's ruling' (*1 Corinthians* 7:10–11; cf. *Mark* 10:9–12). This was less than thirty years after the time of Christ's preaching, and there were many people still alive who from their personal recollections could have challenged Paul, had he attempted to invent statements about Christ's rulings.

5.10 *The Gospel according to John* is, of course, in a different category from that of Synoptics. It is a profound theological meditation, and it represents a later stage and a considerable development of the faith of the Church. Yet even there, it would be unwarranted to suppose that *John* cannot contain authentic original traditions going back to the time of Jesus.[1]

Figure 21   Another mircale of Jesus, as shown on the Andrews diptych: the miraculous multiplication of loaves and fishes to feed the five thousand. (Victoria and Albert Museum.)

5.11   Myth and authenticity

I mentioned earlier a presupposition lying behind much radical criticism of the Gospels, one which lays all the contents of those writings open to suspicion. It is argued that since they relate miraculous and supernatural happenings, which, however credible they may have seemed in past ages, are simply incredible to modern man, the Gospels cannot be supposed to provide reliable

[1] On this point, see C. H. Dodd's *Historical Tradition in the Fourth Gospel* (Cambridge University Press, 1963).

48

testimony about the historical Jesus. Somehow, at some time in the shadowy decades of the early Church, it is assumed that a body of legends and dogmas about Jesus must have grown up and taken shape as the primal myth on which Christianity was founded. This objection provides us with the opportunity of pausing for reflection at this point. You may well have your own views, for or against the position of the critics I have just mentioned. In any case, can you suggest some counter-objections which might be brought against their view?

✠ ✠

5.12   *Points for an answer:* The point I made in § 5.9 about Paul's personal recollections is relevant to discussion of the Gospel record too. When the Gospel was first written down, scarcely more than thirty years had elapsed since Christ's crucifixion. It may reasonably be argued that this is too short a period for the formation of a folk-legend or mythological saga. Over many generations, especially in a primitive society where religious notions are constantly embellished by fantasy and folklore, historical fact can indeed become dissolved in a widening pool of myth; but it is implausible to suggest that the historical facts about Jesus could have been obliterated in a span of about thirty years. C. H. Dodd, one of the most renowned of biblical scholars of this century, once used a homely argument to illustrate this point, referring to the vividness of his own generation's recollections of the beginning of World War I. To adapt his argument to a later generation, it is as if someone today tried to palm off a purely fictitious account of the Battle of Britain in 1940, or tried to get people to accept, as genuine reminiscences, stories about Churchill or Hitler and their conduct of war which bore no relation to the historical truth. There are plenty of us alive today to whom the memory of those years is still fresh and vivid. An invented anecdote about Churchill might easily gain credence, provided it were *ben' trovato* and in keeping with his character. We know that eyewitness accounts of the same events can vary quite widely when it comes to recalling particular details, and that the later historian has to be wary before accepting contemporary war reports at their face value. But it would be impossible to falsify the main pattern of such recent history.

5.13   When we say that the Gospels were not written as history, in our sense of the term, it means that they are not chronicles of events in logical or chronological order; that their first aim is not simply to impart information about past events but to evoke a response of faith in the present; that they are not based on the kind of records and researches that a modern scholar looks for, but on recollections and interpretations current in a closed and intensely fervent religious community; that their authors may indeed colour their narrative with symbolic imagery, using naive and pre-scientific thought-forms; and that they are written with a theological perspective which the historian, *qua* historian, cannot adopt. But it does not mean that they are devoid of validity as sources of authentic knowledge about Jesus of Nazareth, or that they do not preserve any reliable testimonies about what was actually said and done during the period to which they refer. It is possible to admit that the evangelists adapted their message to their audience, and that the Gospels contain symbolic forms of expression, or even legendary accretions, and still recognize in them a bedrock of historical fact.

Perhaps in your answer to my question in § 5.11 you challenged the supposition of the critics who say that 'miracles are incredible to modern man'. You may have objected that it is *a priori* dogmatism to assert that miracles can't happen. It would be more judicious to say that if phenomena are reported which seem to be beyond normal explanation, the evidence must be tested critically; and if the evidence is reliable, an unprejudiced mind will accept that the reported phenomena did occur.

5.14 In the documents available to us, presenting the faith and organization of the Church in the second half of the first century and the early part of the second century, we find no shadow of doubt expressed about the factual foundation of Christianity in the words and work of Christ, no suspicion that the Christian 'good news' was being spun out from the collective self-awareness of the community. The passionate devotion of the Christians to their master and the tenacious conviction of their beliefs concerning him, above all belief in his resurrection, proved capable of steeling them to heroism and martyrdom. Their hostile contemporaries, whose religious tenets were usually more flexible and less demanding, saw their conviction as fanatical obstinacy; but that they held it is a demonstrable fact of history.

5.15 The problems relating to the composition of the Greek Gospels, and the conjectural reconstruction of the elements in the earlier tradition underlying the Gospels, are of absorbing interest, especially to those of us who like literary puzzles. This branch of biblical scholarship has provided occasion for the writing of countless books, learned articles and monographs, and for the display of much ingenuity. But these technical questions need not detain us in this course. The Christian believer is naturally very much concerned to answer the question whether the Gospel texts are reliable records of what Jesus said and did, or whether they are statements of what the developing communities in the primitive Church attributed to Jesus in order to express and satisfy their own spiritual needs. But even if one prefers to leave this question open, one can still study the history of the early Church without being dependent on a definite answer to it. I refer you here to what Dr Nineham has to say on the subject in our thirteenth radio programme.

5.16 The ministry of Jesus

The Gospel story of Jesus lies at the heart of the story of Christianity. Shortly I shall recommend you to take a long pause from reading this course material, to give you the opportunity to read (or to renew your acquaintance with) that story in the pages of the Gospels. The purpose of this reading is to bring home to you what the Christian Church in the later decades of the first century believed and taught about the life, death and resurrection of Jesus.

5.17 Those of you who took the first Arts Foundation Course have already made a fairly thorough study of St Mark's Gospel in the double unit entitled, *What is a Gospel?* You could profitably revise what you studied there, and remind yourself of the content and arrangement of *Mark*. But I should also like to direct your attention to the other two Synoptics. If your time is strictly limited, just read one Gospel, preferably *Matthew* or *Luke*. It is true that *Mark* is of primary interest to biblical scholars. It is the shortest of the Gospels and the reasons for arguing that it was the earliest to be written are persuasive. But for wealth of material and for actual influence in the Church, *Matthew* and *Luke* have a wider historical relevance. We know from evidence of a somewhat later date that *Mark*—probably just because it contained little material that could not be found in *Matthew* or *Luke*—was relatively little read in the early centuries, and hardly any commentaries were written on it by the Church Fathers. *Mark* contains 661 verses; out of these, only 31 are not contained in the other two Synoptics. *Matthew* was the most popular of the Gospels in the Church of antiquity, and therefore the most influential in its early development.

5.18 I will not here attempt to write a 'life of Jesus', but would simply refer you to the pages of the Gospel.[1] Either concurrently with your reading of the Gospel

---

[1] One of the best of modern studies is C. H. Dodd's, *The Founder of Christianity* (Collins 1971), a work of deep scholarly insight yet of masterly simplicity.

or afterwards, read also Chapters 4, 5 and 6 of Filson's book, 'The Galilean Ministry'; 'From Galilee to Jerusalem'; and 'Rejected, Crucified, Risen'. These chapters may serve as a guide for your reading of the Gospel, and will give you useful pointers to further study.

5.19 While you are reading the Synoptic accounts of the ministry of Jesus, I want you to pay special attention to these two questions: (a) What, according to the Synoptic Gospels, was the substance of the **teaching** of Jesus?; and (b) What religious **status or dignity** do they attribute to Jesus? Corresponding to each of these two questions, I will propose an exercise to help you to assimilate the material. The first of these exercises will take up the remaining sections of Part One; the second exercise will be explained in Part Three (§§ 13.0–10), and will take in the data of other New Testament writings as well as the Gospels.

5.20 The teaching of Jesus

The Gospels relate that the teaching of Jesus was expressed not only in exhortations and colourful parables addressed to the crowds who heard him, but also in special instructions to his closer disciples. In the Synoptics the constant theme of Jesus's teaching is 'the Kingdom of God'. (Matthew uses the term 'Kingdom of Heaven', for reasons that are explained by Filson on pages 94–5.) Jesus preached the near approach of this Kingdom, the advent of which would be a crisis and climax for the world. It was vitally urgent for men to enter the Kingdom. **What then was the distinctive character of this religion of the Kingdom of God?** Was it first and foremost a personal religion, a religion of individual conscience, a 'one-to-one' relationship between the believer and God? Or was it a collective movement, requiring a community activity, with specific forms of religious observance, and with recognizable outward marks or even an institutional structure? Or was it something of both? If the latter, where did the emphasis lie? To provide matter for discussion of these questions, I want you in this next exercise to set out briefly some relevant points from the Synoptic Gospels, describing the characteristics of the religion preached by Jesus Christ, under the following two headings: (1) Teaching of Jesus which emphasized **the 'personal' aspect of religion**; (2) Teaching of Jesus which emphasized **the 'community' aspect of religion**. Now, if you have time, settle down to read the text of at least one of the Synoptic Gospels.

A LONG PAUSE HERE
Do not read on until you have worked on the exercise

5.21 **Specimen answers and dicussion**

One answer would be to object to the form of the question. You may retort that neither of my alternatives is applicable, because Jesus was not concerned with the continuance of religion, whether personal or institutional, but only with announcing the imminent approach of the end of the world. According to a thoroughgoing 'eschatological'[1] interpretation of the New Testament writings, the dominant feature of early Christianity was this conviction that the Last Days were close at hand, and that very soon Christ would come again, resplendent in the glory of heaven, to judge the world and to establish his Kingdom. Only when this hope was proved to be illusory did Christians begin to prepare for a longer term, and to substitute the idea of the present Church for that of the eschatological Kingdom. However, I do not think such a negative answer to our exercise adequate. In New Testament Christianity eschatological

---

[1] From the Greek *ta eschata*, 'the last things'. 'Eschatology' refers to what will happen at the end of the world; the term is also used to refer to the ideas of those who think the end of the world is at hand. The classic exponent of the view that Jesus himself was at first carried away by an illusory eschatological enthusiasm was Albert Schweitzer in his book *The Quest of the Historical Jesus* (English trans. 1910).

expectation was certainly intense; but it was quite compatible with concern for bringing individuals to a right relationship with God and for the collective continuance of the mission entrusted by Jesus to his Apostles. The eschatological theme should not be stressed so strongly that other balancing themes are ignored. The apocalyptic pronouncements of Jesus, warning his followers to live in constant readiness for the climax of the world and his own return in heavenly glory, must be taken in conjunction with other of his sayings reported by the evangelists, implying that the Kingdom would be a permanent institution and have an indefinite future, and that it was quite uncertain when the Day of Judgement would be.

Figure 22 Remains of the synagogue at Capernaum on the Sea of Galilee. (Israel Government Tourist Office.)

5.22 You may of course prefer to suppose that these other balancing themes were later strands woven into the tradition to provide the disillusioned Christians with a new anchor-rope when the Last Days and the triumphant return of Christ failed to materialize. There are difficulties in such a theory. But in any case remember that our aim here is not to attempt to distinguish the various strata in the formation of the gospel tradition, but to take that tradition in its formed state and to appreciate how it became normative of the belief and practice of the Church in the subsequent period. My suggested answers to the exercise, then, are as follows:

5.23 **(1) Teaching of Jesus in the Synoptics which emphasized the 'personal aspect' of religion**

(a) All three Synoptic Gospels narrate how Jesus began his public ministry by seeking out the ascetic prophet John the Baptist, the great preacher of personal repentance, and accepting baptism from him (*Matt.* 3; *Mark* 1; *Luke* 3–4). Jesus, too, urgently proclaimed the need for his hearers to 'repent', because the Kingdom of God was at hand (*Matt.* 4:17; *Mark* 1:15.) 'Repenting', for the Jews, meant not merely a change of mental attitude, but a change of outward conduct.

5.24 (b) Jesus taught that God was a loving and caring Father, who watched over his children with a providence that extended to the last detail (*Matt.* 6:25–34); he urged an attitude of filial trustfulness (*Matt.* 7:11).

5.25 (c) Corresponding to the watchful care of the Father over each of his children, the first concern of each man must be wholehearted love of God, with which love of one's neighbour was necessarily bound up (*Matt.* 22:34–40).

5.26 (d) The Kingdom of God, the coming of which was imminent, would bring a divine judgement on the world and on each man. The wicked would be condemned, but there was still time for those who heeded the warning to receive forgiveness as God's free gift. Eternal reward awaited the merciful who fed the hungry, clothed and cared for the outcast, and visited the afflicted; eternal punishment awaited those who failed to do those things. It was Jesus himself whom men served, or failed to serve, in these unfortunates (*Matt.* 25:34–46).

5.27 (e) The Kingdom of God needed no spectacular inauguration; it was not to be recognized 'by observation'. Already 'in fact the Kingdom of God is among you' (*Luke* 17:20–1). The Kingdom could only be entered by those who accepted it with childlike trust (*Luke* 18:16–17).

5.28 (f) Jesus told his followers to pray to the Father 'in secret' and to fast like-wise; 'and your Father who sees in secret will reward you' (*Matt.* 6:5–6, 16–18). He gave them a form of prayer to use to tell the Father of their needs (*Matt.* 6:9–13; *Luke* 11:2–4). He taught them that the prayer which was pleasing to God came from a humble and penitent heart, like that of the publican in the Temple (*Luke* 18:10–14).

5.29 (g) It was not merely outward observance of a code of religious law that counted before God, but inward purity of heart and conscience (*Matt.* 5:27–30; 15:17–20). Each disciple must deny himself, take up his cross daily and follow Jesus. Finding one's own true self was so important that it was better to lose the whole world to gain that end (*Matt.* 16:24–6). Jesus warned his followers against the pursuit of worldly wealth and satisfaction, as contrary to the single-hearted pursuit of the Kingdom of God (*Matt.* 6:19–21; 19:21–34). He pronounced the 'beatitudes' on those who lived in a spirit of lowliness, contrition, gentleness, justice, mercy, purity and peace, and who suffered persecution for the cause of right. 'The Kingdom of Heaven is theirs' (*Matt.* 5:3–10).

5.30 (h) In opposition to pharisaical observance of legal prescriptions, in opposition to the ideal of religious aloofness which characterized most of those who were accounted most godly among his fellow-Jews, in opposition to the prevailing attitude which saw material misfortunes as a sign of God's displeasure, Jesus addressed himself to the common people, mixed with the hated tax-gatherers and sinners, and declared God's special concern for the sick and the maimed, the poor and the outcast (*Luke* 4:18, 7:34, 39–47; 14:12–14, 21; 15:8–32; 18:9–14; 19:1–10).

5.31 (i) Denunciation of outward legalism did not mean that Jesus had no ethical teaching. On the contrary, he laid down for his followers a strict code of conduct —even impossibly strict, it seemed to some. Chapters 5–7 of *Matthew* bring together many of his precepts in the so-called 'Sermon on the Mount'.

(2) Teaching of Jesus which emphasized the 'community aspect' of religion.

5.32 (a) To infer from the points we have just listed that the Synoptic Gospels represent Jesus as preaching spiritual individualism, an anti-institutional religion of purely personal piety, would be a misinterpretation. These points must be set in balance with other aspects of his teaching about the Kingdom of God. Such spiritual individualism would in any case have been quite alien to Jewish religious concepts, which Jesus accepted, and to the Messianic expectations which the evangelists saw fulfilled in him (e.g. *Matt.* 1:16; 21:1–9; 26:63–4; *Mark* 8:29–30; *Luke* 1:68–79; 9:20–1). The sense of community was central in Jewish religion. The People of God were bound collectively to him by a special covenant, and the duty to be faithful to his Law and to worship him by sacrifice and praise was an obligation on the community as a whole.

5.33 (b) The preaching of Jesus about the Kingdom aimed to bind together those who accepted it into a community of love and mutual service, a brotherhood worshipping and serving the heavenly Father together. In a sense the Kingdom was already realized in the mission of Jesus himself, and in his obedience to his Father's will. The Hebrew term for 'kingdom' denoted the king's sovereignty rather than the organization of his realm. The Kingdom of God was present where God's sovereignty was revealed (e.g. *Matt.* 12:28) and where God's will was done (*Matt.* 6:10).

5.34 (c) If some of the precepts and parables of Jesus stressed the decisive role of personal commitment, others showed that the Kingdom of which he was the herald and leader was to be a social body, outwardly visible. It was to grow from small beginnings, like the mustard seed, into a sturdy plant; it was to be like a field of crops, where good seed and darnel were to grow up side by side until the harvest; it was to be as a net cast into the sea of the world enclosing both good and worthless fish, until at the end of time there would be a final separation (*Matt.* 13). It was to be like a vineyard in which labourers were engaged and received their recompense (*Matt.* 20:1–16); it was to be like a wedding-feast to which, when the invited guests refused, lowly strangers would be pressed to come (*Matt.* 22:1–14). His disciples were to be as a city set on a hill, their works visible to all men (*Matt.* 5:14).

5.35 (d) The Gospels describe how Jesus, as well as preaching to great crowds, drew to himself a band of disciples. They were his 'little flock', as Israel had been the 'flock' of Yahweh under the Old Law, and to them the Father chose to give the Kingdom (*Luke* 12:32). From this community of disciples he selected twelve who were to form the inner circle of his new movement. Called his 'Apostles' (that is, 'the men whom he sent'), they were the envoys and missionaries whose task was to proclaim his Kingdom; they were to be 'fishers of men' (*Matt.* 4:19); they were to be received even as he was received (*Matt.* 10:1–11:1; 16:19; 18:18). In the new community there would be leaders with authority. Yet their leadership would not be domination; it would carry the obligation of humble service of all, following the example of Jesus himself (*Matt.*

Figure 23 Jesus raises Lazarus from the dead: another scene from the Andrews diptych. (Victoria and Albert Museum.)

20:25–8; *Luke* 22:24–7). We see from *Acts* that these Apostles continued to form a special group, and that it was considered very important to continue 'this office of ministry and apostleship'—which was the office of giving witness to the life, death and above all the resurrection of Christ (1:17–26; cf. *1 Cor.* 15:5).

5.36 (e) *Matthew* 16:18 relates how Jesus, addressing Simon Peter, announced

his intention of founding a 'Church', which would be built upon a rock. The Greek word which we translate as 'Church' (*ekklesia* = 'congregation') corresponds to Hebrew words (*qahal* and *'edhah*) signifying the gathered community of Israel, 'the assembly of God' (e.g. *Nehemiah* 13:1; *Psalms* 74:2). The word *ekklesia* had already been used in this sense by the Septuagint translators of the Hebrew Scriptures. The term occurs in *Matt.* 18:17, to refer to a local congregation. In *Matt.* 16:18 it evidently refers to 'Church' in a wider sense. The Aramaic word for a rock, *kepha*, here given to Simon as a distinctive personal name (cf. *1 Cor.* 15.5; *Galatians* 1:18), had its semantic equivalent among Greek-speaking Christians in the translation *Petros*, Peter, which also involved a word-play on the meaning 'rock', and which was used by all the evangelists.[1]

5.37   (f)   All the Synoptics give solemn emphasis to the words and acts of Jesus at the Last Supper on the eve of his passion. The Old Covenant between God and the people of Israel, constituting them his own people and giving them their Law and community organization, had been solemnly inaugurated by the performance of a sacrificial rite by Moses (*Exodus* 24:4–8). The evangelists show that Jesus, in deliberate parallelism to that founding of the community of the Old Law, announced the sealing of a New Covenant in his own sacrificial blood. (*Matt.* 26:28; *Mark* 14:24; *Luke* 22:20.) Thus although the word *ekklesia* occurs only in the Gospel of Matthew, all three Synoptic evangelists imply in their Supper narratives that Jesus was inaugurating a new Covenant-people, a new *qahal-ekklesia*, which, at the time they were writing, all their readers would identify as the Christian Church.

5.38   (g)   At the end of Matthew's Gospel it is related how a solemn commission was given to the Apostles, deriving from Jesus's 'full authority'. He bade them to 'go forth therefore and make all nations my disciples', enrolling men everywhere by the baptismal rite (28:18–19).

Figure 24   The Resurrection, by Ugolini. (National Gallery.)

[1] On the text in *Matt.* 16:18, G. Bornkamm writes: 'In the interpretation of the saying on Peter and the Ekklesia Roman Catholic and Protestant theology are nearer each other than they have been for some time (the "rock" means neither Christ—as stated already by Augustine, whose opinion Luther followed —nor Peter's faith or his preaching office, as the reformers thought, but Peter himself, as leader of the church). The two theologies differ, of course, in the opinion of the authenticity of the saying [i.e. several modern Protestant scholars think it was not spoken by Jesus, but reflects a later situation], but they are especially opposed to each other as to whether it is right to transfer the authority given to Peter to the bishop of Rome . . .' (*Jesus of Nazareth*, English trans., 1969 reprint, p. 215.)

So we come to the culmination of the Gospel story, the sequence of events to which everything has been leading up. The end of the Gospel story of Jesus is the beginning of what we call Christianity. All the evangelists give preponderant emphasis to the Passion narrative, in which the arrest, trials, sufferings and death of Jesus are recounted. For two millennia Christians have been retelling the story and meditating on its meaning. No doubt the main lines of that story are very familiar to you. I do not propose to rehearse it here. But I do assume that you have read, or will now read, the Gospel account of the climax of Christ's mortal life. We cannot understand the rise and development of the Christian Church unless we realize that all those Christians looked back to the events there described as the guarantee of their faith and hope. If you read the last two chapters of *Matthew* or the last three chapters of *Luke* you have the substance of the traditional account. The last nine chapters of *John* give it in a variant form, with a considerably larger element of theological interpretation.

5.40   When the evangelists have described the events of the crucifixion and the last cry of the dying man from the cross, it would seem that brutal repression has stamped out the movement led by Jesus of Nazareth. Yet the whole tragic story is told in the light of the mysterious sequel—the resurrection of Jesus to life again after being killed and buried. Nor is it only a spiritual survival of Jesus that is affirmed, or a mere sense of his invisible presence consoling his disciples. The Gospels are emphatic that it is the same body that had been tortured to death, the disfigured corpse from Calvary, that was raised to life anew. The resurrection narratives, almost breathlessly mixed up though they are, stress the reality of the empty tomb as well as of the risen Christ. The evangelists indicate that Jesus himself had previously foretold and accepted his death, that he had attributed to it expiatory value, and that he had also seen it as the prelude to a triumphant resurrection, after which he would be exalted in the power and glory of his Kingdom (*Matt.* 16:21; 17:12, 22–23; 20:17–19; 26:2, 28–29; *Luke* 17:22–25; etc.)

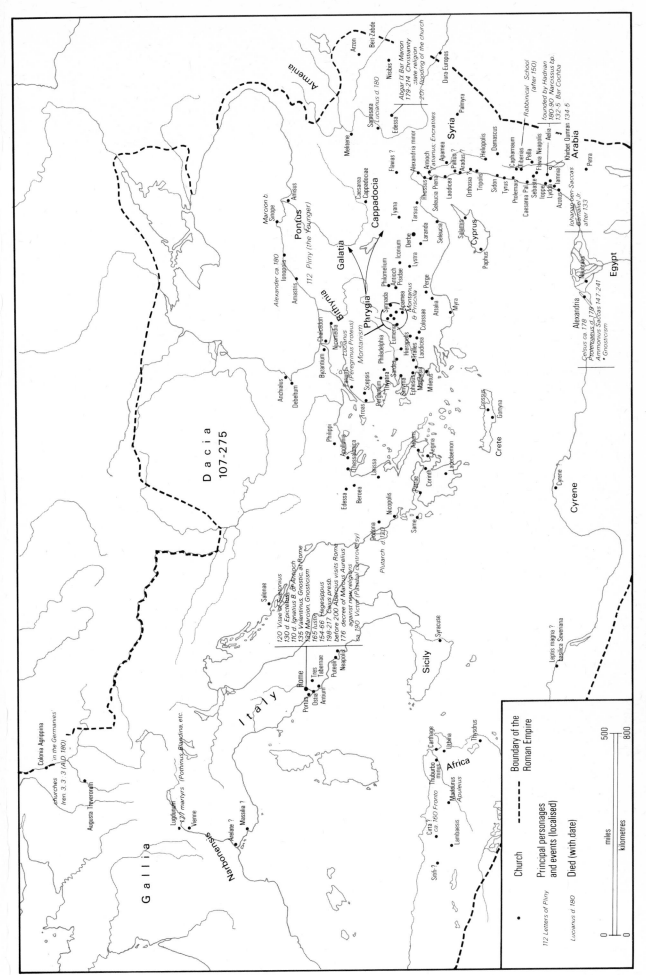

MAP B: THE CHURCH IN THE SECOND CENTURY
(*After the map in Nelson's Atlas of the Early Christian World.*)

PART TWO: PAUL AND THE PAULINE CHURCHES

6.0 (A) HERALDS OF THE RESURRECTION

The source which offers us most particulars about the first phase in the development of Christianity, after the end of the period covered by the Gospels, is the *Acts of the Apostles*. Since ancient times the writer of *Acts* has been identified as 'Luke the beloved physician' (*Colossians* 4:14), who was a companion of Paul. It is clear that *Acts* is by the same author as the *Gospel according to Luke*. In these pages it will be convenient to follow the traditional identification of the author of *Acts*, and to refer to him simply as 'Luke'. In §§ 2.11–14 I noted how well informed he was about the political, social and geographical setting of the Roman empire and Hellenistic world which was the backcloth of his narrative. In his account of Christian origins, however, especially in his earlier chapters, Luke was evidently drawing on earlier sources and traditions, and these were of varied origin and quality. Moreover, he clearly had his theological preoccupations, which affected his handling of his material. We cannot assume that his book gives a plain unvarnished narrative of events in the first Christian communities, in due chronological order. Nevertheless, although due allowance must be made for the editorial colouring of *Acts*, and though its component parts must be subjected to searching criticism,[1] this does not preclude the use of the book as a valuable source for the study of early Church history.

6.1   *Acts* is almost the only source we have for the immediate 'post-resurrection' period, and it is the main source for the study of the subsequent period. Naturally enough, the Christian converts of the second and later generations wanted to know what happened after the point at which the Gospel accounts ended. It was to meet this demand that Luke wrote the book we call the *Acts of the Apostles*, as a sequel to his Gospel. This title is somewhat misleading, for the book by no means gives a full account of the doings of all those who were called Apostles. Of the original Twelve Apostles in the Jerusalem church, only Peter's activities are described at any length—and only a few of those. A missionary journey of John is briefly mentioned, and the martyrdom of his brother James is alluded to. Of the individual 'acts' of the remaining Apostles nothing is said.

Stephen and Philip, who are prominent in the early chapters, were not Apostles in the sense given to the word in the Gospels. Neither was James 'the brother of the Lord', who appears as the leader of the Jerusalem community later on. The fortunes of the Christian community in Judaea are followed only for a dozen years or so. After that the whole interest shifts to the ministry of Paul, 'the Apostle to the Gentiles', who was not one of the original Twelve. The earlier chapters have provided the credentials of Paul and his mission.

6.2   Although the book of *Acts* gave only a limited and selective answer to the question, 'What happened next?', it did provide the developing Church with a heroic saga of its origins. It was this saga that eventually became established as the scriptural account of how the Church was first energized by the Holy Spirit of God (*Acts* 2), and of how it subsequently spread, beginning 'in Jerusalem, and all over Judaea and Samaria, and away to the ends of the earth'.

---

[1] Filson gives a handy short list of works for a critical study of *Acts* in note 22 on page 160. It would be useful at this point to read his seventh chapter, 'Beginnings in Jerusalem', and his eighth chapter, 'Outreach from Jerusalem'.

I say 'eventually', since we do not find clear evidence of direct use of *Acts* in other Christian writings until fairly well on in the second century. By that time the story of *Acts* had become accepted as the substance of what Christians knew about the earliest period of the Church.

6.3 The letters of Paul offer an independent check on some of the data of *Acts*. As we shall see later, these two sources do not always tally. Nevertheless, there is an overall consistency in the picture they give of the new Christian communities which arose in the Jewish Diaspora in the Hellenistic world. Both sources agree about the main areas in which this missionary activity was taking place —though we should not assume that the areas they mention were the *only* ones in which missionary activity was taking place.

6.4 The early chapters of *Acts*, then, provide both a résumé of what happened after Christ's ascension and also a prelude to the story of Paul's apostolate to the Gentiles. Including as they do traditions from the earliest period, they have a special interest for our study. Let us look at the picture they give of the new movement in its infancy, and of its distinctive character at that time. What do those early chapters of *Acts* present as its chief message, and what did it consider the function of the Apostles to be? I think a fair answer would be: Its chief message was that Jesus had risen from the dead and that he was the way for men to reach God; and the function of the Apostles was to be heralds of his resurrection.

6.5 The early chapters of *Acts*: an exercise

Here is an exercise to verify these assertions. Go through the first ten chapters of *Acts* and note passages and texts in which the Christian spokesmen declare their message to those around them. In these statements, **how often do they affirm the resurrection of Jesus as a central point of their belief and preaching?**

A LONG PAUSE HERE
Do not read on until you have worked on the exercise

6.6 **Specimen Answers**

(a)   The first chapter of *Acts* recalls the resurrection and ascension of Jesus, and describes how the vacancy in the number of the Twelve Apostles was filled. The new Apostle, chosen from among the disciples of Jesus, has the function of being 'a witness to his resurrection' (1:22).

(b)   On the day of Pentecost the greater part of Peter's first address to the crowds of pilgrims in Jerusalem is devoted to asserting the resurrection and exaltation of Jesus (2:24–36).

(c)   In the Temple courtyard, after the miraculous cure of a crippled boy, Peter declares to the astonished multitude that this was done by the power of the living Jesus: 'God raised him from the dead; of that we are witnesses' (3:15, 21).

(d)   The companions are arrested by the Temple authorities, who are 'exasperated at their teaching the people and proclaiming the resurrection from the dead—the resurrection of Jesus' (4:2). Peter, as their spokesman, repeats the message of the resurrection and of salvation through the name of Jesus alone (4:9–12). They refuse to be silenced: 'We cannot possibly give up speaking of things we have seen and heard' (4:20).

(e)   Once more they are arrested and brought before the Sanhedrin. Peter again claims a divine mandate for what they are doing: 'We must obey God rather than men. The God of our fathers raised up Jesus whom you had done to death by hanging him on a gibbet' (5:29–30). Flogged and then discharged, they 'went steadily on with their teaching in the temple and in private houses, telling the good news of Jesus the Messiah' (5:42).

(f)   Stephen now stands forth as an intrepid confessor of the new faith. At the end of a long discourse before the Jewish Council he declares that he can see the risen Jesus in heavenly glory, 'standing at God's right hand'. Thereupon he is stoned to death (7:55–60).

(g)   Philip enlightens the eunuch of Ethiopia about the meaning of the Isaian prophecy, and tells him 'the good news of Jesus' (8:30–5).

(h)   The risen Jesus, exalted in heavenly glory, addresses Saul on the Damascus road. Saul in his turn begins to 'proclaim Jesus publicly' (9:3–29).

(i)   In his homily at Caesarea to the household of Cornelius, Peter recalls the works of Jesus, and sums up the good tidings of the risen Christ as follows: 'And we can bear witness to all that he did in the Jewish country-side and in Jerusalem. He was put to death by hanging on a gibbet; but God raised him to life on the third day, and allowed him to appear, not to the whole people, but to witnesses whom God had chosen in advance—to us, who ate and drank with him after he rose from the dead. He commanded us to proclaim him to the people, and affirm that he is the one who has been designated by God as judge of the living and the dead' (10:39–43).

6.7   We shall find Paul's statement of the basic message of the gospel substantially the same as that of the first leaders of the Church in Judaea. He too will be a herald of the resurrection. He will sum up the gospel which he preached to his converts as follows: 'First and foremost, I handed on to you the facts which had been imparted to me: that Christ died for our sins, in accordance with the scriptures; that he was buried; that he was raised to life on the third day, according to the scriptures; and that he appeared to Cephas and afterwards to the Twelve. Then he appeared to over five hundred of our brothers at once, most of whom are still alive, though some have died. Then he appeared to James, and afterwards to all the apostles. In the end he appeared even to me . . .' (*1 Cor.* 15:3–8).

7.0   (B) THE STUDY OF PAULINE CHRISTIANITY

There is a unity of design running through the two-volume work which is made up by *Luke–Acts*. The life, death and resurrection of Jesus Christ, narrated in the Gospel, are the foundation; the primitive Christianity of the Jerusalem church, described in the first dozen chapters of *Acts*, rises on that foundation; and this primitive Christianity of Jerusalem authorizes and validates the mission to the Gentiles, for which the Apostle Paul is set apart by a unique divine choice. The author of *Acts* thus demonstrates that Paul's ministry is duly linked with that of the body of the Twelve accredited Apostles who were entrusted by Jesus with the planting and spreading of the Kingdom of God. But he also shows that Paul is not just a secondary figure, a later convert sent out by the original Apostles as their delegate. No, by a supernatural intervention on the Damascus road he is directly marked out by the risen Jesus himself, and suddenly changed from being a persecutor into an Apostle of the first rank, entrusted with the widest mission of all: 'This man is my chosen instrument to bring my name before the nations and their kings, and before the people of Israel. I myself will show him all that he must go through for my name's sake' (*Acts* 9:15–16). Paul will later insist that he is 'an Apostle, not by human appointment or human commission, but by commission from Jesus Christ and from God the Father who raised him from the dead' (*Galatians* 1:1).

Figure 25   The Crucifixion of Christ, by Raphael. (National Gallery.)

7.1   The sources

We come now to consider the life, deeds, writings and achievements of this man Paul, one of the most remarkable religious leaders in the history of mankind. As sources for this study we shall use, as well as the account of Paul's activity given in *Acts*, the corpus of Pauline letters. Some later apocryphal writings offer further particulars about his life, but their value as historical sources is practically negligible. It is just possible that they contain some grains of remembered fact amidst the legendary chaff—for instance in the description of Paul's personal appearance given in the *Acts of Paul and Thecla*, dating from the later second century: 'A man small of stature, with a bald head and crooked legs, in a good state of body, with eyebrows meeting and nose somewhat hooked, full of friendliness' (Hennecke–Schneemelcher, *New Testament Apocrypha*, vol. 2, p. 354). These facial characteristics are in fact found in representations of Paul in Christian art from the third century onwards.

7.2   Of the thirteen Pauline letters, it is widely agreed that at least nine, and probably ten, were personally written by Paul, or at least dictated by him to amanuenses. (A fourteenth letter, *Hebrews*, was for long ascribed to Paul, but it is clearly by another author. See Filson, p. 325, note 1.) Many scholars do not accept the Pauline authorship of the 'Pastoral Epistles'—namely, the two letters to *Timothy* and the letter to *Titus*, which they think date from a rather later time. Some scholars, while admitting that the letter to the *Ephesians* reflects authentically Pauline ideas, also doubt whether it is directly from Paul. Filson discusses the character of the Pauline letters, and refers to the disputes about the authenticity of some of them, in a number of places in your set book (e.g. pp. 159–60, 238–58, 276–7, 268–88, 291, 309, 391).

7.3 Here and there in his letters Paul makes incidental autobiographical references, and from these, coupled with the data given in *Acts* and from the enduring evidence of his achievements in the churches he founded or instructed, we can piece together something like a 'life' of Paul. Most useful for biographical data of this kind are his letters to the *Romans*, his two letters to the *Corinthians*, and his letters to the *Galatians* and *Philippians*. As I remarked earlier, we do not always find a neat agreement between *Acts* and Paul's letters on points of fact, and there are many tantalizing ambiguities and gaps in the story. But in spite of —indeed, because of—those discordances, the substantial agreement of the two sources about the main lines of Paul's life, ministry and achievements is impressive. We can have a fair measure of confidence that our historical knowledge of this remarkable man is at least as accurate as our knowledge of most of the other great figures of antiquity. Indeed it has been fairly said that of all the characters of antiquity none except Cicero is so intimately known to us as Paul of Tarsus. There is a limpid consistency in the unintended self-portrait of Paul which emerges from his surviving letters, in which he pours out his impetuous thoughts and aspirations.

7.4 In your set book by Filson nearly a hundred pages are devoted to Paul and his work. These pages, comprising Chapters 9, 10 and 11 of the book, give a fairly adequate (if rather uncritical) survey of the subject, and also indicate some of the historical and literary problems which arise. The exercises I will propose are intended to help you to make your own summary, based on the material contained in Filson's book, of the principal features of Paul's career and thought. If you have time, I hope you will also be able to refer to the relevant passages in *Acts* and in Paul's letters, to which Filson gives plentiful references. I propose a simple division of the material: one section of our study to be devoted to **the life and missionary activity** of Paul, and then a second section to **his thought and religious teaching,** as revealed in his letters. It is an over-simplified division, of course, since what Paul believed and taught governed all his activity, and conversely the day-to-day challenges of his pastoral ministry provided the occasion of his writings and determined much of the subject-matter of his letters. But let us adopt that twofold division for our present purposes.

7.5 The biographical pattern

At the back of Filson's book are two maps, the first of which is entitled 'The Journeys of Paul'. It is quite a crowded map, with criss-crossing lines tracing out Paul's itineraries. Three of these are labelled respectively, 'First Missionary Journey', 'Second Missionary Journey', and 'Third Missionary Journey'. The division of Paul's public ministry into these three 'missionary journeys', with the final journey to Rome as their sequel, is a time-honoured one, and is a normal feature of textbooks of Scripture study and Church history. It follows the sequence of Luke's narrative in *Acts*, and provides a useful framework in which to situate Paul's achievements. However, we must remember that Luke presents a schematic version of events, and there are obvious gaps in his narrative. In Paul's letters we find mention of some of his missionary activities not referred to in *Acts*. Perhaps you can give an example?

✠ ✠

7.6   *An answer:* One notable example is *Romans* 15:19, where Paul declares: 'I have completed the preaching of the Gospel of Christ from Jerusalem as far round as Illyricum.' Now Illyricum, or Dalmatia, was the Roman province along the north-east shore of the Adriatic, roughly corresponding to modern Yugoslavia. Yet from *Acts* alone we get no inkling that Paul's missionary penetration in the Balkans went as far afield as that. Then again, Paul told the Christians of Rome that he intended, after visiting them, to go on to Spain (*Rom.* 15:24, 28). Did he do so? We shall see that there are reasons for thinking that he did.

7.7   There are disputes among scholars about the problem of fitting the autobiographical particulars gleaned from Paul's letters into the pattern of Paul's missionary journeys given in *Acts*. In our present study there is no need to enter into the details of these disputes. Given the fragmentary nature of the evidence and the theological *genre* of the writings under consideration, we do not expect them to provide a tidy historical picture. Luke's account, though partly based, it would seem, on a travel diary which he himself kept while in Paul's company, is patently not an exact log of all the journeys Paul made during more than twenty years, nor can it be a complete record of all places, dates and travel-schedules in the story. His presentation of Paul's missionary activities as occurring in three consecutive 'journeys' may be an editorial convention to make the narrative tidier and easier to follow. Moreover, Paul's own references in his letters to his travels and doings are usually recollections put in to illustrate some point of pastoral concern in his argument. We know that memory can telescope events, or single out some happenings to the neglect of others; and where personal issues and controversies are involved the recollections of different parties may be at variance.

8.0   (C)   PAUL'S LIFE AND MISSIONARY ACTIVITY

Instead of following the more usual pattern, which divides Paul's ministry into those three well-defined missionary journeys, I suggest that we group the data from our sources in a rather more general survey. There will naturally be loose ends in the life-story of a man whose career was one long restless series of 'journeyings often'. As he himself summed it up: 'I have been constantly on the road; I have met dangers from rivers, dangers from robbers, dangers from my fellow-countrymen, dangers from foreigners, dangers in towns, dangers in the country, dangers at sea, dangers from false friends' (*2 Cor.* 11:26). Let us take for our next exercise an outline of the main phases in Paul's life, including (where relevant) reference to the places in which he was active, and to the churches which he founded or with which he was associated. From your study of Filson's ninth, tenth and eleventh chapters, with the texts cited there, write down a brief summary of the main biographical facts which emerge about Paul, and about his missionary activity, under the following five main phases of his life. I give in brackets page references to Filson's book where you can find the relevant material.

(1) Paul's early life up to his 'conversion' (pp. 199–203).

(2) The period of reorientation, and Paul's subsequent mission, based on Antioch, to the southern regions of Asia Minor (pp. 203–14).

(3) Paul's missionary activity in Macedonia and central Greece (pp. 217–46).

(4) The Ephesus period: Paul's ministry in proconsular Asia (pp. 246–58).

(5) The climax of *Acts*: Jerusalem, Caesarea and Rome (pp. 259–89).

Figure 26 The conversion of St. Paul, as interpreted by Raphael: a tapestry in the Vatican. (Mansell.)

8.1 Use maps to help you to get an overall picture out of the mass of details. As well as the map in Filson, you have Map A on page 11 of these units, marking localities where Christian congregations are known to have existed at least by the end of the first century. The Pauline churches appear on this map, but you will have to disregard, for the present, the 'non-Pauline' churches shown there, which we shall discuss later (in §§ 11.0–11.16). A useful feature of this map is that it marks the regions of the Diaspora, and thus illustrates the correlation between Paul's missionary strategy and the main areas of Jewish settlement in the north-eastern sector of the Hellenistic world. In your answer try to mention approximate dates where possible. You need not follow Filson's order of treatment exactly or follow him in his various digressions. You will get a clearer summary by picking out the main points and rearranging them as necessary. I will try to do that in my own 'specimen answer', but as usual I will give more detail that I expect you to give in the time available to you.

A LONG PAUSE HERE
Do not read on until you have worked on the exercise

Specimen answers and discussion

8.2 (1) Paul's early life up to his 'conversion'

(a) Born at Tarsus, the principal city of Cilicia, the son of a pious family of Diaspora Jews, Paul (whose Jewish name was Saul) could thus refer to his antecedents: 'Circumcised on my eighth day, Israelite by race, of the tribe of Benjamin, a Hebrew born and bred; in my attitude to the law, a Pharisee; in pious zeal, a persecutor of the church; in legal rectitude, faultless' (*Phil.* 3:5–6). His father, probably a tent-maker as Paul was in his turn, had, rather surprisingly, the coveted privilege of Roman citizenship, a hereditary advantage which his son was able to put to good use in emergencies. Staunchly loyal though he was to the traditions of his race, Saul also had a civic pride in his

64

native city: 'I am a Jew, a Tarsian from Cilicia, a citizen of no mean city' (*Acts* 21:39). Tarsus was a fairly large port at a cross-roads of international trade, renowned for its textiles. It was also a centre of Hellenistic culture, claiming to rival even Athens and Alexandria in its fame for learning. Paul was a child of two cultures. While his Jewish spiritual heritage was the most formative influence, he also knew the ways of the Hellenistic world. While he came from Aramaic-speaking forebears and spoke that language fluently (cf. *Acts* 21:40), he also acquired fluent and flexible use of the *koine* (or 'common') Greek which was to be the medium of his apostolate and of his epistles. He knew the Greek Septuagint version of the Jewish Scriptures through and through, and his own writing was to be impregnated with its phrases.

8.3 (b) According to *Acts* 22:3, Paul declared that although born in Tarsus he had been brought up in Jerusalem, 'and as a pupil of Gamaliel I was thoroughly trained in every point of our ancestral law'. In *Galatians* 1:14 Paul describes 'how in the practice of our national religion I was outstripping many of my Jewish contemporaries in my boundless devotion to the traditions of my ancestors'. When did Paul go to Jerusalem to study? Possibly as a child; he had relatives in Judaea (*Acts* 23:16). His advanced studies at the feet of the highly reputed Gamaliel would have been undertaken before (or possibly even after) the years of Christ's public ministry, for Paul never mentions seeing or hearing of Jesus Christ during his mortal life. From his rabbinical studies Paul acquired mental agility, subtlety in scriptural interpretation, the ardent zeal of the Pharisees, and a deepening of his sense of complete religious dedication to God.

8.4 (c) The first mention of Paul in *Acts* is to describe his presence at the stoning of Stephen (7:58–8:1). That Paul took an active part in persecution of the infant Christian Church is confirmed by his repeated avowals in his letters (e.g. *1 Cor.* 15:9; *Gal.* 1:13; *Phil.* 3:6). According to *Acts*, it was while he was on his way to Damascus, 'breathing murderous threats against the disciples of the Lord' and planning to bring them back captive to Jerusalem, that the whole course of his life was changed by a supernatural intervention of the risen Christ (9:1–19). The same extraordinary episode, with substantially the same circumstances, is twice more related in *Acts* (22:4–11 and 26:12–18). In his letters Paul does not mention the particulars of the blinding experience on the Damascus road, but he does make definite allusions to a decisive encounter with the

Figure 27 A mediaeval mosaic in the Royal Palace at Palermo shows, on the left, St Paul proclaiming his message, and on the right his escape from the walls of Damascus in a basket. (Mansell.)

risen Christ, and to being changed by God's grace from a persecutor into an Apostle (*1 Cor.* 9:1; 15:8–10; *Gal.* 1:11–12; *Phil.* 3:12). In *Galatians* 1:13–17, Paul affirms that God revealed his Son to him while he was actively engaged in persecuting the Church, and he explicitly associates the happening with Damascus, to which he 'afterwards returned'. Whatever the precise circumstances, and whatever the possible explanation of the apparition or revelation, both *Acts* and Paul's own letters are in substantial agreement in attributing his conversion to Christianity to a sudden and direct divine intervention. Assuming that the crucifixion of Jesus occurred about the year 30, the martyrdom of Stephen can be dated about AD 33, and Paul's conversion would be about a year later.

8.5   (2)   The period of reorientation, and Paul's subsequent mission, based on Antioch, to the southern regions of Asia Minor

(a)   *Acts* records that Paul's sight was miraculously restored at Damascus by a disciple named Ananias, and that he was then baptized (9:10–19). Paul was now gripped with a burning conviction that dictated the whole future course of his life. The crucified Galilean whose followers he had been persecuting was not the impostor he had supposed. Jesus of Nazareth was the Messiah and the living Lord who had called his adversary to his service. Paul himself recalled that after the supernatural revelation which revolutionized his life he 'went off at once to Arabia' (*Gal.* 1:17), no doubt to meditate upon what had happened and what it meant. Hitherto he had been intent on meriting God's favour by meticulous devotion to the Jewish Law; now he was overwhelmed by the realization that in his greatest zeal he had been meriting, not reward, but divine wrath and punishment. And yet he had been chosen for God's favour while he was God's enemy. Thenceforward he was to be the herald of God's 'free grace'.

8.6   (b)   After the period of retirement in the desert Paul returned to Damascus (*Gal.* 1:17). *Acts* is silent about the Arabian interlude, but relates that Paul preached his new-found faith with great energy in Damascus, thus provoking for the first time that hostile reaction from the Jews which he was to encounter everywhere. Our two sources agree that he was in mortal peril at Damascus, and that he escaped by being lowered over the city wall in a basket (*Acts* 9:23–5; *2 Cor.* 11:32–3).

8.7   (c)   Three years afterwards (about 36–37) Paul went up to Jerusalem 'to get to know Cephas', that is, Peter. He later recalled that he stayed with Peter for a fortnight and also saw James, the brother of Jesus, but otherwise did not mix with the Christians in Judaea (*Gal.* 1:18–24). Compare this passage with *Acts* 9:26–30, which seems to describe the same episode. In what particulars does Luke's account differ from Paul's?

✠ ✠

Answer: Luke says the brethren in Jerusalem were all afraid of Paul, but Barnabas, a Cypriot who had handed over his wealth to the church's common chest, befriended Paul and introduced him to the Apostles. Paul then moved about freely in Jerusalem, preaching the gospel of Jesus and debating with Hellenistic Jews. When danger arose the brethren escorted Paul safely away.

8.8   (d)   Paul's zeal soon brought him into further danger. He withdrew from Judaea 'to the regions of Syria and Cilicia', returning to his native city of Tarsus (*Gal.* 1:21; *Acts* 9:30). He seems to have spent several years (from about 37

to 44) in those regions. The Judaean congregations heard reports of his evange-
listic ardour and praised God for it (*Gal.* 1:23). It was during those years, to
judge from *2 Cor.* 12:1–10, that he underwent an ecstatic experience which
profoundly affected him. He also contracted a distressing physical disability
which was to remain with him through later years. Eventually Barnabas went
to Tarsus to seek out Paul, with the aim of bringing him to share in the work of
the gospel at Antioch, now a principal centre of Christian activity. Antioch,
with its port Seleucia at the mouth of the Orontes, was a wealthy and populous
centre of communications and commerce. It was the capital of the Roman
province of Syria. At Antioch 'the disciples first got the name of Christians',
and it was there too that significant numbers of Gentiles first became converts.
From Antioch Paul and Barnabas visited Jerusalem to take 'famine relief'
to the needy Christians (*Acts* 11:25–31).

8.9   (e)   It was probably between the years 45 and 48 that Paul and Barnabas
were active in the southern regions of Asia Minor. Luke relates how they
were commissioned for this task by leading members of the Antioch congregation, and in Chapters 13–14 of *Acts* he tells the story of their missionary travels,
first in Cyprus, then in Pamphylia and in cities in the southern part of the province of Galatia: Pisidian Antioch, Iconium, Lystra and Derbe. Luke's record
of the places evangelized is doubtless not complete, for he remarks that 'the
word of the Lord spread far and wide through the region' (*Acts* 13:49).

8.10   The description of events at Pisidian Antioch gives a good illustration of how
Paul normally introduced the gospel by preaching first to the Diaspora Jews
and proselytes in the local synagogue, and then to a wider circle of interested
Gentiles outside. The sermon here attributed to Paul in the synagogue is similar
to others in which Luke sums up the early apostolic preaching about the risen
Christ. He also relates the retort given by Paul and Barnabas to the Galatian
Jews who rejected the Christian message, in words which could serve as a
statement of Luke's own editorial theme: 'It was necessary that the word of

*Figure 28 Paul reproves
Peter at Antioch: a painting
by Guido Reni in the Brera
Gallery, Milan. (Mansell.)*

God should be declared to you first. But since you reject it and thus condemn yourselves as unworthy of eternal life, we now turn to the Gentiles. For these are our instructions from the Lord: "I have appointed you to be a light for the Gentiles and a means of salvation to earth's farthest bounds" ' (*Acts* 13:46–7). Inevitably persecution arose, but many Gentiles were converted. Luke adds a comment which is reminiscent of a key theme in Paul's letters: 'Those who were marked out for eternal life became believers'. Though subjected to physical violence, the missionaries founded fervent congregations in the places they visited, and appointed 'elders' in each. Returning to Antioch, they reported 'how God had thrown open the gates of faith to the Gentiles' (*Acts* 14:27).

8.11 **(3) Paul's missionary activity in Macedonia and central Greece**

(a) According to *Acts*, the great dispute about the observance of the ritual prescriptions of the Jewish Law, and about what obligations should be laid on the Gentile Christians, came to a head at this point in the story and was resolved at what is often called the 'Council of Jerusalem'. However, the allusions to the controversy in Paul's letters show that it was not settled so unambiguously and finally at that time. Many attempts have been made to reconcile the apparently conflicting accounts of Luke in *Acts* and of Paul in *Galatians* 2 about the conference in Jerusalem. On pages 219–20 of his book Filson lists five alternative solutions which have been proposed. Once again, I would voice a caution against expecting our texts to provide a consistent chronology of all Paul's visits to Jerusalem or a record of all the exchanges in this long-drawn-out controversy. At least it is clear that both *Acts* and *Galatians* agree that the liberal policy of Paul and Barnabas towards the Gentile converts was vindicated by a meeting in Jerusalem, at which leading members of the apostolic community, in particular Peter and James the brother of Jesus, recognized the correctness of Paul's attitude. In § 9.20–3 we shall say more about the conflict with the 'Judaizers', one which was to beset Paul's apostolate for many years.

8.12 (b) Paul realized that the chief places of government, culture and trade in the Roman empire were the most advantageous for the purpose of spreading the gospel. In the next main phase of his missionary activity, as described in *Acts*, his prime objective was the Roman province of proconsular Asia. This populous region facing the Aegean Sea had several busy ports and a prosperous hinterland. Ephesus, the metropolis of the province, was the start of a great Roman road to the east. A main line of communication from the east to Rome led westwards from Ephesus across the Aegean and the Adriatic, via Corinth. Landward routes to Europe ran from the north-west of the province across the Hellespont. On his first attempt to reach this important region Paul, who had now parted company from Barnabas, was diverted from his intended route. After passing through Syria and Cilicia and revisiting the places in southern Galatia which he had earlier evangelized with Barnabas, he was 'prevented by the Holy Spirit from delivering the message in the province of Asia' (*Acts* 16:6). Instead, he and his new companion Silas made their way through Phrygia and probably through north Galatia. Again, according to Luke, a supernatural premonition directed their steps away from Bithynia and towards the sea coast at Troas, near the Hellespont. Here a nocturnal vision beckoned Paul across into Europe. His party now included Timothy, a keen young convert from Lystra, and—to judge from the 'we-passages' in *Acts*, which begin at this point in the narrative—Luke himself (cf. Filson, p. 231).

8.13 (c) Paul's ministry in Macedonia and Greece was attended with notable success, as well as with some failures and the usual persecutions. The first

68

congregation he founded in Europe was at Philippi; it was always to be especially dear to him. Others were founded at Thessalonica and Beroea. Then he went on to Athens, where, despite his efforts to suit his message to the sophisticated audience, he achieved little. We hear of individual Athenian converts, but of no continuing church there during Paul's lifetime. When he went on to Corinth, on the other hand, he found many people ready to listen to the message of a religion very different from that of Corinthian Aphrodite, with her thousand temple prostitutes. He made a fairly long stay there, probably about two years, and planted a church which was to have an important place in early Christian history. His ministry was not confined to Corinth; we learn from *Romans* 16:1 that there was a church in the nearby port of Cenchreae. In these Greek cities, as in Asia Minor, Paul preached first in the synagogues, then in public to the Gentiles as well. We find several references to pious and influential women converts. In Corinth the usual violent opposition was stirred up against him and his companions. We have already mentioned this hostility to Paul at Corinth earlier in these units. Because of it we have one of our few fixed points of reference in New Testament chronology. Do you remember how this is so?

✠ ✠

Answer: It was the action of the Corinthian Jews in bringing Paul before the tribunal of Gallio, proconsul of Achaia, that enables us to date Paul's stay in that city fairly accurately, in the years 51–52 or 52–53 (cf. § 2.13 above).

8.14　Luke relates that Paul left Corinth some time after that episode, making his way to Caesarea and Jerusalem, in order to 'pay his respects to the church' and perhaps to fulfil a vow in the Temple (*Acts* 18:18–22). In the years that followed, his congregations in Macedonia and Achaia were constantly in his thoughts. His concern for them is apparent in the letters he addressed to them, some of which survive—two to the Thessalonians, two to the Corinthians, one to the Philippians. The problems of the restless Corinthian congregation caused him particular anxiety. There are references in his letters to further travels in Macedonia and to a sudden extra visit to Corinth. In *Acts* 20 Luke describes a later visit to Macedonia and then a stay of three months in Greece, followed by a return to Philippi for the Passover season. These travels can be dated approximately between the years 55 and 57. We must not forget that visit to Illyricum, alluded to in *Romans* 15:19 but otherwise unrecorded. When was that fitted in? It is because of all these loose ends that I asked you to indicate the main phases and areas of Paul's activity, rather than to attempt to track all his comings and goings during those crowded years.

8.15　(4)　The Ephesus phase: Paul's ministry in proconsular Asia

(a)　Paul's first visit to Ephesus was a short one. *Acts* 18:19–21 tells how he visited the city on his way from Corinth to Caesarea, which would have been about the year 52 or 53. He preached in the synagogue there, but when the Jews of the city urged him to make a longer stay, he declined, saying, 'I shall come back to you if it is God's will'. A year or so later he at last found the way open to achieve his ambition to preach the gospel in proconsular Asia. From his old base at Antioch he set out, first revisiting the congregations in Galatia and Phrygia, 'bringing new strength to all the converts' (*Acts* 18:23). Then, unhindered this time by any providential dissuasion, he was able to travel through the highlands of Anatolia to reach Ephesus.

8.16　(b)　Paul made Ephesus his headquarters for about three years—his longest and most successful ministry in any one place. Luke even asserts that as a result of his preaching 'the whole population of the province of Asia, both Jews and pagans, heard the word of the Lord' (*Acts* 19:10). It must have been during this period that the gospel was spread to the cities of Colossae, Laodicea and Hierapolis by Epaphras, Paul's emissary, whom he called 'a trusted worker for Christ on our behalf' (cf. *Col.* 1:7; 4:12–14). It was from Ephesus that Paul wrote his first letter to the Corinthians (cf. *1 Cor.* 16:9).

8.17   (c)   After the first three months in Ephesus Jewish opposition made it impossible for Paul to preach in the synagogue, so he withdrew his converts and took over a lecture hall, where he discoursed daily. Luke records that he performed miracles and exorcisms, whereupon the whole population of the city was awestruck. Many renounced their magical practices, 'and the name of the Lord Jesus gained in honour'. Even 'some dignitaries of the province were friendly to Paul'. So successful was he in winning men and women over to the Christian way of life that the cult of the goddess Artemis, which was big business in Ephesus, suffered severe loss. This provoked the serious riot which threw the city into an uproar (*Acts* 19:23–41). Some scholars argue that Paul suffered an imprisonment, unrecorded in *Acts*, during this (or a later) stay at Ephesus, and that the so-called 'Letters of the Captivity' (*Philippians*, *Colossians*, *Ephesians* and *Philemon*) were written from there. The more usual opinion, however, is that these letters were written during Paul's later imprisonment in Rome, or, less probably, in Caesarea. (Cf. Filson, pages 276–85.)

8.18   (d)   It was soon after the riot that Paul left Ephesus to resume his travels in Macedonia and Greece. On his return journey, bound for Jerusalem, he purposely avoided Ephesus, summoning the elders of the Ephesian church to

Figure 29 The Acropolis at Athens, with the remains of the Areopagus below. (Mansell.)

meet him at Miletus. In the expectation that they would never see his face again, he renewed his pastoral instructions and exhorted them: 'Keep watch over yourselves and over all the flock of which the Holy Spirit has given you charge, as shepherds of the church of the Lord, which he won for himself by his own blood' (*Acts* 20:15–38). All the same, it is possible that Paul did return to Ephesus at a later date.

8.19   (5)   The climax of *Acts*: Jerusalem, Caesarea and Rome

(a)   The last eight chapters of *Acts* are an account of the climax of Paul's life, as Luke saw it at the time of writing. There is a mounting sense of drama as the Apostle makes his way, amid gloomy forebodings, from Corinth to Palestine, where tribulations and threats to his life await him. The tension rises again as he journeys from Palestine, through further perils and hardships, towards his ultimate goal—Rome. These chapters make up over half of what Luke tells us about the career of Paul. There is a kind of parallelism here to the account of the life of Jesus given in the Gospels, where the last phase in hostile Jerusalem is the most important part of the story. In Chapters 21–26 of *Acts* Luke stresses how Paul bore his witness in Jerusalem and later in Caesarea, and how high-ranking Roman officials found again and again that no just accusation lay against him.

8.20   (b)   When Paul made his 'appeal to Caesar' at the tribunal of the governor Porcius Festus at Caesarea (*Acts* 25:11–12), his bold move made possible what for a long time he had yearned to achieve—to preach the good news of Jesus in the imperial capital itself. When setting out on his last journey from Corinth to Jerusalem he had written to the Roman Christians telling them of his 'eagerness to declare the Gospel in Rome as well as to others', and how he had often planned to go there, but so far without success (*Rom.* 1:11–15; cf. also *Acts* 19:21; *2 Cor.* 10:16). Now he is going to bear his witness in the centre of the world stage. According to *Acts*, while Paul was in mortal danger in Jerusalem the Lord Jesus appeared to him in a vision and said: 'Keep up your courage; you have affirmed the truth about me in Jerusalem, and you must do the same in Rome' (23:11).

8.21   (c)   So Paul is sent to Rome under military guard, accompanied by some faithful disciples, including Luke himself. Finally, after a perilous sea voyage (graphically narrated by Luke in a chapter which is not only a gripping adventure story but also a main source of our knowledge about ancient seamanship), Paul reaches Rome. There he spends two years (until about AD 62) under a kind of house arrest, 'proclaiming the kingdom of God and teaching the facts about the Lord Jesus Christ quite openly and without hindrance'. These are the last words of *Acts*.

8.22   (d)   So *Acts* ends enigmatically, without telling us what befell Paul after his two years' stay in Rome. Several suggestions have been advanced to explain this strange ending to the book.

Can you think of a possible explanation yourself?

✚ ✚

An answer: On pages 285–6 Filson gives four of the explanations put forward by various scholars. The first in his list really combines two possibilities. The simplest explanation is that *Acts* was written at the end of Paul's two-year period in Rome, and so obviously the author could not say what happened later. This theory is logically separable from the further suggestion that *Luke–Acts* were written as a vindication of Paul to help him in his defence before the Roman authorities. I add here another possible explanation, not mentioned by Filson. That is, since Luke wrote his two-volume work, his Gospel and *Acts*, for the purpose of informing one 'Theophilus' (who may well have been a distinguished convert in Rome) of the salient facts in the story of Christianity from the beginning, he did not go on beyond the point at which Theophilus would have personal knowledge of what happened, even though he was writing some years later. On the supposition that Theophilus was introduced to Christianity, and possibly also to Paul, after Paul's two-year stay in Rome was ended, he would know the sequel himself and would need no further information from Luke. Thus the inconclusive ending to *Acts* would mean, in effect—'and you know the rest'. Some scholars think this last explanation is as likely as any. Can you see any obvious weakness in it?

✠ ✠

An answer: A telling argument against it is the following, as expressed by John Ferguson: 'I find it hard to believe that *Luke* and *Acts* were private letters to one man. Surely—like Lucretius's piece of Epicurean evangelizing—they are *public* proclamations, associated with a noble patron?' (See, however, the evangelist's own statement of his purpose in *Luke* 1:3–4.)

8.23   (e) When writing to the Romans at the end of his final visit to Corinth, Paul had declared his intention, after visiting Rome, of pressing on to Spain; he had been longing to go there for many years (*Rom.* 15:23, 28). His missionary strategy, as explained in *2 Corinthians* 10:14–16, was to take as his 'proper sphere' Gentile regions which had not been evangelized by others. When he had completed his work in the eastern half of the Mediterranean world he would go to the west. 'Then', he told the Corinthians, 'we can carry the gospel to lands that lie beyond you.' Paul was a man of iron perseverance and never lost sight of objectives he had once resolved upon. If indeed he was acquitted at the imperial tribunal in Rome and released from surveillance after his two years' stay in the city, it would have been quite unlike him not to pursue his plan to go on westwards in order to spread the gospel in Spain, where other men had not yet laid foundations for it. At the end of the first century the *Letter of Clement of Rome* affirms that Paul 'preached in the east and in the west . . . and reached the furthest limits of the west'—which seems to mean Spain. In the same source there are also indications that Paul was later martyred in Rome; thus the author implies that Paul left the city after the stay recorded in *Acts* and returned there at some later time.

Figure 30 St Paul preaching in the Areopagus at Athens: A tapestry by Raphael in the Vatican.

8.24   Some scholars think that Paul went back to Asia Minor during the years following the date at which *Acts* end. There are passages in the letters to *Timothy* and to *Titus*, which seem to refer to a period of Paul's life and activity subsequent to that covered by *Acts*. Whether these Pastoral Epistles were actually written by Paul himself or not, they may at least be taken as indicating an early belief that Paul had a further period in freedom after his first Roman captivity, and that he was subsequently imprisoned again, with the expectation of death before him (cf. *2 Tim.* 2:9; 4:6–8).

8.25 (f) There seems good reason to accept the tradition that Paul suffered martyrdom in Rome during the reign of Nero. Later I shall be discussing the literary and archaeological evidence indicating that both Peter and Paul were put to death in Rome during the Neronian persecution. Although the site of Paul's reputed tomb under the basilica that bears his name has not yet been scientifically excavated, the constant local tradition relating to his martyrdom and burial is as strong as that relating to Peter's. There is evidence going back to the second century that his tomb was honoured in a roadside cemetery near the Ostian gate of the City. The place of his martyrdom was pointed out at *Aquae Salviae* on the Via Laurentina, which branches off from the road to Ostia. Nowhere is there the slightest trace of a rival to the Roman tradition.

9.0 (D) PAUL'S KEY IDEAS AND THEIR PRACTICAL APPLICATION

After sketching the 'life' of Paul we must say something about his 'thought'. I should make it plain that our aim here is not to explore the depths and details of Pauline theology as it has been elaborated by Christian thinkers in later centuries. For many authors who now write on this subject, chief interest lies in interpreting Paul's message *for our own day*. They are intent to separate what they consider to have been inessential and ephemeral in Paul's teaching, arising from the environment in which he lived, from what they see as the essential and timeless truths he witnessed to. They tend to restrict the central core of Paul's creed to those spiritual themes and values which still form part of their own religious thinking. For those who have such a preoccupation all kinds of problems arise which are not our concern in this course.

9.1 For example, modern theologians who do not believe in the existence of Satan and the dominion of demonic spirits in the world find it an embarrassment that Paul very clearly did believe in them, and that this belief seems to be an integral part of his account of man's religious situation. To defend Paul's religious message for today, they argue that his theology was really quite independent of his demonology and that the latter was one of the dispensable features of his doctrine. They have to apply similar criteria to several other elements of Pauline doctrine, in order to sift what they consider was of abiding worth from what was not. This, however, is not our perspective in this historical study. We want to survey the main lines of Paul's religious thought as they were in the age in which he wrote, and to appreciate, as far as is possible, both the meaning of his ideas for the people he preached to, and also how those ideas influenced the early Church. It is the religious relevance of Paul's teaching *then*, not *now*, that is our primary concern here.

9.2 In studying Paul's thought we almost inevitably impose on it a kind of systematic framework which does not appear in his own writings. He never developed a 'system' of theology. He brought out his theological ideas almost in passing, while dealing in his letters with particular problems of pastoral concern that had arisen in the congregations to which he was writing. The nearest he got to a theological treatise or monograph on a dominant theme was his *Epistle to the Romans*. But I think it is legitimate to set out a statement of basic Pauline themes which are interrelated in one consistent complex of religious thought.

9.3 **What then are 'the key ideas in Paul's teaching',** as they appear in his surviving letters? Any answer to that question will be selective, and both the ideas selected and the basis of selection may be challenged. In a dense paragraph in your set book (from the middle of page 290 to the top of page 291) Filson gives his own summary of what he calls 'great themes not to be ignored by those who want to understand' the theology of Paul. I think it is a useful and judicious summary, though not complete. It represents what Filson takes to be Paul's 'essential gospel', and the omissions perhaps reveal Filson's own judgement on what is essential or inessential. For example, he makes no mention of Paul's emphatic teaching about the world-dominion of the spiritual powers of darkness and evil, or about baptism and the Lord's Supper, those two principal ordinances in Christian life to which Paul attributed a mysterious efficacy. Nor does he mention Paul's eschatological urgency, or his teaching about the resurrection of the body which believers were to look forward to.

9.4 Now I will propose an exercise to help you to fix in your mind a firmer outline of Paul's dominant ideas. At the same time, I want you to try to situate those ideas in the religious thought-world of the first century AD. So we shall have **two aspects** to consider in each of the key ideas we are to discuss: **first, a statement of the doctrine; secondly, how it fitted into the religious setting in which Paul worked.** I suggest that you take Filson's skeleton summary of Paul's 'great themes', rearranging it as you think fit and fleshing it out from what you may have read elsewhere, preferably by referring to Paul's own letters. First write down a list of what you take to be principal themes, with a brief explanation of the meaning of each, adding some supporting references to Pauline texts if you can. Then in each case try to appreciate the relevance of that idea in the age of Paul by asking such questions as the following: 'What were the circumstances in which Paul put forward this teaching? What was its origin, or at least what earlier ideas may have influenced Paul's thinking on the subject? Was he reminding his correspondents of what they already knew and accepted, or was he telling them something that was unfamiliar to them? Did he put it forward as especially relevant to Jewish converts to Christianity, or to Gentile converts, or equally to both? Is there independent evidence to show that Paul's statement of this doctrinal theme and his practical interpretation of it came to be generally accepted in the early Christian Church? Or is there evidence that his understanding of it was disputed or disregarded by other Christian spokesmen?'

9.5 Naturally, you won't have material to enable you to answer all these questions in the case of every one of the key doctrinal themes we are to discuss; but they will at least show you the kind of question to bear in mind while working through this exercise. (**And do please remember the 'word of encouragement' I gave you in § 1.6 about these long and at-first-sight daunting exercises. I do not expect you to do them all, or to spend an excessive amount of time and energy on them.** I propose the exercises in a rather demanding form in order to set the stage for my detailed 'specimen answers'; if you will at least put in some preliminary reflection on the questions before you read my answers, you will find my discussion easier to follow and you will be better able to form your own critical opinion about what I say.) So in the present exercise, to provide an orderly framework for our answers, I suggest that we first set out our list of key ideas, and then after each item write a brief explanation under the following two headings, which correspond to the two aspects I have just explained in § 9.4:

(i) The doctrinal theme.
(ii) The background and bearing of this doctrine.

A LONG PAUSE HERE
Do not read on until you have worked on the exercise

Specimen answers and discussion

9.6   (a)   The sovereignty of God

(i)   **The doctrinal theme:** God, all-holy, all-creative, all-powerful, all-controlling, was the great reality and the first principle of all that Paul thought and wrote. God's sovereign will was the rule of the universe; to worship and serve him was man's life-purpose. 'Source, Guide and Goal of all that is—to him be glory for ever! Amen!' (*Rom.* 11:36; cf. *Rom.* 1:18–25; *1 Cor.* 2:6–7; *2 Cor.* 1:3–4; *Col.* 1:9–12; *Acts* 17:24–8)

9.7   (ii)   **The background and bearing of this doctrine:** This theocratic conception of the rule of God personally controlling the universe and every detail of man's life was, of course, not an original idea of Paul's, but was central to the religion of Israel. It was the inspiration of all Jewish piety, of the devotion to the *Torah*, even of the meticulous legalism of the Pharisees. It dominated the world-picture of Paul, as of Jesus before him. When Paul referred to this belief he could assume complete assent from those of Jewish background. The Stoics likewise had some conception of a personal providence of God. However, it would have been an unfamiliar concept to many converts from a Gentile background, brought up in a culture in which fate, astral influences and a plurality of gods were commonly thought of as the cosmic elements which controlled events and the vicissitudes of man's life.

9.8   Although Paul wrote in one place about the knowledge of God that 'lies plain before the eyes of all men', discernible from the created universe (*Rom.* 1:19–21), so that the heathen were inexcusable in their godlessness, he was not greatly interested in what we should call 'natural theology'. His teaching about God was based on what God himself had revealed. Undoubtedly, the pure monotheism of Israel, which Paul and his fellow-Jews took for granted as the first principle of religion, was one of the 'new' doctrines which had to be assimilated by converts from paganism as Christianity made progress in the Roman empire.

9.9   (b)   The inner predicament: man's sin and its consequences

(i)   **The doctrinal theme:** All men without exception had sinned; sin was an all-pervasive evil which degraded man and alienated him from God, bringing death and other penal chastisements as its consequences; from their birth all men lay under the dreadful judgement of God; all alike stood in absolute need of being saved from this predicament. (*Rom.* 1:18–3:20; 5:12–14; 7:7–25; 11:32; *Gal.* 3:22; 5:19–21; cf. *Eph.* 2:3; 5:6.)

9.10   (ii)   **The background and bearing of this doctrine:** Deep-seated in every observant Jew was an abhorrence of the vices, idolatry and moral abominations of the Gentile world. Paul, with his Pharisaic background, shared this abhorrence to an intense degree. His Jewish converts to Christianity needed no persuasion of the corruption of the pagan world. In the tradition of the *Psalms* and of Hebrew piety generally, Jews humbly acknowledged their own sins and transgressions in the service of God, but they had no thought of equating the regrettable disobedience of Israel with the loathsome wickedness of the Gentiles. Now those who first preached the Christian gospel in Judaea also declared the need for God's people to be saved from their sins. What then was distinctive in Paul's analysis of the situation brought about by sin?

✠ ✠

Answer: His emphatic insistence that Jews and Gentiles were ultimately in just the same case. One and all, even those Jews most zealous for God's Law, were caught in the same predicament of universal sinfulness: **'All alike have sinned, and are deprived of the divine splendour'** (*Rom.* 3:23).

In *Romans* 5:12–19 Paul introduces a theme which can also be found in some Jewish inter-testamentary writings of the period—that of the hereditary transmission of sinful guilt to all mankind as a result of the original transgression of Adam, related in *Genesis*. Did the first Christian communities who read that passage in Paul's letter realize how it would fit into a consistent theological explanation of God's dealings with men? Probably not, but as time went on this doctrine of 'original sin', an evil introduced by the first Adam and nullified by Christ, the second Adam, was recognized as a first premiss in the whole argument.

9.11   (c)   The outer predicament: the menace of demonic powers

(i)   **The doctrinal theme:** The inward perversity of man and his consequent alienation from God was only one aspect of his predicament. The world, and human life in particular, lay menaced by the dark dominion of cosmic powers, envisaged sometimes as elemental spirits or angelic potentates in the celestial realms, sometimes as malevolent demonic forces actively engaged in this world and carrying on ceaseless warfare against mankind and against the forces of good. The arch-demon was Satan, otherwise called by Paul the wily tempter, hinderer, deceiver, the devil (i.e. 'false accuser'), 'the god of this passing age', 'the commander of the spiritual powers of the air'. Collectively and by personal diabolic intervention these hostile powers of darkness held the sinful world in thrall. From their oppressive sway, as from sin and divine condemnation, man needed liberation. (*Rom.* 8:38; 16:20; *1 Cor.* 5:5; 7:5; 10:20–1; *2 Cor.* 2:11; 4:4; 11:14; 12:7; *Gal.* 4:3; *Col.* 1:13–16; 2:15; *1 Thess.* 2:18; 3:5; *2 Thess.* 2:9; cf. *Eph.* 2:2; 6:11–12.)

9.12   (ii)   **The background and bearing of this doctrine:** Much has been written about the antecedents of Paul's ideas concerning spirits and demons. The school of the Pharisees, to which he had belonged, had an elaborate angelology, with a belief in tutelary spirits, good and evil, who from on high exercised influence on the world. These notions were perhaps derived ultimately from Persian sources. Contemporary Jewish apocalyptic writings reflect a similar dualism, and also refer to the cosmic warfare between the forces of light and darkness. In the Gospels themselves there is frequent mention of devils and of the enmity of Satan towards Christ. In other books of the New Testament, especially *Hebrews* and *Revelation*, there is also reference to angelic and demonic powers. *Revelation* 12 describes the war waged by Michael and his heavenly hosts against the forces of Satan.

9.13   The Gentiles, on their side, would have found nothing strange in Paul's references to invisible principalities and powers. They were accustomed to hearing of the activities of numerous gods and supernatural beings. Popular religion accepted that the world of nature was peopled by sprites and demons, and astrological theory asserted the existence of cosmic rulers which controlled the movements of the heavenly bodies, and through them the fortunes of men. On the existence of the elemental powers and demonic forces, Paul was not saying anything original—although he warned the *Colossians* against fantastic speculations on the subject, which were evidently rife among them. His main intent was to assert that all those cosmic spirits, whatever they might be, whether actively malignant to man or at least exercising some kind of occult dominion in the spiritual realm, were now stripped of their power and substance in the new age which had dawned on the world.

Figure 31 The citizens of Ephesus burn their magical books on hearing the preaching of Paul: a painting by Le Sueur in the Louvre.

9.14　(d)　The divine solution: man liberated from all evil and reconciled to God through Jesus Christ

(i) **The doctrinal theme:** God had provided complete deliverance from man's dire predicament, offering it freely to Jews and Gentiles. He had sent his Son, Jesus Christ the Messiah, Redeemer and Saviour, to liberate men from the evil in which they were enmeshed. By the atoning death and life-giving resurrection of Christ, sinful men were reconciled to God and raised to a new kind of existence. Mankind was recreated in the New Adam. Jesus Christ the Lord, exalted in heavenly glory, now held universal sway over all creation, conquering death, sin and all hostile powers. It is needless to give references here to passages in Paul's letters which state this doctrine, for it is the main message of them all.

9.15 (ii) **The background and bearing of this doctrine:** This, the core of the whole Christian message, had already appeared as the substance of the good news which Peter and his fellow Apostles first preached in Judaea, and which Paul faithfully received and handed on in his own proclamation of the word (cf. §§ 6.4–6.7 above). In many ways, however, he sharpened the focus of the message. He showed how the glad tidings of salvation through Christ required, as their sombre foil, realization of the urgent predicament of sinful man without Christ; and he developed in his own distinctive way the doctrine of the atonement through Christ's redemptive death. In the early apostolic preaching the unjust putting to death of Jesus was seen as the prelude to his exaltation, and as part of the sequence of events by which God granted salvation to men. Paul stressed the centrality of the cross and made much more explicit the theme of the saving power of Christ's death.

9.16 *How* did Christ's death bring about the salvation of men? There were two complementary aspects in Paul's thought: on the one hand, Christ's subjective obedience to his Father's will in accepting death called down God's mercy and favour on behalf of mankind; on the other, there was a mysterious objective power, operative through the actual blood, death and resurrection of Christ, by which God nullified all evil and worked salvific effects in Christ's fellowmen. Was it easier for the Gentiles than for the Jews to accept this recondite doctrine? Did the myths of dying and rising saviour gods in pagan religions, and the cultic rites which were believed to canalize the power of those salvific events, provide some kind of analogy in the minds of Gentile converts to illustrate the doctrine of Christ's saving work? It may be, but Paul never alludes to such an analogy—except to express his contempt for the lords and rites of pagan religions, which he saw as diabolical counterfeits (*1 Cor.* 8:4–6; 10:19–21).

9.17 (e)   The transcendent status of the Lord Jesus

(i) **The doctrinal theme:** For Paul, Jesus Christ was the risen Lord, his human achievement crowned by heavenly glorification and by the conferment of a rank that was above all others. But there was still more to be said about his mysterious identity. Before his earthly life, even before the beginning of the world, he had existed as an eternal divine principle, participating in divine creative power. True man though he was on earth, he was also far more than man.

9.18 (ii) **The background and bearing of this doctrine:** Paul's understanding of the personal identity and transcendent status of Jesus must be compared with the general belief of early Christianity on the subject, as shown in the other books of the New Testament. We shall be examining this evidence at some length in Part Three, so I will not say more here. The relevant data from Paul's letters are discussed in §§ 13.34–13.44 below.

9.19 (f)   Justification by faith: the complete gratuitousness of grace

(i) **The doctrinal theme:** By faith each believer apprehended for himself the salvation bestowed on him through Jesus Christ, and so was 'justified' or accepted into God's favour. Nothing that man did or possessed previously, neither good works, nor merits, nor legal rectitude, nor Israelite descent, availed anything at all for earning this favour. Those on whom salvation was bestowed were chosen out beforehand by God's special predilection. To this grace of God, utterly free and undeserved, grateful and obedient faith could be the only counterpart in man. (*Rom.* 3:20–8:39; 9:30–3; *2 Cor.* 3:3–18; *Gal.* 2:15–3:25; 4:21–5:6; *Eph.* 2:1–10; *Phil.* 3:1–10.)

9.20   (ii)   **The background and bearing of this doctrine:** The gospel of 'free grace' and of 'justification by faith', proclaimed by Paul with great emphasis in his impassioned letter to the Galatians, and in his more restrained but no less emphatic letter to the Romans, was a doctrine that had been refined in the crucible of his own spiritual experience. What experience? Can you justify this assertion of mine, by reference to your earlier study of Paul's life?

✠ ✠

Answer: As we have seen (§ 8.5), Paul could never forget that he himself had been singled out for mercy by the amazing grace of God while he was fighting against God and persecuting the Lord Jesus in his members. All his zeal for righteous observance of the Mosaic Law, then, had been merely leading him into enmity with God himself. Yet neither his imagined merits nor his real demerits counted at all in God's mysterious reckoning. Independently of all his deserts he had been predestined by God to be a vessel of election and the Apostle to the Gentiles. He found in his own life a revelation of the meaning of unmerited grace and of the worthlessness of a righteousness based on works.

9.21   Paul by no means supposed that he was the first discoverer of these truths. He claimed that they were contained in the Jewish Scriptures themselves; and although he held that the Law of Moses had been superseded in the Christian dispensation, he was still sure that the Jewish Scriptures were the inspired word of God, and that their true latent meaning was for Christians to understand. Others in the Church, especially Peter after his enlightenment at Joppa (*Acts* 10:1–18), had acknowledged that God was ready to give his Spirit and his favour independently of observance of the sacred Jewish Law, but it was Paul who hammered home this principle to its full conclusions. With all his energy he opposed the men who held that godliness required Christians to accept circumcision and the other prescriptions of the Mosaic Law. At Antioch he upbraided Peter himself before the whole congregation for what he considered to be an unworthy surrender to the prejudices of such men (*Gal.* 2:11–14).

9.22   So we can understand the vehemence of Paul's reaction when the legalistic party among the Jewish Christians began to sow ideas, even among his own Galatian and Corinthian converts, which contradicted the gospel of free grace and saving faith. He denounced those Judaizers as deceivers, sham-apostles, crooked masqueraders, men consumed with dishonest envy, as interlopers who must bear the weight of God's judgement. Why Paul addressed his classic exposition of the doctrine of grace and faith to the distant Romans, whom he had not yet visited, is not clear. Probably he had reason to fear that the contrary doctrine was rearing its head in that most important centre of Diaspora Christianity. Although Paul's teaching about grace and justification was put forward in the context of the dispute about the Jewish Law, he made it clear that it was of universal application. It was not only Jewish legal rectitude, based on the works of the Mosaic Law, that was unavailing; no kind of human virtue or ethical righteousness could justify a man before God. All men, Jews and Gentiles alike, were equally powerless; none could be saved except by God's free grace, received through faith.

9.23   To explain the fuller meaning of Paul's doctrine of grace—just what he understood 'justification' to entail, how he resolved the apparent paradox between the freedom of God's grace and the necessity for man's faith, the distinction to be made between believing that the gospel was true and believing *in* Christ—these and other questions would require a lengthy theological discussion which we cannot enter into here. Filson gives some pointers for such a discussion on pages 261–2. Did Paul's doctrine of grace prevail in the early Church? In the Christian documents of the late first and second centuries we rarely find the distinctive Pauline emphasis on unconditional grace and on the futility of relying on ethical striving in the path to righteousness. Indeed in the *Epistle of James* (2:10–26), we find what seems to be a corrective to an 'antinomian' interpretation of the Pauline doctrine of justifying faith. (This word 'antinomian' is used to refer to the view of those who would claim that Christians are exempt from the obligations of the moral law.) The controversy about the observance of the Mosaic Law lost its edge when the Jewish Christians became an isolated minority group in the Church after AD 70. Nevertheless, the tension between grace-acceptance and ethical righteousness persisted. It is arguable that Paul's message had to wait for later centuries to be understood.

9.24 **(g) The Church as the body of Christ and the new Israel**

(i) **The doctrinal theme:** Paul was convinced that, in mysterious reality, all Christians were members of the risen Lord, making up one corporate body with him. This body was the Church, the 'fullness' of Christ; it was the extension of his risen life and his saving activity into the new age that had come upon the world. The Church was not just an association of like-minded believers, still less was it a merely juridical entity; it was a living organism through which divine life, flowing from Christ the head, pulsated to all the members. Though there were many local churches or different congregations, all believers made up one all-embracing Church which derived its unity from the one Christ.

9.25 Yet this Church, this spiritual organism and mystical fullness of Christ, was also an outwardly discernible institution, with an organization and division of functions between the members. The Church was the new Israel, the new assembly of God's elect, living under the new and perfect covenant sealed in Christ's sacrificial blood. The corporate life of the old Israel under divine protection was a figure of the corporate life of the true Israel, the Christian Church. For the sake of this new congregation of God's people all things were providentially disposed. (*Rom.* 4:16–25; 9:24–9; *1 Cor.* 10:17, 23; 11:18–32; 12:12–27; 15:9; *2 Cor.* 3:6; *Gal.* 1:13; 3:29; 4:24–31; *Eph.* 1:22–3; 3:6; 4:16; 5:23–32; *Phil.* 3:9–10; *Col.* 1:8–24; 2:19.)

9.26 (ii) **The background and bearing of this doctrine:** Taken by itself, the doctrine of justification by faith could suggest an atomistic and non-institutional conception of Christianity, which would thus be simply a spiritual enlightenment of the individual believer dwelling on his own inner relationship with his gracious God. That Paul's conception of Christianity was much more than this appears from his doctrine of the Church. Here again his starting-point seems to have been reflection on his own 'conversion experience'. Can you say how?

✠ ✠

Answer: Paul's personal revelation on the Damascus road, when he realized that in persecuting the Christians he had been persecuting the Lord Jesus himself (cf. *Acts* 9:4–5), convinced him that there was a mysterious unity between Christ and his body the Church.

The Hebrew notion of corporate personality and of the solidarity of Israel in God's plan enabled Paul to make a synthesis of two conceptions of the Church, the mystical and the institutional. There are those who think he drew his ideas here from Stoic metaphors about the body politic, or from Platonist speculations about the participation of the individuals of a species in a transcendent archetypal form. Such notions may have provided Gentile converts with analogues to grasp the Pauline doctrine of the Church, but there is no indication that Paul himself drew either his ideas or his terminology from such sources.

9.27 There is a parallel between Paul's conception of the Church as a living organism united in Christ, and the biological simile related in the *Gospel of John* (15:1-10) by which Jesus compared himself to a vine and his faithful disciples to branches dwelling in the vine and drawing their life from it. This Pauline and Johannine concept was closely linked in the early Church with a realistic understanding of Eucharistic communion with Christ in the Lord's Supper (cf. §§ 9.31-34 below). On the other hand, I think that the institutional conception of the Church, based on the doctrine of the new Israel, had more influence in the early development of a hierarchical system than is generally realized. The *Letter of Clement of Rome* (Chap. 40-2; cf. § 15.5 below) explicitly points a parallelism between the Jewish hierarchy of High Priest, priests, levites and people, on the one hand, and the organization of the Christian Church on the other.

Figure 32 Some remaining masonry of the ancient harbour at Caesarea. Here Paul landed on his final journey to Jerusalem, and from here he embarked on his voyage to Rome. (Matson Photo Service, California.)

9.28 (h) Life in Christ and in the Spirit

(i) **The doctrinal theme:** Bound up with Paul's understanding of the Church as the body of Christ was his teaching about the new spiritual dimension in which Christians now existed. It was a new creation, a new spirit, a new birth, a new life, an abiding 'in Christ' or 'in the Spirit'. The Holy Spirit, sometimes called the Spirit of God, sometimes the Spirit of Christ, was visualized as an energizing principle poured into the hearts of the faithful making them capable of Christian witness, love and godly conduct. They formed 'the temple of the Holy Spirit'. (*Rom.* 7:5-6; 8:9-28; *1 Cor.* 2:9-16; 3:16-17; 6:19-20; 9:19; 12:3-13; *2 Cor.* 3:17-18; 6:16; 13:14; *Gal.* 2:20; 4:6-7; 5:16-25; 6:1, 8; *Phil.* 1:27; 2:1-2; *Eph.* 2:18; 4:4, 30; *Col.* 3:3-4; *1 Thess.* 4:8.)

9.29 (ii) **The background and bearing of this doctrine:** Once more Paul's own intense spiritual experience dominated his description of the new sphere of being in which Christians existed. 'The life I now live is not my life, but the life which Christ lives in me' (*Gal.* 2:20); this was his habitual state of mind. However, his doctrine of the Spirit came not only from his personal experience but also from the Hebrew Scriptures and the Jewish Wisdom literature, where the Spirit of God was presented as a creative, holy and all-pervading principle of divine operation in the world. Old Testament prophecy of an outpouring of the Spirit in the final Day of the Lord was seen by Christians as fulfilled in the extraordinary events at Pentecost (*Acts* 2:1–39).

9.30 This spiritual energy could have some disconcerting side-effects. There were those strange phenomena, including '*glossolalia*', or ecstatic utterance in unknown tongues, which were regarded as marks and manifestations of the Spirit. There is no reason to doubt that these phenomena occurred, for they have been reliably reported at many times from that day to this. One of the problems Paul had to deal with in the Corinthian church was an excess of this ecstatic utterance. While claiming to excel in such spiritual ejaculation himself, he realized that its indiscriminate exercise reduced congregational worship to a state of confusion. So in discussing the gifts of the Spirit he urged his readers to seek first the higher gifts, especially the highest of all—love, which was the source of kindness, courtesy, generosity, compassion, truthfulness, endurance and fidelity to God's will (*1 Cor.* 14:1–39).

9.31 (i) Paul's sacramentalism

(i) **The doctrinal theme:** We have seen that in Paul's theology there were two complementary aspects of the new human condition brought about through Christ. On the one hand there was a new relationship of the believer to God, depending on God's unsearchable decision to grant his merciful favour to those he had chosen; on the other there was that mysterious participation of Christians in the corporate reality of Christ's body, the Church, involving a new mode of being in which the Spirit possessed and directed the whole body and each of the individual members. Corresponding to those two complementary aspects, Paul gave **two complementary explanations** of the process by which the new state was conferred upon men. On the one hand there was **the preaching of the gospel** by Christ's accredited Apostles and their assistants, eliciting the response of justifying faith in the elect; on the other, there was **the mysterious efficacy of baptism**, which incorporated the believer into the reality of Christ's Church-body.

9.32 The baptismal experience refashioned believers in a new spiritual birth, and communicated to them the power both of Christ's death and of his resurrection. One might describe it as a kind of 'homoeopathic cure' of the deadly corruption of sin in man, through sacramental contact with Christ in his purifying death; and at the same time it was a spiritual resuscitation of the believers to new godlike life, through sacramental contact with Christ in his resurrection. This new life was further nourished by partaking of the Lord's Supper. By eating and drinking the sacramental bread and wine, declared to be Christ's body and blood, his followers constantly showed forth his sacrificial death and entered into communion with him and with one another. (*Rom.* 6:3–11; *1 Cor.* 1:13–7; 6:11; 10:1–4; 10:14–22; 11:23–32; 12:12–13; *Gal.* 3:27; *Eph.* 4:5; 5:25–7; *Col.* 2:12–13; cf. *Tit.* 3:4–6.)

9.33 (ii) **The background and bearing of this doctrine:** *Matthew* 28:18–20 shows that the early Church believed that baptism, already in use during the earthly ministry of Jesus, had been enjoined by the risen Christ as the means of

enrolling disciples into his Kingdom. *Acts* 2:41 relates that baptism was conferred on some 3,000 people who responded to Peter's preaching after the outpouring of the Spirit on the day of Pentecost. Afterwards the baptismal rite is frequently mentioned in *Acts* as the normal means of initiation into the Church. Paul's letters reflect this general practice, and his reference in *1 Corinthians* 11 to the current celebration of the Lord's Supper attests that in the use of the Eucharistic rite, too, the churches he had founded were following an already established custom. Nevertheless, Paul's interpretation of the inner meaning of these two sacraments marks a new stage in the development of Christian doctrine. (Our English word 'sacrament' comes from the Latin *sacramentum*, the word used in the Latin version of the Bible to translate the Greek term *mysterion*, or 'mystery'. Paul himself did not apply the latter term to baptism and the Lord's Supper; that usage is first found in Christian writers over a century later.)

9.34 Some authors conjecture that Paul must have derived what I have called his 'sacramentalism' from the ideas and practices of the mystery religions in the contemporary pagan world. You will hear what I have to say about this conjecture in Radio Programme 14. (See also §§ 4.23–4 above.) An interesting parallelism to the Pauline teaching about baptism and the Lord's Supper is to be found in the *Gospel of John*. Although the author of that Gospel uses quite different categories and terminology, there is an unmistakable affinity between his sacramental realism and that of Paul. It is clear from the documents of the second century that this belief concerning the mysterious efficacy of the sacraments of baptism and the Eucharist became a very important element in early Christian piety. (cf. §§ 17.15–18 below.) Sacramental *practice* entered far more deeply into the experience of ordinary men and women than did theoretical explanations of doctrine.

9.35 (j) The eschatological perspective

(i) **The doctrinal theme:** When he wrote his two letters to the Thessalonians, the earliest of his surviving writings, Paul confidently predicted that the

Figure 33 Original Roman paving stones on the Appian Way, just south of Rome. A party of Roman Christians travelled down this road to meet Paul at Appii Forum, and it was by this road that Paul entered the City. (J. Allan Cash.)

glorious second coming of Christ, which would bring the apocalyptic end of the world, would occur within the lifetime of himself and of his first converts. He still held this view when writing his first letter to the Corinthians, and there he added a long defence of the doctrine of the resurrection of the righteous dead. Already, however, the apocalyptic tone was muted, and Paul was accepting a longer perspective. The final conflict with the forces of evil was not a sudden occurrence to be expected in the near future; it was already in progress in the age in which Christians found themselves. Christ's final triumph had already been achieved in principle, and only awaited its working out in his body, the Church.

9.36 Paul continued to speak often of the ultimate goal, towards which he and his fellow-Christians were moving, as the spectacular 'Day of the Lord'. At the same time he now assumed that the last age was already inaugurated; its duration was indefinite, but during the time of waiting for the world's destiny to be unfolded each individual would continue to meet his personal destiny by passing through death. Paul evidently visualized a personal fulfilment even before the final resurrection. To die would be 'to depart and be with Christ' (*Phil.* 1:23). An 'eternal glory' awaited Christians in heaven; better to 'leave our home in the body and go to live with the Lord' (*2 Cor.* 4:17–5:10). On Paul's eschatology in general, see *1 Thess.* 2:19; 3:13; 4:15–18; 5:23; *2 Thess.* 1:6–10; 2:1–12; *1 Cor.* 1:7–8; 3:12–5; 4:5; 5:5; 6:2–3; 11:32; 15:12–58; *Phil.* 1:6, 10–11, 23; 3:9–14, 20–1; 4:5; *2 Cor.* 1:14; 4:14; *Rom.* 2:5, 16; 8:18–25; 13:11–12; 14:8–9; *Col.* 1:26–7; 3:4; *Eph.* 5:6.

9.37 (ii) **The background and bearing of this doctrine:** Paul's earlier teaching about the end of the world faithfully reflected the eschatological perspective that we find in the Synoptic Gospels (cf. § 5.21 above), and also echoed the vivid expectations of Jewish apocalyptic writings. In his teaching on the resurrection of the dead Paul built on the tenets of the Pharisees. He was familiar with the Jewish Wisdom literature, which reflected Hellenistic notions about the survival of the disembodied soul after death (e.g. *Wisdom* 3:1–9); but his conception of survival was not based on the Platonist notion of the soul as a separate and temporary inhabitant of the body. Although he changed his emphasis as time went on, and was no longer sure that the '*Parousia*' or triumphal coming of the Lord was imminent, I think he never ceased to hold that it *might* come in the near future. In the first century, and in the second too, this eschatological perspective was common among all Christians. Belief in an afterlife, with heavenly bliss for the just and punishment in hell for the wicked, was a powerful motive in the lives of Christians. Some pagan religions also promised personal survival and an other-worldly paradise, but in general the ancient world was agnostic or unhopeful about what lay beyond death. (Cf. Units 10–11, § 5.9.)

9.38 (k) The new law of liberty

(i) **The doctrinal theme:** At first sight, the gospel of free grace and of the worthlessness of human works might seem to do away with the need or possibility of regulations and of a code of conduct for Christians. But that was very far from Paul's understanding of the Christian way. 'I am not in truth outside God's law, being under the law of Christ', he said (*1 Cor.* 9:21). Elsewhere he called it 'the life-giving law of the Spirit' (*Rom.* 8:1). Although personally diffident, Paul had no doubts about his own right and duty, by virtue of his commission from the Lord, to exercise authority in the churches he had founded, to interpret the will of Christ, to make decisions which the faithful were bound to obey, to regulate their discipline and worship, and to exhort them to moral rectitude. Likewise in the local congregations, which had their own leaders, he insisted that 'all be done decently and in order'.

9.39 Nevertheless Paul was careful to remind Christians that it was the Holy Spirit that ruled and directed their lives, and it was the gifts of the Spirit that office-holders in the Church possessed. His constant exhortations to well-doing and his stern denunciations of wrong-doing were based on the premiss that those who followed Christ must not prevent the Spirit from working their sancti-fication. 'You, my friends, were called to be free men; only do not turn your freedom into licence for your lower nature, but be servants to one another in love. For the whole law can be summed up in a single commandment: "Love your neighbour as yourself". . . . If the Spirit is the source of our life, let the Spirit also direct our course.' (*Gal.* 5:13–14, 25; cf. also *Rom.* 12:1–15:13; *1 Cor.* 1:10; 4:6–7, 15; 5:1–7:40; 10:14–11:34; 13:1–13; 14:1–40; *2 Cor.* 2:9–10; 3:1–6; 6:14; 10:8; 13:5–10; *Gal.* 5:13–6:10; *Phil.* 1:27–2:18; 3:17–4:9; *1 Thess.* 4:2–12; 5:12–22; *2 Thess.* 3:6–15.)

9.40 (ii) **The background and bearing of this doctrine:** Some commentators think that there was a fundamental paradox in Paul's account of the Christian life in the Spirit: a paradox which sprang from two incompatible ethical atti-tudes, one of which Paul held in theory, the other which he found inevitable in practice. On the one hand, they say, there was the ethic of sheer grace, of the 'new creation' in which the believer, justified by faith, was possessed by the Spirit and learned the worthlessness of works; on the other, Paul's letters show a recurring strain of moralism as he reacted to the day-to-day exigencies of his pastoral ministry, in which he had laboriously to chide, correct, guide and exhort his often very refractory Gentile converts towards a more fitting way of life. Was the acute moral conflict which Paul described so feelingly in *Romans* 7:21–5 an admission that even the conviction of justification by saving faith did not free one from torments of conscience? Was Paul then an antinomian in theory and an earnest moralist in practice? While he proclaimed his gospel of unmerited grace, was he after all unable to rid himself of the mentality of ethical striving so deeply ingrained in him from his rabbinical upbringing? Do you think there was this internal contradiction in Paul's ethic?

✚ ✚

9.41 *My answer:* I do not think so. In Paul's eschatological perspective, the new age in which he and his fellow-Christians lived was a time set between the resurrection and the final consummation which would come with Christ's triumphant return. In this in-between time the spontaneous surge of the Spirit produced the fruits of godliness in believers, but it was still a time of trial and temptation. Christian life involved a struggle against the lower self and the world without, as well as personal co-operation in the process of being conformed to Christ. When Paul rejected the legalism of the Pharisees he did not reject their affirmation of man's free responsibility.

9.42 Paul was well aware that his doctrine of grace and justification was endangered on both flanks. His letter to the Galatians shows that not only were there Jud-aizers insisting on justification through the works of the Law, but there were also antinomians ready to return the freedom of the gospel into licence. There was no contradiction between what he said about grace and what he said about the law of Christ. It was quite consistent to hold, on one side, that the believer was first justified by grace through no merits of his own, and, on the other, that he did not cease thereafter to be responsible for his conduct. The law of Christian liberty meant not the abandonment of morality but the acceptance of a higher morality, based not on fear but on love. This higher ethic is described by Paul in some detail in Chapters 12–15 of *Romans*, and summed up in *1 Corinthians* 13:1–13.

Figure 34 Mediaeval relief in the crypt of St Peter's Basilica, Rome, showing St Paul being taken to martyrdom. (Mansell.)

9.43   (1)   The place of Israel in God's plan

(i)   **The doctrinal theme:** What I have put last in this summary of Paul's key ideas had a central place in his own thinking. God's original choice had been of Israel to be his own 'peculiar people'. He had revealed himself in a unique manner to the Hebrew race, had freed them from slavery, had established his covenant with them, had shown his loving-kindness to them, and throughout their history, despite all their backslidings, had continued to remain faithful to his promises to them. It was from Israel that God raised up his Son Jesus Christ the Saviour; and it was within the house of Israel that the Christian Church was first founded. In God's plan, Paul was convinced, salvation through Christ was first to be offered to the Jews, and thence to the rest of mankind. Mysteriously, even though the Jews as a nation had rejected the offer, their providential destiny remained. (*Rom.* 1:16; 3:1–4; 9:1–11:36; *2 Cor.* 11:22; *Gal.* 3:14.)

9.44   (ii)   **The background and bearing of this doctrine:** We have seen that Paul's consistent method of spreading the gospel throughout the Diaspora was first to go to the synagogue, where he preached to the Jews and to the 'God-fearers' who were versed in the Jewish Scriptures. Only after that first step did he then preach to the Gentiles of the place. He felt an obligation to offer first to the Jews the opportunity that was theirs by right of the divine promises; and when they refused it he felt free to conduct his main mission to the Gentiles. This interpretation of the apostolic vocation was distinctively Paul's. Although he was conscious of his special responsibility as Apostle to the Gentiles, and although he denounced the obduracy of the Jews and warned them that their physical descent gave them no personal privileges in the spiritual order, he never forgot the priority of Jews before Gentiles in the divine plan. From this doctrinal principle flowed his practical concern to get the Hellenistic churches to collect alms for the Jewish Christians in Jerusalem. 'Indeed they are in debt to them, for if the Gentiles have come to share in their spiritual

86

blessings, they ought also to be of service to them in material blessings' (*Rom.* 15:27). The leaders of the Jerusalem church seem to have regarded such contributions as tribute fittingly paid (*Gal.* 2:10).

9.45 Some preachers seem to have claimed that the Jewish Christians had superiority or even authority over the Gentile Christians by virtue of their Hebrew lineage, and by virtue of the dominion which Jesus, the Son of David and the Messiah of Israel, had established over the nations in the new age. James himself, the respected kinsman of the Lord and eventually the leader of the Jerusalem community, may have held this view (*Acts* 15:14–18). Paul's understanding of the priority of the Jews in God's plan was very different, and he firmly opposed any such religious chauvinism.

9.46 The Jewish-Christian claims were in any case no longer a live issue after the disaster which overwhelmed Israel in the war of AD 66–73. The Jerusalem congregation was dispersed and already the Church was preponderantly Gentile in its composition. Although from that time onwards the place of Israel in God's providential plan became only a secondary point in Christian doctrine, it had meant very much more to Paul. The strange climax in the history of his own race which he loved so dearly, and the apparent frustration of its collective destiny, perplexed and saddened him. 'In my heart there is great grief and unceasing sorrow. For I could even pray to be outcast from Christ myself for the sake of my brothers, my natural kinsfolk' (*Rom.* 9:2–3). Yet as he meditated on the purpose of God in history he was buoyed up by a sure confidence that in the end the whole of Israel would accept the salvation brought by their own Messiah (*Rom.* 11:25–32).

10.0 (E) THE PLACE OF PAUL IN THE EARLY CHURCH

There was something ambivalent in Paul's relationship with the other leaders and missioners in the early Church, and in his attitude to the parent church in Palestine. The Jerusalem brethren recognized Paul as an authentic minister of the gospel and as a successful colleague in the service of Christ—yet at times it seemed to be an almost grudging recognition. Paul in his turn acknowledged the eminent standing of Peter, James, John and the other Apostles (with whom James the Lord's brother soon took a leading place). Those 'Twelve' had been the first witnesses of Christ's resurrection, the foundation pillars of his Church, and the first preachers of the word. Paul describes how he had laid before them for approval an account of the gospel he preached to the Gentiles, 'to make sure that the race I had run, and was running, should not be run in vain' (*Gal.* 2:2). Yet on the other hand we can detect a separateness and independence in his attitude to them, with even a surprising note of irony in his references to 'those reputed pillars' and 'those superlative apostles' (*Gal.* 2:9; *2 Cor.* 11:5). 'I am a free man and own no master', he said boldly when comparing his apostolate with theirs (*1 Cor.* 9:19).

10.1 Fundamentally at one with them in faith and loyalty to Christ, and in his conviction of the indivisible unity of the Church in which Christ's Spirit dwelt, he could still criticize them, quarrel with them, and on occasion tell them 'that their conduct did not square with the truth of the gospel'. The Judaean brethren praised God for the fruits of Paul's preaching among the Gentiles, yet repeatedly we detect a reserve, at times even suspicion, in their attitude to him. His notoriety for disregard of the Jewish Law was a serious embarrassment to them (cf. *Acts* 21:18–25). That this tension never developed into schism was perhaps due in no small measure to Paul's constant care to provide for the material necessities of 'the saints' in Judaea from the resources of his congregations in Gentile lands.

Figure 35 Bronze relief on the doors of St Peter's Basilica, Rome, showing the martyrdom of St Paul at Aquae Salviae. (Mansell.)

10.2 I think that in Paul's own mind there was a kind of analogy between his relationship to the original Apostles and the relationship of the Christian Church to the old Israel. The Israelites had been chosen and prepared for the Messianic destiny; yet in the event it was not the Jewish nation as such who proved to be the true elect and the true heirs of God's promises, but the unexpected offshoot from Israel—the Christian Church with its large Gentile contingent. There was something similar in the way God had brought the gospel to the nations of mankind. Jesus had carefully chosen and prepared his own Twelve Apostles to preach his message and to carry on his saving work; to these Apostles his resurrection was first revealed and they were the witnesses authorized to proclaim it. And yet in the event it was none of the Twelve whom God's grace marked out to be the chief herald of the gospel to the Gentiles. Paul was humbly penitent when he recalled what he had been, but he was unhesitantly proud when he affirmed what God had made him. His own words explicitly invited his readers to see an analogy between, on the one hand, the free and disconcerting grace with which God had chosen for his favour the new believers rather than the old Israel, and, on the other, the free and disconcerting grace with which God had chosen Paul, an upstart and a late-comer in the Church, to be his Apostle to the nations, rather than any of the original founding pillars of the Church:

> In the end he appeared even to me; though this birth of mine was monstrous, for I had persecuted the church of God and am therefore inferior to all other

apostles—indeed not fit to be called an apostle. However, by God's grace I am what I am, nor has his grace been given to me in vain; on the contrary, in my labours I have outdone them all—not I, indeed, but the grace of God working with me (*1 Cor.* 15:8–10; cf. *2 Cor.* 4:1).

10.3 Of course the analogy I have indicated applied only in one respect: namely, that in both cases there was an unpredictable divine choice of an unexpected recipient of grace in the execution of God's plan. But in another important respect the analogy did *not* apply. Reflect for a moment and say what it was.

✠ ✠

Answer: Paul had no thought of pressing the analogy to the extent of implying that the original Apostles and the Jewish-Christian trunk of the Church had rejected Christ's message, and that he himself and the newly engrafted growth of the Pauline churches had been chosen instead. In the passage just quoted he goes straight on to say: 'But what matter, I or they? This [namely, the gospel of the risen Christ] is what we all proclaim, and this is what you believed.'

Figure 36 A sheet of what is probably the oldest surviving manuscript of Pauline writings. The upper half of the page contains the conclusion of the Epistle to the Hebrews, *and the lower half shows the beginning of* 1 Corinthians. (*Papyrus from the Chester Beatty Library, Dublin.*)

10.4 Not altogether surprisingly, we find traces of a severely critical judgement on Paul in some Jewish-Christian circles in the generations after his death. (References in Hennecke–Schneemelcher, *op. cit.*, vol. 2, pp. 71–2). In the Church at large, however, and in Rome in particular, he was ranked next to Peter in esteem. There can be no doubt of the formative influence of Paul's letters on the development of Christian doctrine. We get a hint of the authority they soon acquired in the letter which is known as *2 Peter*, which probably dates from the first quarter of the second century. The pseudonymous author referred to the wisdom with which Paul was endowed and ranked his letters with 'the other Scriptures'. This judgement was confirmed by the usage of other second-century Christian writers, for we find them too citing texts from Paul's letters as they would cite texts of the Old Testament (cf. §§ 15.9 and 15.24 below).

10.5 Yet already in that passage from *2 Peter* we find allusion to the problems of interpretation to which Paul's central teaching about salvation gave rise:

> Bear in mind that our Lord's patience with us is our salvation, as Paul, our friend and brother, said when he wrote to you with his inspired wisdom. And so he does in all his other letters, wherever he speaks of this subject, though they contain some obscure passages, which the ignorant and unstable misinterpret to their own ruin, as they do the other scriptures. But you, my friends, are forewarned. Take care, then, not to let these unprincipled men seduce you with their errors (*2 Peter* 3:15–17).

In fact the Gnostics of the second century seized on some key elements of Paul's teaching, particularly about spirit, grace and law, and wrested them to support their own dualistic and antinomian theosophy. In reaction against such Gnostic distortion of these Pauline themes, orthodox Christian writers would tend to neglect or weaken their authentic meaning. To follow up those later developments I would refer you to Professor Maurice Wiles's work, *Divine Apostle: The Interpretation of St Paul's Epistles in the Early Church* (Cambridge University Press 1967).

Figure 37   A coin struck by the Emperor Vespasian to commemorate the Roman victory in the war against the Jews, culminating in the destruction of Jerusalem in AD 70. The obverse of the coin has the words 'Iudaea capta'—'Judeae vanquished'—and the downfall of the Jewish people is symbolised by the mourning woman seated beneath a palm tree. (Ashmolean Museum, Oxford.)

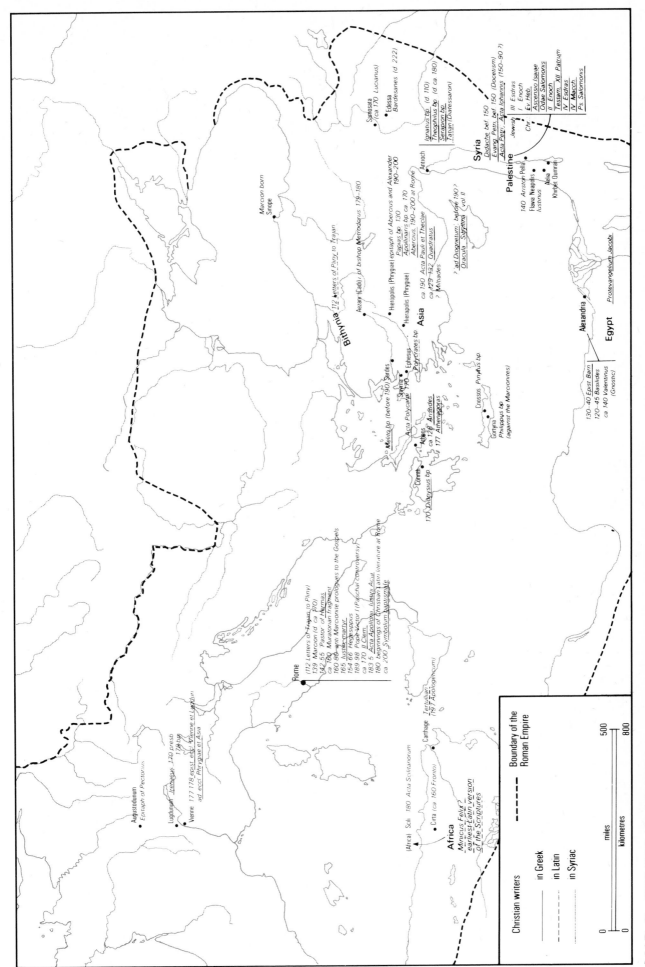

MAP C: CHRISTIAN WRITERS OF THE SECOND CENTURY
(*After the map in Nelson's Atlas of the Early Christian World.*)

PART THREE: THE DEVELOPING CHURCH

11.0 (A) OTHER FOUNDATIONS

One-third of the New Testament consists of the Pauline letters, and the greater part of the longest book in the New Testament, the *Acts of the Apostles*, is about Paul and his work. It is possible to get the impression that the story of Christianity after the departure of Jesus was almost entirely the story of Paul and the Pauline churches. It would seem that the Jewish-Christian church, inward-looking and conservative, sharing the habits of thought of the closed community of Israel, lacked the missionary dynamism to spread the new faith far afield; that, without Paul, the 'sect of the Nazarenes' would have remained an obscure movement in Judaea, hardly heard of in the wider world; and that without Paul's original speculative genius, the simple beliefs of the primitive Jerusalem church would never have been transformed into a theological system of subtle complexity and coherence. Is this a true picture?

11.1 From what you have already studied, I think you will agree that it is not. In this section I should like to discuss the question of non-Pauline missionary expansion, leaving the question of non-Pauline theological development for later consideration. In section (C) below you will have opportunity to compare Paul's doctrine about Christ with independent statements of Christian theology by other New Testament authors; it will be seen that Paul's explanations of the Christian tenets were only part of a wider development of Christian belief.

11.2 For your next exercise I propose that you note down items of evidence to show that during the period from Pentecost to the end of Paul's career **other missionary activity was proceeding in the Church, concurrently with Paul's but independently of it.** This evidence will come mainly from *Acts* and from the letters of Paul himself, but you may find a few other clues from your reading of Filson. Probably you can already list several reasons for arguing that the missionary expansion of Christianity was not all Paul's doing—though undoubtedly Paul played the most influential part in it. **Who else was active in that first expansion of Christianity, and where?** In §§ 16.0–16.39 we shall be discussing the later phases of the Church's geographical expansion, from the closing years of the first century to the later part of the second century. In this present exercise we are dealing only with the earlier period, covering the lifetime of the Apostles. Both *Acts* and Paul's letters mention a large number of individuals, converts of Paul, who were his assistants and 'fellow-workers' in spreading the gospel. Do not include any of these in your answer, for their ministry can be regarded as part of the one wide-ranging Pauline mission. Only include missionary initiatives that were clearly independent of Paul's direction.

A LONG PAUSE HERE
Do not read on until you have worked on the exercise

Specimen answers and discussion

11.3 Non-Pauline missionary activities

(a) The first preaching of the gospel to people from far afield is described in *Acts* 2. The Jewish pilgrims who were among the first hearers of the Apostles' message on the day of Pentecost are said to have included 'Parthians, Medes, Elamites; inhabitants of Mesopotamia, of Judaea and Cappadocia, of Pontus and Asia, of Phrygia and Pamphylia, of Egypt and the districts of Libya around Cyrene; visitors from Rome, both Jews and proselytes, Cretans and Arabs'. The holy city of Jerusalem was a cross-roads for visitors from all parts of the Jewish Diaspora, and some at least of them would have taken back to their homelands tidings of the new movement that had aroused such a stir in Judaea.

11.4   (b)   *Acts* 6 refers to 'the inspired wisdom' with which Stephen, a chief spokesman of the Hellenist section of the Christian community in Jerusalem, argued with Greek-speaking Jews from the Diaspora, including 'Cyreneans and Alexandrians and people from Cilicia and Asia'. Among the latter it is quite likely that the still unconverted Paul was included.

11.5   (c)   The first phase of expansion outside Jerusalem was occasioned by the persecution which arose at the time of the martyrdom of Stephen. Now the faith was spread in 'the country districts of Judaea and in Samaria'. It is related that Philip, another of the Seven elected from among the Hellenist Christians, converted many of the Samaritans, a people who were shunned by orthodox Jews. Peter and John went down to Samaria to follow up Philip's success. The first recorded baptism of a foreigner from afar was that of the eunuch of the Queen of Ethiopia (*Acts* 8).

11.6   (d)   Soon the Christian message was spread to Damascus in Syria, where men and women were already 'following the new way' at the time of Paul's conversion (*Acts* 9). We know the name of one of these first believers in Damascus—Ananias, who came on the scene when Paul was to be restored to strength and baptized (*Acts* 9).

11.7   (e)   Groups of believers are next mentioned in Galilee, Lydda and Joppa. The break-through which brought the Judaean brethren to accept that 'God has granted life-giving repentance to the Gentiles also' was the enlightenment of Peter at Joppa and the consequent conversion at Caesarea of the household of the Italian soldier, Cornelius, who was already a 'God-fearer' devoutly worshipping the God of Israel (*Acts* 10).

11.8   (f)   Meanwhile, other expatriate Jewish-Christians had taken the gospel to Diaspora Jews in Phoenicia, Cyprus and Antioch. Some of them, 'natives of Cyprus and Cyrene', took the decisive step at Antioch of preaching to pagans as well, thus anticipating Paul's ministry. Barnabas was sent from Jerusalem to report on this new development; he heartily approved of it (*Acts* 11).

11.9   (g)   All the missionary activities we have noted so far were carried out before Paul began his ministry. There were many others after that date which were not dependent on Paul's direction. For example, after Paul and Barnabas had parted company, a separate mission was undertaken in Cyprus by Barnabas, accompanied by John Mark (*Acts* 15:36–9).

11.10   (h)   An interesting character who was not a convert of Paul's, and who exercised a quasi-independent ministry, was Apollos, the eloquent Bible-scholar from Alexandria in Egypt. Although he preached in the Pauline mission-field of Achaia, and 'watered the seed' Paul had planted, his version of the Christian message was sufficiently distinctive for there later to be a party in Corinth of those who said, 'I am for Apollos', when others said, 'I am Paul's man' (*Acts* 18:24–8; *1 Cor.* 1:12; 3:4–5, 22).

11.11   (i)   The same partisan spirit alluded to by Paul in his first letter to the Corinthians suggests the possibility that Peter too may have preached in Corinth and elsewhere in the Diaspora. As well as the 'Paul party' and the 'Apollos party', there were those who said 'I belong to Cephas'. After narrating the escape of the Apostle Peter from the death planned for him by Herod Agrippa I, Luke cryptically remarks that Peter then 'departed and went to another place' (*Acts* 12:17). We hear nothing more in *Acts* of his movements during the following twenty years, apart from his important intervention at the Jerusalem conference about the middle of the century (15:7–11). Later traditions speak of an extended missionary activity by Peter during that period, which is probable enough, for if Peter was at liberty he would not have been idle. We do know from *Galatians* 2:11–14 that he visited Antioch while Paul was there, and at first disregarded the kosher laws, taking meals with the Gentile Christians—which suggests that he was already familiar with communities less rigoristic than those of Judaea. When Paul arrived in Jerusalem for his fateful last visit, about the year 57, James evidently ranked as chief leader of the community there; Luke makes no mention of Peter, who had been so prominent in the affairs of the Jerusalem church in earlier years (*Acts* 21:18). It seems evident that Peter was no longer there. (Incidentally the Christians of Judaea must have been very successful propagators of their faith; *Acts* 21:20 mentions their 'many thousands of converts among the Jews'.)

11.12 Paul testified that Peter had a God-given commission to be 'an Apostle to the Jews', as he himself had a similar commission to be an Apostle to the Gentiles. (*Gal.* 1:8). These words are more easily understood if Paul was aware that Peter had an extended ministry among the Diaspora Jews, and did not confine his attention to the Jews of Judaea and the neighbouring regions. Whether Peter visited Corinth or not, Paul's words in *1 Corinthians* about the 'Peter party' at least indicate that other, non-Pauline, preachers were active there, who put Peter's authority above Paul's. A hundred years later a bishop of Corinth, Dionysius, claimed that both Peter and Paul had ministered to the Corinthians.

11.13 (j) At all events some person or persons had brought Christianity to Italy independently of Paul. His respectful letter to the Romans, about the year 57, testified to the existence of a well-established and highly reputed congregation of believers in the imperial capital (*Rom.* 1:7–14). Paul later found hospitable fellow-Christians at Puteoli, near Naples, when he landed there on his way to Rome, and he was also met on the Appian Way by welcoming Christians from Rome itself (*Acts* 28). You may wonder about two places marked on the map on page 11 as having early Christian congregations—Herculaneum and Pompeii, which were both destroyed by the eruption of Vesuvius in AD 79. True, these places were near Puteoli, and may well have contained Christians. It has been suggested that a wall-mark and a kind of altar-table found in the excavations at Herculaneum were of Christian origin, but I remain sceptical about this. The evidence for Christianity in Pompeii is even more inconclusive (cf. §§ 2.30–2.31 above).

11.14 (k) Paul himself avowed that the gospel had been preached in the Hellenistic world by others before him, or at least independently of him. He wrote: 'It is my ambition to bring the gospel to places where the very name of Christ has not been heard, for I do not want to build on another man's foundation' (*Rom.* 15:20); 'And we do not boast of work done where others have laboured, work beyond our proper sphere' (*2 Cor.* 10:15). He does not say where those others had laboured and laid other foundations, and we can only conjecture, in the light of later developments, which those places were. Obvious possibilities, given the pattern of the Diaspora in the Greek-speaking half of the empire, were Egypt, Cyrenaica, Crete and the Aegean islands, the Black Sea coast and Cappadocia. The letter to *Titus* does indeed refer to a ministry entrusted by Paul to Titus in Crete (and *2 Timothy* also refers to a journey of Titus to Dalmatia), but we hear nothing of these activities during the main period of Paul's ministry. It is not likely that the large and populous island of Crete was completely neglected by Christian preachers, at a time when churches were springing up in Greece and Asia Minor, and in the island of Cyprus. We need not assume that the other foundations which Paul refers to were in regions quite different from his own mission fields, for some of the 'other men' may well have planted the faith in regions where there were also Pauline plantations. In §§ 16.15–16 below I shall say something about ancient traditions which link the Apostle John and other prominent members of the Palestinian church with Ephesus and neighbouring places.

11.15   (l) If, as I think not improbable, *1 Peter* dates from this period, it provides evidence of the contemporary spread of Christianity into those very areas of eastern and northern Asia Minor to which Paul did not penetrate. The inscription of the letter is to God's scattered people 'in Pontus, Galatia, Cappadocia, Asia, and Bithynia'. Of these five provinces, Pontus, Cappadocia and Bithynia were non-Pauline mission-fields. The author refers to 'preachers who brought you the Gospel in the power of the Holy Spirit from heaven' (1:12), and he clearly implies that many of those he is addressing were converts from paganism (2:9–10). We saw earlier that Pliny refers to some who had been Christians in Bithynia in the reign of Domitian (§ 2.9 above).

11.16   (m) In your answer you may have mentioned an ancient tradition, mentioned by Origen in the early third century, to the effect that when the Apostles were dispersed to preach the gospel Thomas took as his mission territory Parthia, a kingdom stretching over Mesopotamia and Persia, and Andrew took Scythia, the region to the north of the Black Sea. Another Egyptian tradition asserts that Pantaenus, a missioner who went to India in the later second century, came across churches there which had been founded by the Apostle Bartholomew. The apocryphal *Acts of Thomas*, dating from the third century, assert that the Apostle Thomas preached the gospel in Persia and then in India, where he was martyred. A tomb said to be his is venerated by Indian Christians at Mylapore, near Madras, to this day. Another tradition, dating from the second century, links Philip the Apostle (or perhaps 'Philip the evangelist' mentioned in *Acts*) with the city of Hierapolis, which became the chief church in Phrygia. There may well have been some historical bedrock on which these and other similar traditions about early apostolic activity were founded, but nothing definite can be said about their origin. One may safely add that there must have been many other missionary activities in that first period of the Church's expansion of which no record has survived (cf. § 16.2 below.)

Figure 38 Relief from the Arch of Titus, Rome, commemorating the conquest of Jerusalem by Titus in AD 70. A triumphant procession bears the spoils of conquest, including the Menorah, or seven-branched candlestick from the Jewish Temple. (Mansell.)

We have seen that the earlier letters of Paul, although reflecting a more developed stage of Christianity than the Synoptic Gospels, were the first to be written of all the books which were later collectively called the New Testament. It is probable that the other New Testament writings were almost all composed during the last four decades or so of the first century. We cannot date them exactly, nor can we be certain where they originated. We know that it was the custom in the early Church to copy out the letters of Paul, and later of other prominent Church leaders like Clement of Rome, Ignatius of Antioch or Polycarp of Smyrna, and to send copies to other Christian congregations. The evidence of the manuscript transmission indicates that the Gospels were also being copied and circulated in the same way.

12.1 The first three Gospels and the *Acts of the Apostles* may be roughly dated as originating some time between the sixties and the eighties of the first century, and the *Gospel of John* probably soon after the end of that period. There may have been other 'gospels' in circulation, or at least written materials concerning Jesus. The author of the *Gospel of Luke* referred to such writings in the preface which he addressed to 'Theophilus':

> Many writers have undertaken to draw up an account of the events that have happened among us, following the traditions handed down to us by the original eyewitnesses and servants of the Gospel. And so I in my turn, your Excellency, as one who has gone over the whole course of these events in detail, have decided to write a connected narrative for you, so as to give you authentic knowledge about the matters of which you have been informed.

12.2 Whatever those many other writings may have been, most of them did not survive for posterity. However, a permanent body of writings did begin to acquire special authority among the congregations of Christians which were springing up in the cities and trading centres of Syria, Asia Minor, Greece, Italy and elsewhere. As well as the Pauline letters and the four Gospels, there were also some letters attributed to James, Peter, John and Jude, a letter to some '*Hebrews*' and the *Revelation* of John, which seems to have originated during the persecution of Domitian, about the year 95. There were other contemporary or nearly contemporary Christian writings which were also held in high repute, as we shall see later. Papias of Hierapolis, who wrote in the first half of the second century, showed knowledge of most of the books which were eventually included in the canon of the New Testament. He also said that he valued the oral tradition about Jesus even more highly. (Cf. Filson, p. 82, note 35.)

12.3 The first Christians were a 'People of the Holy Spirit' rather than a 'People of a Holy Book'. After Pentecost they testified that the Spirit of God, or of Jesus, had fallen on them and was energizing them with power. It would be an anachronism to imagine that Bible-reading, the reading of the New Testament writings in particular, played the same part in early Christianity that it did in later centuries, especially in the Protestant Churches. The copying and circulation of manuscripts was a slow process and literacy was limited. Most Christians would have to rely on having passages read to them at their communal meetings. The establishment of the New Testament canon was still in the future (see §§ 17.12–13 below), and the relative value to be accorded to different Christian writings was by no means clear in the first hundred years or so of the

Church's expansion. Christians knew the Jewish Scriptures, of course. They used them especially for the apologetic purpose of demonstrating how Christ fulfilled what was foreshadowed under the Old Law.

13.0 (C) THE BELIEF OF THE EARLY CHURCH CONCERNING THE DIVINITY OF JESUS CHRIST

Although they are not the only relevant documents, the New Testament writings are of first importance for understanding the history of the developing Church. We can take them as reflecting the generally accepted beliefs, while remembering that there were dissident minority groups who differed, to a greater or less degree, from the doctrines and usages of the majority. Central to those generally accepted beliefs, as we have seen, was an emphasis on the role and dignity of Jesus Christ, considered not merely as a past founder and teacher, but as the risen and present Lord. Now it is time to study more closely just what the Church of the New Testament believed and taught about the person and status of Christ, and to try to appreciate how this belief and teaching gave a unique character to the Christian religion in its formative stage.

13.1 I will begin by recalling the passage from the letter of the Younger Pliny to the Emperor Trajan, written about the year 112. In that letter (quoted in Lewis and Reinhold, pages 582–3), Pliny reports 'the sum and substance' of the Christians' observance, as he has learned it by interrogation of suspects. The first point he mentions is that the Christians 'are accustomed to meet on a fixed day before dawn and sing responsively a hymn *to Christ as to a god*'. I have italicized the last six words to give you the theme of what we are to discuss. Here, some eighty years after the crucifixion of Jesus of Nazareth by a Roman governor, another Roman governor in a remote province has to report to the emperor that a man thus executed by Roman justice was being widely honoured as a god. Now there were many stories about deified men in the ancient world. Why would this attribution of deity to Jesus appear especially surprising?

✠ ✠

Figure 39   Jerusalem today, from the Mount of Olives. The domed building in its enclosure is the Dome of the Rock Mosque, which is built on the site of the Jewish Temple. (J. Allan Cash.)

13.2 *Points for an answer:* Jesus of Nazareth was a Jew who appealed to the traditional Law and faith of Israel, and his first followers were all likewise Jews. The exclusive monotheism of Israel, the worship of the one true God, was the central tenet of the faith which the Jews defended with such uncompromising zeal (*Deuteronomy* 6:4–8). Nothing was more abhorrent to them than the Gentile cults—the worship of idols and strange divinities, and especially the blasphemous attempt, made alike by the Seleucid kings and the Roman emperors, to propose deified men as objects of worship. The Jews certainly expected the advent of a Messiah, as a great prophet and national leader to be sent by God to save Israel. Christians claimed that Jesus was that Messiah. (You know, I expect, that the word 'Christ', which soon came to be used as a kind of surname for Jesus, was originally the Greek translation of the Hebrew word, 'Messiah', meaning 'the anointed one'.) However, Jewish orthodoxy never for a moment supposed that the Messiah would be a god; that would have contradicted the first principle of the faith of Israel. There were other Jews who claimed to be the Messiah, and who gained a following—for example, Bar-Kochba, who led a revolt against Rome in AD 132–5. But no one accused those claimants of blasphemous usurpation of divine dignity, nor did their followers attribute to them the status of anything more than that of mere men. It was because of the Christians' claim that Christ was more than human, even that he had the attributes of God himself, that the developing Church came into irreconcilable conflict with the Jews, and also with the conservative Judaeo-Christian groups, who accepted Jesus as the Messiah but recoiled from doctrines that would attribute deity to him.

Figure 40 Tombstone of Nunnius, a slave who was a forester or gamekeeper of the Emperor Nero. The discovery of this and several contemporary tombs in the Vatican City confirms that the Vatican Hill was used for burials in the first century. There is an ancient tradition that the Apostle Peter was buried on the Vatican Hill after his martyrdom in the persecution of Nero. (Societäts-Verlag, Frankfurt-am-Main.)

13.3 Is it really credible that the Christian Church, which originated in the milieu of the strictest Jewish monotheism, could have come to give divine honour to the Galilean carpenter whom they looked to as their founder? However strange this may seem, Pliny's report was essentially accurate, and it is confirmed by contemporary statements by Christian spokesmen. For example, Ignatius of Antioch, martyred in Rome about the same time that Pliny was writing to Trajan, sent a series of letters to fellow-Christians in different localities, in which he several times calls Jesus Christ simply 'God'. His letter to the Church of Ephesus contains four passages in which he does so (e.g. 'Our God Jesus Christ was carried in the womb by Mary'.) Similar expressions are found in other second-century Christian writings, declaring the general belief of the faithful. Then how had this come about? We can seek an answer to that question by asking how the writers of the New Testament books regarded the figure and person of Jesus Christ, and what status they accorded to him. For our next exercise I propose that you look for that answer in their writings. Theologians employ the technical term 'Christology' to refer to the study of the doctrine concerning the person, nature, dignity and work of Jesus Christ. It is a handy label, and I will use it in the following pages.

13.4 Christology: an exercise

This is an ambitious exercise, for obviously it calls for considerable reading and reflection. Some of you will already have a fair knowledge of the New Testament, and in that case the exercise will not be too formidable a task. But those of you who do not have much familiarity with the New Testament need not be deterrred from attempting at least a part of the exercise. To give you some headings to work from, I suggest that you tackle it in the following form:

> Give references to and briefly comment on evidence in the New Testament which indicates that the Christians of that time **attributed a more than merely human status to Christ, that they credited him with divine attributes, and even that they regarded him as God.** Set out your answer under the following headings:
>
> (i) Data from the **Acts of the Apostles** reflecting the Christology of the early Palestinian Church;
> (ii) Data from the **Synoptic Gospels;**
> (iii) Data from the **Pauline letters;**
> (iv) Data from the **Fourth Gospel;**
> (v) Data from the **other books** of the New Testament.

13.5 Countless learned books and articles have been written on this theme, but I do not want you to spend time seeking out and studying such works now. I want this exercise to be an incentive to you to study the New Testament writings themselves. Those of you who are unfamiliar with the New Testament will have to cut your cloth according to measure, and naturally your answers to this exercise will not be as complete as those of students who already have some competence in this field. I quite realize that if you have to start from scratch, without previous knowledge to draw on, this exercise could take you a very long time—many more hours than you have available for study at present. So in order to cut the exercise down to a realistic size and to make it more flexible, I suggest that you choose to collect data under only *one* of the five headings given in § 13.4. Take any one of those sections, and leave the rest to read about later. I will offer you 'specimen answers' in §§ 13.11–55, and you will then be able to compare your answers with mine, and to see what I say about the sections you have had to omit. (Of course if you *do* have time and inclination to tackle more than one section of the exercise, all the better!)

13.6   If you object that I have set you a task in theology, I grant you that it looks like that. But theologians presuppose belief in the principles on which they base their reflections, and the task I have set you does not demand that you should believe the Christology of the New Testament to be true. Even if you think it is not, you can still try to enter with empathy into the beliefs of the writers, and to appreciate how those beliefs gave early Christianity its energy to develop, expand and eventually to conquer the Roman world. It is one thing to show that the New Testament writers attributed a divine or supernatural dignity to Christ, another to ask whether and how their different statements can be unified in a coherent theological scheme, in a way that does not contradict the basic monotheism which Christians shared in common with Jews. This second question was to be the object of intense theological activity and controversy in the Church in later centuries. I do not want you, however, to enter into these later Trinitarian and Christological controversies here.

13.7   Using the terminology of Greek metaphysical thinking, the later Church Councils of Nicaea, Constantinople, Ephesus and Chalcedon, in the fourth and fifth centuries, defined dogmas about Christ in terms of 'substance', 'nature' and 'person'. They spoke of his consubstantiality with God the Father and the unity of his two distinct natures, divine and human, in one person. Christological speculations have continued within the Christian Church all down the centuries. The starting-point of these controversies was in the New Testament data. It would be unhistorical, however, to make the New Testament writings adopt the perspective of those later controversies. Although in theology it may be legitimate to assume a transcendental factor giving believers a special insight into the orthodox meaning of the Scriptures, the historical method we are using in our course demands that we should interpret the New Testament documents in their own context. We must not here interpret them in the light of the theological formulae of later centuries, however great the authority given to those formulae within the Christian Church.

13.8   If this exercise achieves nothing else, I hope it will at least enable you to become more familiar with those source documents of Christianity, which were taken as the warrant for all its later development. It should also enable you to realize more clearly what an extraordinary claim Christians did in fact make about Christ, and how belief in that claim was fundamental to their religion and a principal factor in its survival and spread. Remember that the aim of the exercise is not to prove that Jesus Christ was God, nor is it to decide whether such a claim was invented within the Christian communities in the period after his death. **It is to verify whether the claim of divine status for Christ is contained in the various New Testament writings, and in what sense.**

13.9   Some prefer to hold that the story of Jesus Christ *must* have been falsified or clothed in mythological form during the course of the first century. Others accept that the New Testament does give an authentic account of Christ, while allowing that the literary forms in which the story is told must be carefully analysed, so that the essential content may be duly separated from the envelope of symbolic or poetic expression. Some judge that it is self-evidently false, and a contradiction in terms, to assert of a man that he is also God. Others point to the theological speculations of great thinkers who have found no contradiction in such an assertion, and who have proposed ways of making its mysterious meaning more intelligible to the human mind. You are not asked here to pronounce judgement on these or other theories.

Whatever the answer may be to questions about the ultimate credibility and factual foundation of Christian belief, we may legitimately restrict our attention here to an objective study of the content of that belief, in the developed form it had assumed by the end of the first century.

13.10 Investigation of the New Testament data

All the relevant texts have been exhaustively studied for centuries, but we cannot here go deeply into points of exegesis or linguistic criticism.[1] Nor is that necessary for our present purpose, for the Christians of that early period usually read the New Testament writings with a direct literal interpretation. To appreciate how they understood the texts relating to the person and dignity of Jesus Christ, it is the more obvious and uncritical interpretation that we must look to, rather than the more scholarly and technical criticism to which a modern biblical theologian would submit them. So when you have taken time to study the New Testament data in the light of the question I have put to you, try to group the points you have noted under the headings given in § 13.4. Filson gives some very brief indications on pages 326–7 which may help to show you the kind of New Testament passages that are relevant in your answer.

A LONG PAUSE HERE
Do not read on until you have worked on the exercise

13.11 **Specimen answers and discussion**

An adequate answer to this exercise would require a lengthy tome, so we must try to select and condense. I will make my answers much fuller than I expect yours to be, and will add some commentary and explanation of the passages in their wider context, which you could not be expected to know from a reading of the text alone. My rather lengthy discussion of this question may also serve as an overall survey of the New Testament writings and indicate some of their distinctive features not touched on elsewhere in this course.

13.12 (i) Data from *Acts* reflecting the Christology of the early Palestinian church

Although written at a relatively late date, after the Gospel of Luke, *Acts* preserves in its first dozen chapters a less developed Christology. These chapters, especially the speeches attributed to Peter and Stephen, have an archaic character, retaining many 'semitisms' (i.e. phrases reflecting an Aramaic original) which suggest that the author is using an authentically early source. Although Luke must have been well acquainted with Paul's more developed Christology he does not interpolate it into the early preaching that he reports in *Acts*. As an example of this 'archaism' of the first chapters of *Acts*, there is the identification of Jesus with the atoning 'Suffering Servant' of Yahweh (*Isaiah* 52:13–53:12; cf. especially *Acts* 8:30–8), a theme which to a large extent dropped out of sight in the later more explicit Christology. It is reasonable, then, to take these chapters of *Acts* as giving the most primitive form of teaching about Jesus Christ that we can discern in the history of the early Church.

13.13 This earliest *kerygma*,[2] or proclamation about Jesus, is reflected in the words of

---

[1] For deeper study later I recommend two works directly on our theme: Oscar Cullmann, *The Christology of the New Testament*, English trans., S.C.M. Press 1963; and R. H. Fuller, *The Foundations of New Testament Christology*, New York 1965.
[2] Note Filson's comment, pp. 171–2, on the now customary contrast between *kerygma* and *didache* in the primitive Church.

Peter to the crowd at Jerusalem on the day of Pentecost, related in *Acts* 2:22–36. The passage does not assert any divine pre-existence of Jesus. It does assert that Jesus has been exalted by God to a heavenly status which makes him the source of the extraordinary powers and phenomena then manifest to Peter's hearers: 'I speak of Jesus of Nazareth, a man singled out by God and made known to you through miracles, portents and signs, which God worked among you through him, as you well know. . . . Exalted thus with God's right hand, he received the Holy Spirit from the Father, as was promised, and all that you now see and hear flows from him. . . . Let all Israel then accept as certain that God has made this Jesus, whom you crucified, both Lord and Messiah.'

13.14 Similar preaching by Peter, referring to a heavenly status and power awarded to Jesus as a sequel to his resurrection, and looking forward to his expected return to earth, is recorded in *Acts* 3:12–26: '. . . The God of our fathers has given the highest honour to his servant Jesus. . . . Repent then and turn to God, so that your sins may be wiped out. Then the Lord may grant you a time of recovery and send you the Messiah he has already appointed, that is, Jesus. He must be received into heaven until the time of universal restoration comes.' In *Acts* 4:9–13, Peter affirms that Jesus in his exalted state is now the universal saviour: 'There is no salvation in anyone else at all, for there is no other name under heaven granted to men, by which we may receive salvation'.

13.15 So too in *Acts* 5:31, Peter declares to the High Priest and the Sanhedrin: 'He it is whom God has exalted with his own right hand as leader and saviour, to grant Israel repentance and forgiveness of sins'. Peter tells Cornelius: 'He is the one who has been designated by God as judge of the living and the dead' (*Acts* 10:42; cf. 17:31). These extraordinary powers and dignities—to be the saviour of men, the forgiver of sins, the sender of the Holy Spirit, the object of faith, the one in whose name miracles are worked, the judge of the living and the dead, 'the author of life' (*Acts* 3:15)—were in the Jewish Scriptures properties of God alone. The attribution of them to Jesus in these early discourses of Peter implies that he has been invested with a share of the divine prerogative. But note that according to these passages the supra-human dignity appears to have been conferred by God on the man Jesus; it is not stated that he already possessed it eternally.

13.16 In the account of the interrogation and martyrdom of Stephen, in Chapter 7 of *Acts*, it is related that he looked up to heaven and 'saw the glory of God, and Jesus standing at God's right hand'. He then declared what he saw, using the phrase, 'I see the Son of Man standing at God's right hand'. This is regarded as blasphemy by his adversaries, who thereupon stone him to death. The apparently vague expression, 'Son of Man', is found to be charged with considerable significance for Christology, as will be argued in §§ 13.21–27. I mention it here because, as we shall see, it can imply the notion of a heavenly pre-existence of Christ. As Stephen is stoned to death he cries out, 'Lord Jesus, receive my spirit'. The prayer is from the *Psalms* (30:5), where it is addressed to the God of Israel. In *Luke* 23:46 it is the dying cry addressed by Jesus to God his Father. Finally, as he falls, Stephen prays to Jesus as 'Lord' once more (*Acts* 7:60). (Note that, according to *Acts* 9:5–16, Saul and Ananias also addressed prayer to Jesus; and Jesus gave commands to them in supernatural visions.)

13.17 **The use of the title 'Lord'** (in Greek, **Kyrios**) in the early apostolic preaching recorded in *Acts* (e.g. 2:36, 'God has made this Jesus whom you crucified, both Lord and Messiah') is noteworthy, in view of the employment of this term by Paul, and in the Greek-speaking churches generally, as a title implying the world mastery of the risen and glorious Christ, as we shall see in §§ 13.38–40 below. In the Synoptic narratives of the earthly ministry of Jesus it seems to be merely a title of respect given to him as a teacher; but in the early chapters of *Acts* it evidently means more than that. Peter tells Cornelius that Jesus Christ is 'Lord of all' (10:36). Some have argued that the application of the title *Kyrios* to Christ first occurred in the Hellenistic churches, and was an importation from pagan religions or from the civic cult of the Roman emperors. Against this theory stands the significant fact that the Hellenistic churches preserved an invocation of Christ as Lord in an Aramaic phrase, *Maranatha,* transliterated in Greek characters in *1 Cor.* 16:22. It expressed the yearning for the return of Christ—'Come, Lord'. The Aramaic phrase is also found transliterated in the early Christian document called the *Didache.* It is translated into Greek in *Revelation* (22:20). Why is it so significant that the phrase *Maranatha* was used in the Gentile churches?

✠ ✠

Answer: The fact that this manner of addressing the risen Christ as Lord was preserved *in Aramaic* even by Greek-speaking congregations, to express worship of Christ and longing for his triumphant return, strongly suggests that the special use of the title originated in the earliest Judaeo-Christian community at Jerusalem, before the Gentile mission began and before Aramaic, the original Christian language, gave place to Greek. Thus the exalted sense of the title 'Lord' may well be implied in the early chapers of *Acts.*

13.18   (ii)   Data from the Synoptic Gospels

The Christology of the first three Gospels is of special interest. Some authors have argued that the early traditions concerning Jesus preserved by the Synoptics show him simply as a great and good man, a religious teacher of genius, but not as anything more than a man. The belief that he was a divine being is thus supposed to be a later elaboration of the story. Is there such a variance between the Synoptics and the later strata of the New Testament? In the sayings of Jesus recorded by the first three Gospels there is, indeed, no explicit claim to be God, nor do the evangelists make any explicit assertion of a divine status in their narrative and commentary on events. Nevertheless, there are many texts in those Gospels which converge with remarkable coherence to convey an implicit claim that Christ possessed a rank and power far above that of a mere man. I give references in most cases to *Matthew,* as the fullest Gospel and the one which was the best known in antiquity; you can easily find the parallel passages, where applicable, in the other two Gospels. On the theme that we are investigating there is really no substantial difference of doctrinal emphasis between the three Synoptics, although *Matthew* and *Luke* do give more picturesque details in their 'infancy narratives', describing the miraculous circumstances of Christ's birth. I summarize the data under three sub-headings, as follows.

13.19   (a)   According to the Synoptics, Jesus claims for himself **power and prerogatives that belong properly to the God of Israel.**

— Jesus declares that he will be the universal Judge of the good and the wicked at the Last Day (*Matt.* 13:39–42; 24:30–1; 25:31–46). In the 'great commission' to his Apostles at the end of *Matthew,* he claims: 'Full authority in heaven and on earth has been committed to me' (28:18). In all three Gospels *his* 'Kingdom' is identified with 'the Kingdom of God'.

— He claims to be lord of the Sabbath, which, for the Jews, was a sacrosanct ordinance of God, and also to have superior right over the Temple, which was regarded as the place of God's presence, where alone sacrifice could be offered to him (*Matt.* 12:6, 8).

— He teaches as a master who has authority equal to that of the God who gave the Law to Moses on Mount Sinai: e.g. *Matt.* 5:27–8, 31–2. He even amends or improves this God-given Law: e.g. *Matt.* 5:33–4; 38–9. For the Jews, the Law or *Torah* was not merely a code of religious regulations; it had a divine dignity. Indeed in rabbinic teaching the *Torah* was identified with the eternal wisdom of God.

— Unlike other miracle-workers described in the Old Testament, Jesus is described in the Gospels as working miracles in his own name and with his own authority (e.g. *Mark* 1:41; *Matt.* 9:28–30; 13:25–7).

— He forgives sins on his own authority—again, a divine prerogative, for sin is offence against God. *Mark* relates that when lawyers and Pharisees accuse him of blasphemy for this very claim, saying, 'Who but God alone can forgive sins?', he works a miracle of healing to convince them that he has the right to forgive sins (*Mark* 2:5–12). According to *Matthew* 1:21, the name 'Jesus' (=Saviour), was originally given to the child of Mary 'because he will save his people from their sins'—a function which in the Old Testament is attributed to God alone.

— Jesus claims everlasting force for his teaching: 'Heaven and earth will pass away; my words will never pass away' (*Mark* 13:31).

13.20 (b) According to the teaching of Jesus in the Synoptic Gospels, **men's religious and moral life must be centred on himself**—which implies a claim to divine dignity.

— He declares that he must be loved and followed before all else, even to the loss of life itself (e.g. *Matt.* 10:37–9; 17:24–7; 19:29).

— He promises eternal reward to those who have faith in him and suffer for his sake, and he threatens eternal damnation to those who reject him (*Matt.* 5:11–12; 10:32–3; 24:9–31; 25:31–46; *Mark* 9:41–2; 15:16–17; *Luke* 23:42–3). His twelve special disciples will share with him the joys of heaven and will, as his deputies, judge the twelve tribes of Israel on the Last Day (*Matt.* 19:27–8; *Luke* 22:28–30).

— He assures those who centre their religious life on him that he will aid them and they will have treasure in heaven (*Matt.* 11:28–9; 19:21). The *Gospel of Matthew* concludes with Jesus's promise to be with his followers always, to the end of time. (28:20).

13.21 (c) The Synoptics use **titles** to refer to Jesus—especially 'Son of Man' and 'Son of God'—in a sense which implies a mysterious **heavenly pre-existence and transcendent status.**

'Son of Man'. In the Synoptic Gospels a number of titles are applied to Jesus, including that of 'Messiah'. *Mark* 8:29–30 and *Matt.* 16:20 indicate that he did not disclaim the latter title, but the evangelists never put it on the lips of Jesus himself. They consistently record that he (and he only) used the term 'Son of Man' as a usual title for himself. It occurs 30 times in *Matthew*, 14 times in *Mark* and 25 times in *Luke*. Apart from the one usage by Stephen in *Acts* that we have already noted, it also occurs 13 times in the Fourth Gospel, twice in *Revelation*, but nowhere else in the New Testament. It is significantly absent from the Pauline writings. This suggests that in their use of this

expression the Synoptic evangelists were repeating the testimony of a very early tradition, even though the expression had lost its force in Gentile Christianity. 'Son of Man', which in ordinary Hebrew and Aramaic usage would mean simply 'a human being', seems a lowly enough title. (It occurs frequently in *Ezekiel*, where it is the form of address used by God when giving instructions to the prophet.) Since it is the only title that Jesus applies to himself, according to the first three Gospels, it would seem to limit his own claims strictly to the purely human sphere. However, in the light of apocalyptic expectations current in Judaism, the title 'Son of Man' proves to have a much more exalted reference.

13.22   *The Book of Daniel*, probably written during the persecution of Antiochus Epiphanes (*c.* 167–164 BC; cf. § 3.5 above) contains an account of a mystic vision in which the prophet sees 'one like a son of man', coming with the clouds of heaven, who is presented before 'the Ancient of Days' and is given 'dominion and glory and kingdom' which are to last for ever, so that all peoples should serve him (7:13–14). This imagery may reflect a notion which the author of *Daniel* found already current, possibly derived from Babylonian and Persian sources. This was the notion of a 'heavenly man', perhaps a prototype of all men, who was thought of as a kind of grand vizier or high chamberlain at the throne of God. There was also the notion that each nation had its own 'guardian angel' or heavenly protector who guided its destiny. Daniel's vision may also be compared with that of the prophet Ezekiel, who stands at the beginning of the Jewish apocalyptic tradition. As an exile in Babylonia, Ezekiel saw above a throne 'a being that looked like a man' who was resplendent with 'the likeness of the glory of Yahweh' (*Ezek.* 1:27–8). In *Daniel* the vision of 'the one like a son of man' is subsequently interpreted in such a way that the mysterious personage is seen as a symbol of the 'saints of the Most High', the nation of Israel which will be raised up to triumphant sovereignty in the coming new age.

13.23   Scholars dispute whether in *Daniel* the heavenly son of man is to be interpreted solely in a collective sense, or whether—as I think more probable—the author presents him both as an individual and as a collective symbol. However this may be, it is clear that in later Jewish apocalyptic writings, especially in the *Similitudes of Enoch* (dating from the first century BC), the Danielic 'Son of Man' is taken to be an individual personage. In these writings he is presented as a pre-existing heavenly dignitary who existed with God before the creation of the world and who will appear as an eschatological saviour and judge in the last days, coming in the clouds of heaven. It was as a heavenly redeemer in this form that some Jews (though not the official leaders and teachers) expected the Messiah to come. It seems that it was the author of the *Similitudes of Enoch* who first applied the technical term 'Messiah' to the coming deliverer of Israel, and he expressly identified this Messiah with the celestial Son of Man. The same expectation appears in the Syrian *Apocalypse of Baruch* and in 4 *Ezra*, both dating from the second half of the first century AD, in which the Messiah is seen as a superhuman king of Paradise. There are also echoes of it in the Jewish *Sibylline Oracles* and in rabbinical traditions.

13.24   It seems certain that such ideas had some currency in the time of Jesus. The Gospels relate that he made repeated references to his own role and future eschatological appearance as 'the Son of Man coming in the clouds of heaven with great power and glory' to execute judgement (e.g. *Matt.* 16:27; 24:30 and parallels; *Luke* 17:22–30, etc.). The evangelists also imply that the High Priest was well aware of this expectation of a quasi-divine Son of Man, current in some Jewish circles, when they record the climax of the trial of Jesus before the Sanhedrin:

13.25   The High Priest then said, 'By the living God I charge you to tell us: Are you the Messiah, the Son of God?' Jesus replied, 'The words are yours. But I tell you this: from now on, you will see the Son of Man seated at the right hand of God and coming on the clouds of heaven.' At these words the High Priest tore his robes and exclaimed, 'Blasphemy! Need we call further witnesses? You have heard the blasphemy. What is your opinion?' 'He is guilty,' they answered; 'he should die' (*Matt.* 26:63–6).

Does this passage remind you of another text which we have already considered on an earlier page?

✠ ✠

Answer: In § 13.16 we noted that, according to *Acts* 7:56–7, Stephen was likewise accused of blasphemy and stoned to death for claiming to see Jesus as the Son of Man in the circumstances described in the passage just quoted.

13.26   Since the Synoptic evangelists record the use of the 'Son of Man' title only as a description used by Jesus of himself, and in other contexts they use other titles, it can be argued that Jesus chose to use that everyday Aramaic expression, *bar-nasha*, in an esoteric sense, derived from the Danielic vision and the Jewish apocrypha which developed the idea, in order to express a mysterious claim about his own mission and his consciousness of his eschatological role. In his teaching, however, the theme took a form rather different from that of the Jewish apocalyptic expectations, for it included an insistence that the Son of Man must *suffer*. This is an element absent from the apocryphal writings in question, and it links the Son of Man with the Suffering Servant in Deutero-Isaiah (cf. § 13.12 above).

13.27   Some scholars would accord considerably less significance to the 'Son of Man' title than I have done here, taking it simply as a circumlocution for 'I' on Jesus's lips, or in some instances as no more than an assertion of his function as representative of the people of God. They would restrict the interpretation of the Danielic Son of Man (as also of the Isaian Servant of the Lord) to the theme of corporate representation of Israel. There are theologians who, perhaps for apologetic reasons, look askance at the idea that Jesus or the evangelists could have adapted a bizarre mythological notion to refer to his mission. There are other theologians, however, who see the Son of Man concept in Jewish apocalyptic as a providential *praeparatio evangelica*—that is, as an evangelical 'preaching aid', one of several concepts and illustrations drawn from contemporary culture to convey the meaning of a divine revelation which would otherwise have been scarcely intelligible.

13.28   The term **'Son of God'** occurs in several places in the Gospels, and it is not easy to decide the precise significance it is meant to convey in different contexts. This title was not in itself an obvious assertion of divinity. It was common usage in the Old Testament to apply it to those who were considered to be especially favoured by God—e.g. to the people of Israel collectively (e.g. *Exodus* 4:22; *Hosea* 11:1), or to the anointed king (*2 Samuel* 7:14; *1 Chron.* 17:13; 22:10; 28:6; *Ps.* 2:7), or to the angels (*Ps.* 29:1; *Job* 1:6; cf. *Genesis* 6:2). Indeed, all God-fearing Israelites were 'children of God' (*Deuteronomy* 14:1; *Isaiah* 1:2; 30:1; *Jeremiah* 31:20; *Hosea* 1:10, etc). Pious Pharisees prayed to God as 'Father'. There are also many instances of the use of such terms in ancient polytheistic religions, with their stories of men being begotten by gods or of men being endowed with divine powers by virtue of which they were called 'sons of gods'. Some critics hold that these notions infiltrated into Hellenistic Christianity from its pagan environment. But once again it seems that the 'Son of God' passages are inextricably woven into the early Palestinian traditions about Jesus.

13.29   In the earlier traditions preserved by the Synoptic evangelists, is the term 'Son of God' used in the exalted sense found in the Pauline and Johannine writings, or still in the humbler sense of the Old Testament? The answer seems to be that in the Synoptics the term is already applied to Jesus not simply as *a* son of God, but as *the* Son of God in a unique sense, as a title of majesty. Jesus is shown as conscious of a unique relationship to God as his Father, with a unique mission to be carried out in obedience to his Father. He makes a clear distinction between the relationship of his disciples to God ('your Father') and his own relationship to God ('my Father'): e.g. *Matt.* 6:32 and 7:21; 10:29, 32; *Luke* 2:49. In the parable of the wicked husbandmen Jesus distinguishes between all God's other messengers and representatives, the prophets, whom he describes as 'servants', and himself, the true son and heir of the Father (*Luke* 20:13; *Matt.* 21:33–42).

13.30   All three evangelists give solemn importance to the account of the baptism of Jesus in the Jordan by John the Baptist, relating that the descent of the Holy Spirit on him was made manifest, and that the voice of God was heard from the heavens proclaiming Jesus as his well-beloved Son. (Some have even inferred from this passage that the Gospels here suppose an elevation of Jesus to the status of divine sonship at that moment.) The title 'Son of God' is given solemn significance in the confrontation between Jesus and the High Priest, already referred to in § 13.25, and in the avowal of Peter at Caesarea Philippi. In the form of this episode given by *Matthew*, Jesus asks the question: 'Who do you say I am?', and Peter replies: 'You are the Messiah, the Son of the living God'. This is hailed as a special enlightenment of Peter from on high, disclosing a hidden truth about the identity of Jesus: 'You did not learn that from mortal man; it was revealed to you by my heavenly Father' (*Matt.* 16:13–17).

13.31   Finally, in *Luke* 10:22 (and *Matt.* 11:27) a divine sonship in an extaordinary sense is claimed by Jesus. It involves an intimate relationship between himself as Son and God his Father, so mysterious that the true identity of the Son is hidden from men and known only by God: 'Everything is entrusted to me by my Father: and no one knows who the Son is but the Father, or who the Father is but the Son, and those to whom the Son may choose to reveal him.' This assertion of a divine sonship, involving complete mutual awareness with God at a level above human experience, is so akin to the Christology of John in the Fourth Gospel that it has been called 'a meteorite from the Johannine heaven fallen in the Synoptic earth'. It can at any rate be taken as one more indication that the Christology of the Synoptic Gospels is by no means simple and rudimentary, as some have supposed.

13.32   The first three Gospels certainly present Jesus as the Messiah, but they also present him as much more than the merely human Messiah expected by most Jews. There are a few texts in the Synoptic Gospels which could be brought as objections to belief in the divinity of Christ—for instance, his ignorance of the day of judgement (*Matt.* 24:36). These may be theological difficulties, but the total effect of the evidence we have been considering still remains. It is plain that in the sources and traditions which the evangelists used, divine prerogatives were already attributed to Jesus. Their coherent testimony on this point is the more remarkable, because it is not stressed as an explicit theme but emerges almost unobtrusively from their texts.

13.33   Some critics of an earlier generation liked to fasten on *Mark*, as the earliest Gospel, and to contrast its supposed primitive and down-to-earth Christology with the later Pauline and Johannine notions about Christ's divinity, which they saw as Hellenistic adulterations of the first Palestinian gospel. On this theory, *Matthew* and *Luke* reflected the later beliefs, *Mark* the earlier. But closer study of *Mark* shows that this distinction cannot be sustained. As Vincent

Taylor remarks in *The Gospel according to St Mark* (Macmillan 1932, p. 121), 'Mark's christology is a high christology, as high as any in the New Testament, not excluding that of John'. When, for example, Mark relates the story of the miraculous stilling of the storm, he concludes with the question, asked by the disciples, which must evidently raise in the minds of his readers the ultimate question about the mysterious identity of Jesus: 'Who can this be whom even the wind and the sea obey?' (4:41).

Figure 41 The Marble Street in the ruins of Ephesus. (J. Allan Cash.)

13.34 (iii) Data from the Pauline letters

You have already studied several aspects of Paul's teaching in Part Two. Here we are reviewing the Pauline teaching about Jesus Christ, not to decide how far Paul was the originator of it and how far he was passing on what he had received from others, but to appreciate the body of Christological teaching which the post-apostolic Church had before it in the Pauline letters which were read regularly for the instruction of the congregations.

13.35 The Christology of Paul is primarily dynamic and functional, rather than static and speculative. That is, his first concern is with the saving work and present power of Christ. He does not set out to give a metaphysical treatise on the nature, status or substance of Christ. His Christology is dominated by two ideas which for him are inseparably linked: the atoning death and the vitalizing resurrection of Jesus Christ. Nevertheless, since what Christ has done and still does for mankind depends ultimately on who and what he is, Paul also has an objective Christology which appears in many places in his letters. He presents Christ as a pre-existent divine being, who, sent by God for the salvation of the world, lived a truly human life among men, died upon the cross and rose again, thereupon to be exalted afresh by God to a sublime divine dignity as Lord of all. I summarize Paul's teaching on these points under five sub-headings, as follows:

13.36 (a) Paul affirms that Christ **pre-existed** before the creation of the world, and attributes to him **divine creative power**

'For us there is one God, the Father, from whom all being comes, towards whom we move; and there is one Lord, Jesus Christ, through whom all things came to be, and we through him' (*1 Cor.* 8:6). 'For the divine nature was his from the first; yet he did not think to snatch at equality with God, but made himself nothing, assuming the nature of a slave' (*Phil.* 2:6). 'He is the image of the invisible God; his is the primacy over all created things. In him everything in heaven and on earth was created, not only things visible but also the invisible orders of thrones, sovereignties, authorities and powers: the whole universe has been created through him and for him. And he exists before everything, and all things are held together in him. . . . For it is in Christ that the complete being of the Godhead dwells embodied. . . .' (*Col.* 1:15–17; 2:9; cf. *2 Cor.* 4:4). Some of what Paul says about Christ's role in creation has affinity to Jewish speculations about divine creative and all-pervasive wisdom, such as are found in *Proverbs* 8:1–36 and especially in the *Book of Wisdom* (e.g. 7:22–7) and *Ecclesiasticus* 23:1–34. Paul also affirmed repeatedly that Christ was the Son of God, in a unique sense (*1 Cor.* 15:28; *2 Cor.* 1:19; *Gal.* 2:20; *Col.* 1.13, etc.). This Son pre-existed with God, who carried out his purpose 'by sending his own Son in the likeness of sinful flesh' (*Rom.* 8.3; of *Gal.* 4.4). 'God did not spare his own Son' (*Rom.* 8.32).

13.37   (b)   Paul declares that God **conferred on the risen Christ** supreme divine power and dignity.

'God raised him to the heights and bestowed on him the name above all names, that at the name of Jesus every knee should bow—in heaven, on earth and in the depths—and every tongue confess, "Jesus Christ is Lord", to the glory of God the Father' (*Phil.* 2:9–11; cf. *Isaiah* 45:23 where God declares, 'To me every knee shall bow'). The 'name that is above all names' is, in Hebrew usage, the glorious and ineffable dignity of God himself. *Ephesians* develops this Pauline theme, extolling the mighty power which God 'exerted in Christ when he raised him from the dead, when he enthroned him at his right hand in the heavenly realms, far above all government and authority, all power and dominion, and any title of sovereignty that can be named, not only in this age but in the age to come. He put everything in subjection beneath his feet, and appointed him as supreme head to the Church, which is his body and as such holds within it the fullness of him who himself receives the entire fullness of God' (1:20–3. cf. also *Rom.* 1:4).

13.38   (c)   Paul applies the **Kyrios name** to Christ as a title of majesty

For Paul the distinctive title signifying the majesty of the risen and glorious Christ is *Kyrios*, Lord. It occurs some 200 times in the Pauline letters, applied both to God the Father and to Jesus Christ. Christ is referred to 44 times as 'Lord' or 'The Lord', and 43 times as 'Our Lord'. The Hebrew word *Adonai*, 'Lord', was used in Jewish worship and Scripture-reading as a substitute for the name of God, *Yahweh*, which was considered too sacred to pronounce. *Kyrios* was the corresponding translation used for the name of the Lord God in the Greek Septuagint version of the Scriptures. The word was used by Greek-speaking Jews in their worship, and it was natural that it should also be adopted by Gentile Christians.

13.39   In its ordinary secular usage *Kyrios* implied high rank; it was also commonly used as an honorific form of address, rather like our 'Sir'. (There is a similar multivalence of the word for 'Lord' in modern Italian or Spanish: 'Signore' or 'Señor' can be the title of God, or of an aristocrat, or it can have an everyday usage, equivalent to 'Mr'.) The Gentile Christians were aware that the same title *Kyrios* which they gave to Christ was given to pagan deities in the Hellenistic religions of the world around them (cf. *1 Cor.* 8:5). It was also used with quasi-religious reverence to refer to oriental rulers and to the Roman emperor himself. The Jewish and Christian usages of the term were, however, clearly distinct from those other usages.

13.40 As we have seen (in § 13.17) the Aramaic word for 'Lord' was already in cultic use in the primitive Church as a special term of veneration for the risen Christ, in the phrase *Maranatha*, faithfully transliterated by Paul at the end of *1 Corinthians*. In Paul's letters 'The Lord' is the characteristic title to refer to Christ in his state of exaltation at the right hand of God, continuously exercising supreme power over the world for the sake of his Church and his faithful ones. The conferring of the *Kyrios* name corresponds to the new supreme status conferred upon him by God. To confess 'Jesus is Lord' (*Rom.* 10:9; *1 Cor.* 12:3; *2 Cor.* 4:5; *Phil.* 2:1) was in the early Church a solemn expression of faith in this divine majesty and power of Jesus. Other New Testament writings show that this special usage of *Kyrios* was not limited to Paul and the Pauline Churches.

13.41 (d) According to Paul, Christ is **the object of men's worship,** life-purpose and right conduct, and he is also **the source of their spiritual life and power:** all this implies divine status

Paul addresses personal prayer through Christ to God (*Rom.* 1:8; 7:25; *2 Cor.* 1:20; *Col.* 13:14), and directly *to* Christ (*2 Cor.* 12:8; *1 Thess.* 3:12; *2 Thess.* 2:16). He links Christ with God the Father in blessings calling down divine favour (e.g. *1 Cor.* 1:3; *2 Cor.* 13:14; *Gal.* 1:3, etc.). Christians everywhere 'invoke the name of the Lord' (*1 Cor.* 1:2; cf. *Acts.* 9:14, 21). This implies worshipping Christ, for in Old Testament usage 'invoking the name of the Lord' was to worship God (e.g. *Genesis* 4:26; 12:8; *1 Chronicles* 16:8). In *Rom.* 10:12–13 Paul directly applies to Christ the words of *Joel* 2:32 about the God of Israel: 'Everyone who invokes the name of the Lord will be saved'. (cf. the 'doxology', or praise of divine glory, addressed directly to Christ the Lord in *2 Tim.* 4:18). Paul claims to derive his spiritual authority not from a human source but from Christ and the Father (*Gal.* 1:1).

From your earlier study of Paul's theology of salvation, in Part Two, can you indicate other points in his doctrine which imply a transcendent and suprahuman status of Christ?

✠ ✠

13.42 *Answer:* Several sections from Part Two are relevant here, especially §§ 9.19, 9.24, 9.28 and 9.31–2. We saw that, according to Paul, attaining right relationship with God depended on faith in Christ Jesus. 'The grace of the Lord Jesus Christ' was the same as 'the grace of God' which saved men. Men received this salvation initially by being incorporated into Christ through baptism. Christ was the mysterious and ever-present reality in whom Paul and all the faithful lived. Paul uses the expression 'in Christ Jesus' 164 times to refer to a new manner of existence in the sphere of this supernatural reality.

13.43 (e) The term **'God' in Paul's vocabulary**

It is true that in Paul's theological vocabulary, which he seems to follow consistently, the term 'God' is applied strictly to God the Father, who sent his Son, Jesus, and this God the Father is the God of whom the Hebrew Scriptures speak. It is not certain that Paul ever applies the Greek name *Theos*, 'God', to Christ by direct predication. It is true that almost all Christian tradition and not a few modern theologians think he does so in *Romans* 9:5. The question of the meaning of the Greek text there hinges on a point of grammar and punctuation; the more natural reading would take 'God' to refer directly to Christ. If so, this would be a departure from Paul's consistent phraseology elsewhere.

The translators of the *New English Bible* do not accept the traditional reading. However, in their rendering of *Titus* 2:13 they agree that the author of that letter calls Christ Jesus 'our great God'.

13.44   In any case it is clear that in Paul's theology there is no absolute identification of Christ, the Son, with God the Father. Although he clearly attributes to Christ divine pre-existence, majesty and power, and asserts that Christ shares the attributes and even the nature of God the Father, he also clearly marks a distinction between them. Indeed, in Pauline theology there is undoubtedly a subordination of the Son to the Father, at least in God's revelation and saving action through Christ, which is the central theme of that theology (cf. especially *1 Cor.* 15:27–8). Moreover, the sublime status of the risen Christ often appears as a *consequence* of his resurrection and entry into heavenly glory, and as a reward bestowed on him by God. These aspects of Paul's Christology were to provide matter enough for speculation and controversy in later centuries. The heresy known as Arianism was to fasten on them as support for the notion that Christ was a second and subordinate deity, an emanation or archetypal creature of the supreme God. In reaction against Arian ideas the Church Councils were to define the dogma that is still recited in the Nicene Creed: '. . . Lord Jesus Christ, the only-begotten Son of God, begotten of his Father before all ages, God of God, Light of Light, very God of very God, begotten not made, being of one substance with the Father . . .' To discuss this formulary, however, would take us too far afield. Our task here, we have agreed, is to set out the basic New Testament data, not to study how theologians in later centuries harmonized those data.

Figure 42   Two early Christian frescoes from the Crypt of Lucina, in the Roman catacombs. They symbolize the Eucharist. The casket contains loaves of the Eucharistic bread, and in the original coloured design there appears a glass phial of red Eucharistic wine, set in the basket underneath the platter of loaves. The fish symbolizes Christ, according to a well-known acrostic in which the letters of the Greek word for fish, ichthus, formed the initial letters of the phrase, 'Jesus Christ, Son of God, Saviour'. These frescoes are among the oldest examples of Christian art. (The Hamlyn Group: photo, John R. Freeman and Co.)

13.45   (iv)   Data from the Fourth Gospel

If Paul's ruling preoccupation is with 'soteriology', that is, with the doctrine of the salvation brought to men by the life, death and resurrection of the Son of God and with the enduring action of the risen Lord in his Church, John's[1] ruling preoccupation, within the same general theological framework, can be said to be with the self-revelation of the central figure himself. The Fourth Gospel, written in simple and unadorned Greek, is a work of consummate artistry without apparent use of art, and is also the first full-scale treatise in Christology.

---

[1] On the authorship of the Fourth Gospel, see §§ 16.15–16 below, and Filson, pp. 370–9.

13.46   There are two terms between which the Gospel narrative of *John* is set. The first is the solemn prologue (1:1–18), a paean of praise of the mysterious *Logos*, the Word of God, who existed before the beginning of the world, who was with God, who was God, through whom all things came to be. This *Logos*, the Son of God, who 'became flesh' amongst men, witnesses to and imparts God's light, grace and truth out of his own divine fullness. He is Jesus Christ, the very source of life. The second term, the climax of the Gospel, comes at the end of Chapter 20 (the natural ending of the Gospel; Chapter 21 has the character of a postscript). It is the dramatic exclamation by which Thomas, confronted with Jesus risen from the dead, acknowledges what and who he really is: 'My Lord and my God' (10:28). Acceptance of this stupendous truth about Jesus marks out as blessed those who have not seen him in the flesh but have believed; the evangelist declares that he has written his Gospel with the object of instilling this belief (20:29, 31). Some of John's readers might well contrast Thomas's confession with another contemporary use of the very same expression—the demand of the Emperor Domitian to be acknowledged as *Dominus et Deus*, 'Lord and God'.

13.47   Why the author of *John* used the *Logos* title, in what sense, and where he drew it from, are questions much discussed. Not a few modern commentators think he derived it from Greek philosophy, especially from Stoic thought, in which it was a basic concept for the interpretation of man and the world (cf. Units 4–5, § 7.2). But Stoic philosophy never presented *logos*, the divine principle of reason in the universe, as a person; and for his part John shows not the slightest interest in any philosophical explanation of the world. Others suggest that the Johannine concept of the Logos was developed from the Jewish reflections about divine widom, as found in *Job*, *Proverbs* and especially in the deutero-canonical *Book of Wisdom*; or that it was borrowed from the speculative thought of later Alexandrian Judaism. The exegete Philo expressly uses the term in a theological sense. In these sources, however, there is nothing really comparable to the *Logos*-Son of God-Jesus of the Fourth Gospel. Others again link the *Logos* with the word of God, to which a creative and all-powerful role is attributed in the Old Testament. Indeed, the very first phrase of the Fourth Gospel, introducing the *Logos*, seems to be modelled on the opening phrase of *Genesis* about God's original creative act. However, in the Hebrew Scriptures God's utterance is never objectified into a distinct personal agent.

13.48   It may be that some at least of these influences contributed to the Johannine conception of *Logos*. Whatever the ultimate derivation of the term, it cannot be assumed that the first Christian usage of the *Logos* title of Jesus was in *John*. Applying the methods of literary form-criticism to the text of the Fourth Gospel, some biblical scholars have concluded that in his prologue the author used and adapted an already current *Logos*-hymn. If so, this Christological title would have been already known to those for whom he was writing.

13.49   At the time the Fourth Gospel was written there was already a challenge from incipient Gnosticism, which threatened to make a radical distortion of the Church's belief about Christ. As we saw in § 4.28, Gnosticism held that matter was evil and only spirit was good. It also proposed a theory of emanation of *aeons* from the supreme good God, to explain how spiritual goodness filtered downwards from the higher spheres of being to the lower. Because of their anti-material philosophy, Gnostics denied the true reality of Christ's human nature. Those called Docetists (or 'Apparitionists') held that he was a spiritual emanation appearing on earth in a phantasmal body. In counteracting these notions *John* stressed the true humanity of Jesus. The divine *Logos* really and materially 'became flesh'. At the same time the evangelist stressed the unity in Godhead of the Son with the Father. The *Logos* was not a demigod or a subordinate divine being, he was not a second God beside the first God, but he was the revelation of the only God.

13.50 In many different ways *John* asserts the deity of Jesus in the fullest sense, not only explicitly in the prologue and in the climax of the Gospel, but implicitly throughout the work. The mysterious identity of Jesus, constantly referred to in veiled allusions, misunderstood by his enemies and gradually dawning on his followers, is the theme of the narrative. Among many allusive expressions which recur frequently throughout the Gospel is the phrase on the lips of Jesus, *ego eimi*—'I am', or 'It is I'. The phrase evokes the mysterious name of God revealed in answer to Moses's question on Horeb: 'God said to Moses, I AM WHO I AM. And he said, Say this to the people of Israel, I AM has sent me to you' (*Exodus* 3:14–15). So in the Fourth Gospel, when Jesus declares, 'In very truth I tell you, before Abraham was born, I am' (8:58), his enemies attempt to stone him for blasphemy. God the Father, Jesus declares, has made his incarnate Son coequal with himself in dignity. His enemies were 'still more determined to kill him, because he was not only breaking the Sabbath, but, by calling God his own Father, he claimed equality with God' (5:18). Jesus replies that all he is, has and does comes from the Father; nevertheless, 'the Father does not judge anyone, but has given full jurisdiction to the Son; it is his will that all should pay the same honour to the Son as to the Father' (5:22–3). Throughout the Fourth Gospel this claim is repeated. The followers of Jesus are required to give to him the same kind of devotion that is due to God: they must direct to him their faith (6:29–47; 11:26; 14:1), their trust (14:13–14; 15:5–7), and their love (14:21, 28).

13.51 Although the primacy of God the Father and his distinction from the Son whom he has sent is clear, the *Gospel of John* insistently asserts that there is also an absolute unity between Jesus and God his Father, with whom he coexisted in divine glory before the creation of the world. 'My Father and I are one' (10:29). Again his Jewish opponents reach for stones to strike him down for blasphemy, because, 'You, a mere man, claim to be God' (or, 'a god'). The long discourse of Jesus to his disciples in Chapters 13–17 develops this theme: 'Anyone who has seen me has seen the Father. . . . Believe me when I say that I am in the Father and the Father in me. . . .' (14:9, 11); 'Father, glorify me in thine own presence with the glory I had with thee before the world began' (17:5).

13.52 In *John* the expression that most closely approaches our abstract noun 'divinity' is the word translated as 'glory'. In the Hebrew Scriptures 'the glory of God' is the resplendent radiance of God and the crushing weight of his power and majesty, often manifested in the phenomena of nature. This Old Testament concept of God's glory is transferred to Christ in the New Testament. In the Synoptic Gospels it is mentioned chiefly in an eschatological context—the vision of the Son of Man coming in glory in the clouds of heaven. In the Fourth Gospel it is the permanent state or being of Christ. It is announced in the prologue: 'So the Word became flesh; he came to dwell among us, and we saw his glory, such glory as befits the Father's only Son, full of grace and truth' (1:14); the theme recurs throughout the Gospel (e.g. 2:11; 12:41; 13:31; 16:14). The 'hour' of Christ's glory is especially the sequence of events of his passion and death, leading on to his resurrection (17:2–5).

13.53 (v) Data from other books of the New Testament

The remaining books of the New Testament contain several other testimonies to belief in Christ's deity; it is evident that this was a generally accepted doctrine, not an interpretation put forward by certain teachers or in certain groups only.

The *Epistle to the Hebrews*, which may have been written by Apollos, the learned Jew from Alexandria (*Acts* 18:2), begins with a proclamation of the sublime dignity of Christ, a passage which equals the prologue of *John* in the grandeur of its expression and the boldness of its claims. The author's theme throughout his treatise is to prove the superiority of the New Covenant over the Old. At the outset he proves this superiority by appealing to the divine transcendence of Christ. Under the old dispensation God spoke only through human intermediaries, the prophets: 'But in this the final age he has spoken to us in the Son whom he has made heir to the whole universe, and through whom he created all orders of existence: the Son who is the effulgence of God's splendour and the stamp of God's very being, and sustains the universe by his word of power.' As well as being a pre-existent creative principle, the Son has also been vested with a supreme dignity by virtue of his atoning ministry: 'When he had brought about the purgation of sins, he took his seat at the right hand of Majesty on high, raised as far above the angels, as the title he has inherited is superior to theirs' (*Heb.* 1:1–4).

13.54 After citing a text from *Psalm* 45 to show that the Son, who is Jesus, is to be ·addressed directly in the vocative, 'O God' (1:8–9), the author of *Hebrews* goes on to make a direct application to Christ of other Old Testament texts which, in their original context, applied solely to God, the creator of heaven and earth (1:10–11; cf. *Psalm* 102:25–7). This transference to Jesus of Old Testament texts referring to Israel's Lord and God appears elsewhere in the New Testament (e.g. *1 Peter* 3:14–15; cf. *Isaiah* 8:12–13. So too, *John* 12:41; cf. *Isaiah* 7:10). Can you give another notable example of it, which we have already mentioned more than once in these pages?

✠ ✠

Answer: We have seen that the *Kyrios* title itself, which was in general use in the New Testament communities as the title of majesty for Christ (cf. §§ 13.17 and 13.38–40), is an instance of this transference. It is found in all the New Testament writings except *Matthew, Mark, Titus,* and the Johannine epistles.

13.55 In the shorter writings of the New Testament there are incidental testimonies: e.g. to the heavenly dignity of the risen Christ in *1 Peter* 3:22. *2 Peter*, a later work, refers to 'our God and Saviour Jesus Christ' and to 'his divine power' (1:1, 3). *1 John* declares that in Jesus Christ 'the eternal life which dwelt with the Father was made visible to us' (1:2–3; cf. 5:20, 'This is the true God, this is eternal life'). The only major testimony still to be mentioned is that of the author of *Revelation*, the last book in our canonical New Testament. In his strange apocalyptic imagery he refers to Jesus in his heavenly glory, and ascribes to him titles, honours and functions that belong to God. He describes adoration given jointly to God and to Christ, 'the Lamb that was slain', who shares the throne of God. Christ is 'King of kings and Lord of lords'; he has 'a name known to none but himself'; he is the 'one like the son of man', glorious as in the Danielic vision, but now vested with the same appearance that Daniel attributed to the Ancient of Days (*Rev.* 13–16; cf. *Dan.* 7:9, 13)'; he is 'called the Word (*Logos*) of God'; he is 'the Alpha and the Omega, the first and the last, the beginning and the end' (*Rev.* 5:12–14; 7:10, 17; 17:14; 19:12–13, 16; 21:22; 22:1, 3; 22:13).

13.56 Christology and monotheism

The Christological concepts we have been considering in the New Testament writings are quite varied and contain much that is obscure. They are not systematized into one theological synthesis, yet there is a remarkable underlying co-

Figure 43 A tombstone from the Roman catacombs. It commemorates in Latin a deceased woman, Licinia, and bears also the Greek phrase 'Ichthys zonton'—'The Fish of the living'. See note to Figure 42. The anchor was a common Christian symbol of hope, and the fish design was also commonly used by Christians. Tertullian, a Christian writer from North Africa, referred to this symbolism. Christ, he said, was the Fish, and Christians were the little fishes finding life from the waters of baptism. Note that this tombstone, almost certainly Christian, still bears the conventional superscription D M, an abbreviation for 'Diis Manibus', which was originally an invocation to the tutelary gods and spirits. (Benedictine Sisters of the Catacomb of Priscilla, Rome.)

herence between them. The early traditions preserved in the Synoptics and in *Acts* already witness to a belief in Christ's supra-human dignity. The more developed Christologies of Paul, of John and of the author of *Hebrews*, although expressed in different thought-patterns, do not contradict one another and indeed have a basic harmony. From our survey of the documents of the New Testament, it does appear that there was an evolution of Christology during the period of its composition. The assertion of the full divinity of Jesus Christ is explicit in a later book like *John* and less definite in the earlier strata of the tradition. Does this prove that the doctrine was a later invention or a mythologizing of the primitive gospel? There is no obvious discontinuity in belief. We have seen that, even in the earliest strata discernible in the New Testament tradition, attributes were ascribed to Christ that belonged properly to God. If there was an evolution towards more explicit assertion of his deity, it may still be argued that it was an organic development of doctrine, as a seed develops into a plant; that with the passing of the years the inner meaning of the doctrine became more manifest and the religious understanding of it deeper.

13.57 Certainly, there were formidable intellectual problems in a faith which contained elements seemingly so difficult to reconcile. To begin with, while asserting the identity of the man Jesus of Nazareth, the son of Mary, with a pre-existent divine person who was also the present Lord of glory and the future eschatological Judge, the New Testament writers saw an evident difference between his human and divine modes of existence. In his human life he was subject and obedient to God, and even his exalted resurrection-status is presented as a reward bestowed upon him as man by God. But there was a further paradox: in his pre-existent and everlasting divine status he was 'with God', 'in the form of God', 'in the Father', 'one with the Father', 'equal to God', and was himself 'God'; yet always a distinction is marked between him and the Father.

13.58 Now the basic religious presupposition common to Jesus, to his disciples, and to all the New Testament writers, was, as we have seen, the absolute monotheism of Israel: there was one God, and there could be no other gods beside him. Although the New Testament writers did not state in so many words the theological problem raised by the apparently conflicting elements in their beliefs about Christ (indeed, they showed no concern to provide a rational apologetic for their faith), they did show a care to avoid anything that would suggest 'ditheism', or a doctrine of the existence of two Gods. Paul and John used metaphors which implied that there was no absolute separation between the Son and God the Father. The Son was 'the image of the invisible God' (*Col.* 1:15); he was 'the likeness of God' (*2 Cor.* 4:4); he was as a word (*Logos*) uttered by a speaker (*John* 1).

13.59 We saw in § 13.53 that the author of *Hebrews* used two metaphors to express the relationship. Christ in his divine pre-existence and creative power was both 'the effulgence of the glory of God', and also 'the stamp of God's very being' (*Heb.* 1:3; cf. *Wisdom* 7:26). The first metaphor alone might suggest that he was simply an aspect of divine glory, like the radiance of the sun by which men apprehend the sun itself; the latter might suggest that he was a separated image of God, patterned on the supreme Deity as a wax seal reproduces the form of the original die. Taken together the two metaphors could be taken as complementary, avoiding either extreme. Such metaphors, of course, did not remove the obvious difficulties which the New Testament Christology presented to human understanding. In the later Trinitarian controversies all the subtlety of Greek metaphysical thinking would be brought to bear on the question—with the further complication that, with the development of dogmatic theology, the third divine person—the Holy Spirit—had to be included in the same systematic solution of the theologians. (See §§ 14.0–2 below.)

13.60 In your answer to the exercise which I proposed in § 13.4 you may have included some further texts and arguments which I have not mentioned in my own lengthy answer. In such a wide field it should not be difficult to point out aspects of the question which I have not touched on, and naturally there is scope for variant interpretations of the texts I have discussed. In any case, my summary survey of the texts was not meant to provide a full account of what the New Testament writers say about Christ and his work. It singled out one aspect, which though of central importance is not treated in the New Testament as an isolated subject. Indeed, in concentrating on the scriptural passages which testify to the deity of Christ, it is possible to give a misleading impression. The texts which assert Christ's eternal pre-existence, his creative power, and his enthronement with God in heavenly majesty, are evidently the most significant for the purpose of the particular question we have been discussing. However the emphasis, at least of the Synoptic and Pauline writings, is not there, but rather on 'functional Christology'. As we have seen (§ 13.35), this expression refers to the mission and salvific work of Christ, and to its effects in the life of the Church and the faithful.

13.61 The preaching of the early Church about Christ did not begin with an abstract dogma about a pre-existent *Logos*, or about the divinity of the figure who would eventually appear in eschatological splendour from the clouds; it was founded on conviction about an actual intervention by God in human experience. That intervention was seen to be manifest in the events of the life, death and resurrection of Jesus of Nazareth. These events, and above all the fact of his resurrection, were attested by eyewitnesses who devoted their lives to proclaiming what had happened and who were prepared to die for what they proclaimed. This conviction was what gave Christianity its first energy and power of expansion. However, it is too much to say, as some authors do, that the Church of the New Testament was *only* concerned with 'functional Christology', and not at all with the question of who and what was the person who stood at the centre of their faith. By later reflection on the implications of their 'salvation history', and on the clues given them in veiled language by their Master himself, Christian thinkers began to work out theological statements about the being on whom they centred their religious life.

13.62 We have been concentrating on those passages of the New Testament which testify to a belief in the divinity of Christ; it would have been possible but hardly necessary to set you an exercise to find evidence that the Christians of the New Testament period also believed that Christ was truly a human being. This would be a simple matter to demonstrate. Clearly the authors of the four Gospels and Paul were convinced that Jesus was a real man. Although they also attributed to him properties belonging to God, they stress that he lived a real human life, that he truly suffered and died. It was Docetic Gnosticism, not mainstream Christianity, that would represent Christ as a heavenly apparition in human guise, who only appeared to be man and whose sufferings and death were illusory. What we have seen is that mainstream Christianity, while affirming that Christ was truly man, *also* affirmed that he was truly God.

13.63 You may be aware that in some theological circles today there is a desire for a critical re-thinking of traditional Christology. Some modern theologians are uneasy about the attribution of divinity to Christ, which has been so prominent a feature of Christianity throughout the centuries. They consider that today it is the humanity of Christ that needs to be stressed. How far do you think this question is relevant to our present study?

✠ ✠

13.64 *My answer:* At the risk of labouring the point, I would again urge you not to allow present-day religious concerns to cloud the issues we are investigating here—however valid those concerns may be in their own place. It is natural enough if a believing Christian is more interested in the New Testament writings as a sourcebook for his belief, conduct and devotion, rather than as historical documents throwing light on a remote past. A biblical theologian may be chiefly intent on getting behind the letter of the text in search of the original religious meaning and values of the Christian message. With this aim in view, he may consider it very important to distinguish between what Jesus said of himself and what the evangelists and second-generation members of the Church said about him. Other divines and preachers may be preoccupied with the problem of 'demythologizing' the New Testament, in order to discover a Christ who is religiously meaningful to modern man, and to preach a gospel which has authentic relevance to present-day life. These, however, are not our preoccupations here. Those of you who study the New Testament primarily with a view to discovering what its message is to the Christian of today will need to remind yourselves constantly of the more restricted approach we are adopting in this course. We accept the New Testament writings as documents of their time, which reflected and moulded the belief of the early Church, and we have been asking how those writings represented Christ to those Christians in that age. It is no part of the aims of this course to decide whether traditional Christology can now be restated in a way that is more acceptable to modern man.

As a kind of postscript to this discussion, perhaps I ought to add a word here about the doctrine of the Holy Spirit and of the Trinity, since you are no doubt well aware that traditional Christian teaching not only asserts that Jesus Christ is a divine 'person' coequal with the Father, but that the Holy Spirit is also a distinct divine 'person' coequal with Father and Son. The term 'Trinity', though now so familiar in Christian usage, is in fact not to be found in the New Testament. (The earliest known use of it is in Theophilus of Antioch, about AD 180.) Throughout the Bible there is indeed frequent mention of the Spirit of God. In the Old Testament this expression refers to divine creative power, wisdom and life-breathing energy (e.g. *Genesis* 1:2; *1 Samuel* 10:10; *Ezekiel* 37:8 seq.; *Joel* 3:1–2). In the New Testament special functions of sanctifying, enlightening, guiding and strengthening Christians are attributed to a power coming from God which is called either 'spirit', or 'holy spirit' or '*The* Holy Spirit' (e.g. *Luke* 1:15, 35, 41, 67; 2:25–6; 4:14; 12:12; *Acts* 1:8; 2:2–47; 5:3–4; 10:19–20; 8:29, 39; 13:2, 4; 16:6; 15:28; 20:28). We have seen that for Paul the Spirit was the source of authentic Christian living. Dwelling within Christians, this spiritual principle made them children of God and enabled them to witness to God in their words and deeds. (See § 9.28 above.)

Figure 44 A typical gallery in the early Christian catacombs of Rome. These passages were hewn out of the soft but sturdy rock called tufa. *The bodies of the dead were placed in the rectangular recesses called* loculi, *which were then covered in with the sealing slab. These graves, in the Catacomb of Panfilo, were plundered in past centuries. (Pontifical Archaeological Commission, Rome.)*

14.1 In some New Testament passages the term 'Spirit of Christ', or 'Spirit of the Lord' was used interchangeably with the term 'Spirit of God' (e.g. in *Romans* 8:9); but there were other texts which were interpreted in the early Church to imply that the Holy Spirit was a distinct divine principle. Particularly influential in this respect was the baptismal formula given in *Matthew* 28:19:

'Go forth therefore and make all nations my disciples; baptize men everywhere in the name of the Father and of the Son and of the Holy Spirit . . .' Similar threefold formulae were found in *2 Cor.* 13:13; *Titus* 3:4–6, etc. There were also the suggestive texts in the Fourth Gospel which attributed to the Spirit a distinctive personal function as counsellor and teacher, and (using the personal pronoun) spoke of him in a manner which, while associating him with Christ and the Father, nevertheless indicated a distinction between him and them (*John* 14:16, 25–6; 16:7–15).

14.2   In the period we are studying, up to the closing decades of the second century, the Church had certainly not yet formulated the dogma of the Trinity, as it was to be later defined. Some Christian authors, indeed, made assertions which do not square with later orthodoxy on this subject. Yet there were already signs in that period that the New Testament texts referred to above, especially the baptismal formula which had so great a practical importance in Christian life, were being interpreted in a sense which was leading towards the future Trinitarian definitions. By the beginning of the second century the divine triad were being linked together as a joint object of religious devotion, and called upon in one common attestation. In the *Letter of Clement of Rome* to the Corinthians is this phrase: 'As surely as God lives, as Jesus Christ lives, and the Holy Spirit also—on whom are set the faith and hope of God's elect—so surely the man who keeps the divinely appointed decrees . . . will be exalted . . .' etc. Similarly Ignatius of Antioch wrote to the Magnesians: 'May everything you do, worldly or spiritual, go prosperously from beginning to end in faith and love, in the Son and the Father and the Spirit . . .'. A process of doctrinal development was already at work which would eventually lead the Fathers and Councils of the Church to acknowledge the Holy Spirit, not simply as an indeterminate divine energy, but as a personal principle distinct from and coequal with both the divine Father and the divine Son, yet united with them in one Godhead.

(E)   CHRISTIAN LITERATURE OF THE SUB-APOSTOLIC AGE

15.0   In the footsteps of the Apostles

For a study of the history of the Church in the second century you should know something about the Christian literature of the sub-apostolic period. 'Sub-apostolic' is an adjective used to describe the period following that of the lifetime of the Apostles. Applied to early Christian literature, it may be taken to refer to those writings, other than the books of the New Testament, which originated in the hundred years or so after the close of the period covered by the *Acts of the Apostles*. You may find this slightly puzzling, since, as we saw earlier (§ 2.23) the most esteemed writers of that period are commonly called 'the Apostolic Fathers'. This term does not mean that they were Apostles or companions of the Apostles, but it can be taken to mean that they wrote in a time when the memory of the Apostles' teaching was fresh, and that they faithfully followed the apostolic tradition and spirit. The time divisions are not hard-and-fast here, and some of the early non-canonical writings we shall be considering (i.e. writings not contained in the canon of the New Testament) originated about the same time as, or in some cases even earlier than, the later books of the New Testament.

Figure 45 The apotheosis of the Emperor Antoninus Pius and his wife Faustina. The imperial couple are shown being carried up to heaven by a winged spirit, with eagles in attendance. This relief, from a monumental column of the second century, is in the Cortile della Pigna, in the Vatican. (The Hamlyn Group: photo, Alinari.)

15.1 The sub-apostolic Christian writings are of unequal value. Some few of them—notably the *Epistle to Diognetus*—show deep religious insight and power of expression. Many of them, however, when compared to the letters of Paul, the Gospels, the Johannine writings and the *Epistle to the Hebrews*, seem mediocre. (In fact, the 'sub' in the 'sub-apostolic' conveys a nuance of meaning that this period was a step down from the heights of the Church of the Apostles.) Their authors seldom show the spirit of original religious genius. Even prominent Church leaders among them are evidently conscious of treading in the footsteps of masters whose teaching they cannot improve on but must faithfully repeat and try to understand.

15.2 Some of the writings of the period have survived only in fragmentary form, or are known to us only through quotations or references in later works. Some, belonging to the category of 'apocrypha and pseudepigrapha' (cf. § 2.24), reflect Gnostic notions or the particular outlook of Judaeo-Christian groups who stood apart from the Gentile majority in the Church. All of them, whether 'orthodox' or otherwise, are of interest to the historian. But here we have space only to refer to those writings which came to acquire some general repute in the Church, and which can thus be taken as more representative of the common belief and practice. Some of them were accorded so great an authority that they were ranked with the New Testament books during the period before the scriptural canon became generally fixed. The authentic text of most of these writings has been preserved in a satisfactory form. Some passages have survived by being incorporated into later works, especially in the *Ecclesiastical History* of Eusebius, a diligent fourth-century bishop who preserved much early material for posterity.

15.3 Survey of the post-apostolic writings

You cannot be expected to read through those early Christian writings now, but some day when you have more time I hope you will read the more important of them; for example, in the Penguin translation by M. Staniforth, *Early*

Christian Writings: The Apostolic Fathers (1972 reprint). For the more advanced student the two-volume edition in the Loeb series, *The Apostolic Fathers*, gives the original texts and translation by Kirsopp Lake; this edition contains some writings omitted in the Penguin translation. At the end of your set book Filson gives references to places in which he has quoted or referred to the writings of those who are included in the class of 'Apostolic Fathers'. In the course of the book, especially in Part Five, Filson also refers to a number of other second-century writers, such as Justin Martyr, who are not usually called 'Apostolic Fathers', because they wrote somewhat later in the second century.

15.4 The information Filson gives about the early Christian literature is only sketchy, but for the purpose of the next exercise you can use it as far as it goes, and perhaps supplement it from what you have read elsewhere. You may find useful here Map C on page 91 of these units, showing the geographical distribution of Christian writers of the second century. The exercise is as follows:

> **List the more important non-canonical Christian writings** up to about the end of the reign of Marcus Aurelius (AD 180), giving an approximate indication of the **date** of each, a note about its **authorship,** and a very brief indication of its **contents.**

A LONG PAUSE HERE
Do not read on until you have worked on the exercise

Specimen answers and discussion

I have included in my list some writings which Filson does not discuss, and also some which, though they survive only as fragments or in quotations by Eusebius, are of particular interest. All the writings mentioned were written in Greek, unless otherwise indicated.

15.5 (a) **1 Clement,** the name given to a letter from the church of Rome to the Christians of Corinth, was written about AD 96. The author has from very early times been identified as Clement of Rome—was he the 'fellow-worker' mentioned by Paul in *Philippians* 4:3? He writes on behalf of the Roman community, urging the Corinthians to heal a rift in their church by restoring to office some ministers whom they have deposed. The letter, which is a firmly worded exhortation to unity and obedience, stresses the divinely instituted authority of the Church's ministers, which is derived by succession from the Apostles of Christ. This letter acquired great authority, and can be seen as a milestone in the rise of the Roman church and bishop to pre-eminence.

15.6 (b) **The Didache,** or 'Teaching of the Twelve Apostles', is a short work, probably compiled in Syria in the first half of the second century, but incorporating archaic material which may well go back to a very early date. It consists of a discussion of 'two ways', the Way of Life and the Way of Death, then some regulations about church practice and worship, and finally a concluding section which shows that, at the time of writing, expectation of the Last Days and of the proximate return of Christ was still very much in the forefront of Christian thinking. The *Didache* reflects a period when Church organization was still rudimentary. I have always been intrigued by one of the instructions concerning baptism in the *Didache*: 'Baptize in running water in the name of the Father and of the Son, and of the Holy Spirit. If no running water is available, baptize in still water. If no cold water is available, baptize in warm water' (no. 7). Where on earth, one might ask, would the latter conditions be verified?

✠ ✠

My answer: Where there were hot springs or geysers. I remember coming across hot springs and steaming pools, with streams of hot water running from them, in the Yarmuk gorge through the mountains to the east of the Lake of Galilee, and wondering whether the *Didache* regulations may have originated in some such locality. A very ancient tradition asserts that at the time of the Jewish revolt, when the destruction of Jerusalem in AD 70 was imminent, the Christian community fled from Jerusalem to the region of Pella, east of the Jordan. This is not very far from the Yarmuk gorge; some at least of the refugee Christians may have settled in those parts.

15.7 (c) **The letters of Ignatius of Antioch** date from the reign of Trajan. Ignatius was bishop of the church in the sprawling metropolis of Antioch in Syria, which had been a chief base for the original missionary expansion of Christianity. His seven letters, the genuine text of which has been established beyond reasonable question, were written while he was a captive on his way to execution, knowing that he was to be thrown to the beasts in the amphitheatre in Rome. Eusebius says that Ignatius was martyred in the eleventh year of Trajan's reign, which would put the date at about 109. One of the letters was addressed to the Christian community in Rome, one to Polycarp of Smyrna, and five to Christian churches in the Roman province of Asia, which by the end of the first century had become a main 'heartland' of Christianity.

15.8 The letters of Ignatius are vibrant with zeal and piety, and contain many valuable indications about the contemporary beliefs and practice of the churches with which he was in communication. He was anxious to counter the Docetist heresy (cf. § 4.23) and above all to foster unity and love between Christians. He attests the growing prevalence (at least in Asia Minor and Syria) of what is called 'monepiscopacy', or the rule of a single bishop over a local church, with a closely-knit group of presbyters and deacons around him. Some think that Ignatius himself was largely influential in furthering this system.

15.9 (d) **The Epistle of Polycarp** was written at some date after the martyrdom of Ignatius, to which it refers. Polycarp was bishop of Smyrna, and he and his flock had welcomed the captive bishop of Antioch during his halt there on his way to Rome. Ignatius afterwards wrote to Polycarp in terms of warm affection and fatherly advice. Polycarp's letter, his only surviving writing, was sent to the Christians of Philippi in Macedonia, giving spiritual exhortations and vigorously condemning the Docetist heresy. It is notable for its verbatim quotations from *Matthew*, from several of Paul's letters and from *1 Peter*, which were evidently already accepted as equivalent to Scripture in Christian eyes. According to Irenaeus, who as a child had heard him speaking to the people, Polycarp had in his own youth listened to the preaching of the Apostle John.

15.10 (e) **The Epistle of Barnabas** can be dated some time after AD 70 and before 132. The author was certainly not the Barnabas who was a companion of Paul (*Acts* 13–14). His aim in writing was to counteract Judaizing tendencies among Christians, by completely discrediting the Jewish interpretation of the Law and denying the claim of the Jews to be the people of God's covenant. He reinterprets the Old Testament in a Christian sense, using fanciful allegory.

15.11 (f) **'The Apologists'** is the name collectively given to those who wrote tracts presenting the Christian faith and way of life in a persuasive manner, hoping to break down prejudice and to win a favourable hearing from non-Christian readers. An *apologia* meant a defence or vindication of one's position, not an expression of regret. The Apologists are often regarded, rather artificially, as a coherent group, who took up the torch from the Apostolic Fathers and played an important role in the development of Christian theology by bringing it into intellectual encounter with Greek thought. Some critics say that they 'hellenized' Christianity in the process, but if this means that they changed its basic nature and doctrines, it is too much to say. Their interpretation of Christianity was indeed adapted to the needs of controversy, but it was not essentially different from that of their predecessors. Perhaps it is a fair criticism to say that most of them—Justin is a notable exception—seem more concerned to commend Christians than Christ to their pagan contemporaries.

15.12 The earliest of these 'apologies' was addressed to the Emperor Hadrian about the year 125 by an Athenian called Quadratus; a fragment of it is preserved by Eusebius. It is possible that this was the same work as the elegantly written *Epistle to Diognetus*, which decries the follies of paganism and Judaism and paints an attractive picture of Christian ideals and conduct. Another Athenian apologist, Aristides, follows the same method in a rather clumsy work which was also addressed to an emperor—probably Hadrian again. A Jewish-Christian apologist was Ariston, who wrote a *Dialogue concerning Christ* about the middle of the second century.

15.13 The most famous of all the apologists was Justin of Samaria, who was martyred in Rome about AD 165. Using the skills and some of the ideas of contemporary philosophy, especially of Stoicism and Platonism, he addressed an *Apologia* to Antoninus Pius and his son Marcus Aurelius about 150. It was followed by an appendix, sometimes called Justin's *Second Apology*. Justin also wrote a long *Dialogue with Trypho the Jew*, and an anti-Gnostic work, now lost, called *Against all Heresies*. His writings are a valuable source of knowledge about the way in which Christian beliefs and worship were developing. A disciple of Justin, the Assyrian Tatian, wrote an *Address to the Greeks* in mocking vein, hardly calculated to win friends and gain influence. He is better known for his *Diatessaron*, a harmonized conflation of all four Gospels. He later left the main Church.

15.14 At the end of the period we are considering, about 180, Theophilus, bishop of Antioch, wrote a more persuasive account of the Christian religion, addressed to his non-Christian friend Autolycus. About the same time Athenagoras of Athens addressed to Marcus Aurelius and his son Commodus the most polished of all the second-century apologetic works. He disproved the calumnies commonly brought against the Christians, and presented the Christian religion as the noblest and purest philosophy. At the end of the second century an *Apology* was written in Latin, by Tertullian. Another was the *Octavius* of Minucius Felix. There are extracts from both in Lewis and Reinhold, pp. 584–9.

15.15 (g) **The Shepherd of Hermas** is a work datable from the beginning of the reign of Antoninus Pius, probably about 140. It is a peculiar composition, partly apocalyptic, partly (it would seem) autobiographical. The author, a freedman engaged in trade, was a brother of Pius, bishop of Rome. The *Shepherd* is clumsily composed, is often obscure and abounds in strange imagery. Yet it gained so great esteem in some circles that it was ranked with the New Testament writings. Its author's chief preoccupation is with righteousness of Christian living, and the point usually singled out for comment is his teaching about ecclesiastical penance and forgiveness of sins. He holds that after baptism there can be one more remission of sins, but only one. The same practical concern 'to keep the flesh pure and the seal of baptism unsullied' is shown in a homily of about the same date, known as the **Second Epistle of Clement.** It is so called because it was for long mistakenly ascribed to the author of *1 Clement*.

15.16 (h) **The Martyrdom of Polycarp,** the earliest authentic example of narratives of the sufferings of the martyrs, which were eagerly circulated for the edification of the faithful in other communities, was written just after Polycarp had been done to death in the arena at Smyrna. The date can be fixed with strong probability as 155. Nearly half a century had elapsed since Ignatius, on his way to martyrdom in Rome, had written to Polycarp. The venerable bishop of Smyrna was now eighty-six years old, as he declared under interrogation. Apart from two legendary details, which may be later additions, this fervent account gives a vivid and convincing glimpse of conditions during a ruthless pogrom of Christians by direction of the Roman provincial authorities. Another authentic account of martyrdoms describes the ordeal of the Christians of **Lyons and Vienne** in Gaul, in the year 177. There is a fairly lengthy extract in Lewis and Reinhold, pages 591–3.

15.17 (i) Among works which we know of only from **surviving fragments** or the reports of others, the writings of Papias, bishop of Hierapolis, probably dating from the reign of Hadrian, have a special interest for New Testament scholars. Eusebius quotes some remarks of Papias about the authorship of the Gospels and about oral tradition. He also describes him as 'a pupil of John and a companion of Polycarp', but does not think much of his intelligence. Perhaps one day a manuscript of the lost five books of Papias's *Exposition of the Sayings of the Lord* may turn up somewhere, or perhaps even a collection of the *logia*, the sayings of the Lord to which he referred. A famous fragment is the **Muratorian Canon** (named after the scholar who discovered it), which goes back to the latter part of the second century. It gives the earliest extant list of New Testament books which the 'Catholic Church' (as distinct from Gnostic or separatist groups) considered to be authentic, and which could thus be publicly read in church. It includes most of the books that were eventually to be universally accepted as canonical.

15.18 (j) If we included all the apocryphal and pseudepigraphical books of Christian origin, and also all the **anti-Gnostic works** written by defenders of the Catholic position in the later part of the second century, our catalogue of early Christian literature would be lengthy indeed. Some of the apocrypha for which the attempt was made to claim apostolic sanction by use of the Apostles' names (for instance, *The Revelation of Peter*) date from the first half of the second century (cf. § 2.24 above). Preoccupation with the threat of Gnosticism runs all through the Christian writings of the later decades of the second century, especially after the rise of a formidable Gnostic leader and teacher, Marcion, who went to Rome about 140 and eventually set up a rival Church with widely ranging organization and membership. Among the many writers who took up the pen against Gnosticism, pre-eminent was **Irenaeus of Lyons,** a native of Asia. His *Against Heresies*, written about the end of the reign of Marcus Aurelius, was the classic work on the subject. Eusebius mentions several others who wrote against Gnosticism during this period, including three bishops, Dionysius of Corinth, Melito of Sardes and Philip of Gortyna. At the end of the second century Clement of Alexandria, one of the first great speculative theologians, opposed Gnosticism on its own ground, by presenting faithful Christians as possessors of the true *gnosis*.

15.19 Two representative testimonies

After this cursory survey of the post-Apostolic writings, I suggest that we take two fairly representative selections from them for discussion. I will cite a passage from the *Letter of Polycarp* to the Philippians, and another from *The Epistle to Diognetus*. For our next exercise I suggest that you comment on these two passages, writing brief answers to the following questions:

(a) Is there a difference in 'tone' between the two passages, reflecting a difference in the aim and outlook of the two authors?

(b)   Both writers refer to opposition which the Christians have to encounter. Is the same opposition envisaged in both cases?

(c)   Do you find links between these two passages and the New Testament writings?

15.20   From the *Letter of Polycarp*[1]

If we pray to the Lord to forgive us, we ourselves must be forgiving; we are all under the eyes of our Lord and God, and every one of us must stand before the judgement-seat of Christ, where each will have to give an account of himself. Therefore let our serving of him be marked by that fear and reverence which he himself, no less than the Apostles who brought us the Gospel, and the Prophets who foretold the Lord's coming, has enjoined upon us. Let us have a real ardour for goodness, taking every care to avoid giving offence, and refusing all association with false brethren and those hypocritical bearers of the Lord's name who only lead empty heads astray.

To deny that Jesus Christ has come in the flesh is to be Antichrist. To contradict the evidence of the Cross is to be of the devil. And to pervert the Lord's words to suit our own wishes, by asserting that there are no such things as resurrection or judgement, is to be a first-begotten son of Satan. So let us have no more of this nonsense from the gutter, and these lying doctrines, and turn back again to the word originally delivered to us. Let us be sober and watch unto prayer, earnestly adjuring the all-seeing God to lead us not into temptation—since, as the Lord has told us, though the spirit is willing, the flesh is weak.

Let us never relax our grasp on the hope and pledge of our righteousness; I mean Jesus Christ, who bore our sins in his own body on the tree; who did no sin, neither was guile found in his mouth, who steadfastly endured all things for our sakes, that we might have life in him. Let us imitate that patient endurance of his; and if we do have to suffer for his name's sake, why then, let us give glory to him. For that is the example he set us in his own person, and in which we have learnt to put our faith.

15.21   From *The Epistle to Diognetus*[2]

The difference between Christians and the rest of mankind is not a matter of nationality, or language, or customs. Christians do not live apart in separate cities of their own, speak any special dialect, nor practise any eccentric way of life. The doctrine they profess is not the invention of busy human minds and brains, nor are they, like some, adherents of this or that school of human thought. They pass their lives in whatever township—Greek or foreign—each man's lot has determined; and conform to ordinary local usage in their clothing, diet, and other habits. Nevertheless, the organization of their community does exhibit some features that are remarkable, and even surprising. For instance, though they are residents at home in their own countries, their behaviour there is more like that of transients; they take their full part as citizens, but they also submit to anything and everything as if they were aliens. For them, any foreign country is a motherland, and any motherland is a foreign country. Like other men, they marry and beget children, though they do not expose their infants. Any Christian is free to share his neighbour's table, but never his marriage-bed. Though destiny has placed them here in the flesh, they do not live after the flesh;

[1] §§ 6–8; Staniforth, *op. cit.*, pp. 146–7.

[2] § 5; Staniforth, *op. cit.*, pp. 176–7.

their days are passed on the earth, but their citizenship is above in the heavens. They obey the prescribed laws, but in their own private lives they transcend the laws. They show love to all men—and all men persecute them. They are misunderstood, and condemned; yet by suffering death they are quickened into life. They are poor, yet making many rich; lacking all things, yet having all things in abundance. They are dishonoured, yet made glorious in their very dishonour; slandered, yet vindicated. They repay calumny with blessings, and abuse with courtesy. For the good they do, they suffer stripes as evil-doers; and under the strokes they rejoice like men given new life. Jews assail them as heretics, and Greeks harass them with persecutions; and yet of all their ill-wishers there is not one who can produce good grounds for his hostility.

Now write your comments in the form of answers to the three questions I put to you in § 5.19.

A LONG PAUSE HERE
Do not read on until you have worked on the exercise

Specimen answers and discussion

15.22 (a) The two passages are evidently of different character, reflecting the difference between the aims of the writers and the difference between the readers for whom they were written. *The Epistle to Diognetus* is an apologetic work, written to give a general description of the Christian creed and way of life to a non-Christian inquirer of high rank. Its author expresses his plea in elegant language, seeking to allay prejudice by reasoned argument and by emphasizing the nobility of Christian ideals and conduct. Polycarp, on the other hand, is writing a fervent exhortation to fellow-Christians of another community, who have asked for his fatherly counsel. He is reminding them of what they already know, warning them of spiritual dangers and urging them to steadfastness.

15.23 (b) Both writers refer to persecution and physical suffering for which Christians have constantly to be prepared. Doubtless the persecutions referred to were those carried out by local civil authorities, like the persecution in Bithynia mentioned in Pliny's letters. The apologist is evidently referring to penal action of this kind when he writes: 'For the good they do they suffer stripes as evil-doers.' There was also the constant danger of popular intolerance spilling over into mob violence. In addition to these persecutions from pagans, other opponents are referred to in the two documents. Polycarp earnestly warns the Philippians against 'false brethren and hypocrites', and especially against the heterodox Christianity of the Docetists, who, because of their Gnostic rejection of matter as the root of evil, denied the material reality of Christ's flesh and of his passion. *The Epistle to Diognetus* mentions opposition that Christians have to encounter from the Jews, who 'assail them as heretics'.

15.24 (c) The passage from Polycarp's letter includes several allusions to New Testament teaching, including some verbatim quotations. If you know the New Testament well, you may have noted references to the following texts: *Matt.* 6:12; *2 Cor.* 5:10; *Phil.* 2:12; *1 John* 4:2–3 (and *2 John* 7); *1 Peter* 4:7; *Matt.* 6:13; *Matt.* 26:41; *1 Peter* 2:22, 24, 21. The passage from *The Epistle to Diognetus* is likewise clearly inspired by texts and ideas from Paul's letters. Although there is less verbatim quotation the author paraphrases Paul's words, and makes a direct use of *2 Corinthians* 6:10 and *Philippians* 3:20. Other relevant texts include: *Rom.* 8:13; 12:14; *2 Cor.* 4:8–11; 6:4–9; 10:3; *1 Cor.* 1:23; 4:11–13; *Eph.* 2:19.

(F) THE GEOGRAPHICAL EXPANSION OF THE CHURCH

16.0 Bridgeheads and the first advance

In Unit 12, when studying the story of the Roman occupation of Britain, you saw how fragmentary is the surviving evidence about it, and how hard it is to write a connected history of what happened and what followed. From Tacitus and Dio we can glean only vague and laconic information about the military subjugation of the island, and then there is hardly any literary record at all of the process of Romanization of Britain during the two centuries after the invasion fleets crossed the Channel in the reign of Claudius. Nevertheless, we can draw a pretty fair map of Roman Britain, and we know a great deal about life there, from the archaeological data, from the topography of Roman Britain in later times (which casts considerable light backwards on to the history of the earlier period), and also from our wider knowledge of imperial Rome, which gives the context for understanding Roman rule and civilization in individual provinces like Britain.

Figure 46 The Temple of Hadrian, in the ruins of Ephesus. (J. Allan Cash.)

16.1 To some extent this provides a simile to illustrate the problems that confront us when we try to trace the history of the expansion of Christianity from its first bases. During the same decades that the legions of Claudius, Nero and Vespasian were steadily advancing the area of Roman rule in Britain, consolidating their position and imposing the Roman way of life on the Celtic tribes, the Christian Church was carrying forward its very different invasion and peaceful penetration of Roman provinces elsewhere, which was eventually to bring the message and the spiritual sway of Christ to all parts of the Roman world. As in the story of Roman Britain, we know the starting-point of the Christian invasion, and we are much better informed about its first bridgeheads, which, as we have seen earlier, can be located on the map in Syria, Asia Minor, the Aegean, Macedonia, Greece and Italy. After that, however, it becomes impossible to write a connected narrative of the steady advance and consolidation of Christianity in the provinces of the Roman empire, although we know it was going on. The evidence is fragmentary and imprecise, and there are big gaps in our knowledge which can only be bridged by conjecture. True, we have far more literary documents relating to first and second-century Christianity than we have relating to the contemporary Romanization of Britain. But the character and aim of those documents was primarily religious; only incidentally do they provide some solid historical facts enabling us to say when and how Christianity arrived and developed in particular places and regions.

16.2 In the beginning, and probably for several decades afterwards, the founding members of the local Christian churches were drawn mainly from the communities of Jews and their proselytes in the seaports and trading centres of the Mediterranean. At first Christianity was almost everywhere an urban religion, except in the more remote provinces, like Bithynia and eastern Syria. We know the names of hardly any of those who were the pioneers of the Church's missionary advance in the century following the period covered by the *Acts of the Apostles*. No doubt merchants and mariners were in many cases the first to bring the Christian message to far places, as well as itinerant evangelists sent specifically for that purpose. The cosmopolitan character of the Jewish Diaspora would make it easy for the first Christian missionaries to make contacts. We know that there was frequent interchange of letters and visits between the scattered Christian communities.

16.3 Casting light backwards

Although we cannot write a continuous chronicle of the advance and consolidation of Christianity, we can say quite a lot about church activity in certain localities. By piecing together the historically relevant items extracted from the religious writings, by illuminating what is obscure in one region by clearer evidence of usual Christian practice elsewhere, and by intelligent use of later documents to cast light backwards on the earlier period, we can sketch a general outline of the expansion of Christianity in the second century. (See Map B.) At the same time, we must point out the large blank spaces in our knowledge.

16.4 In his twelfth chapter Filson gives an outline of the general historical background during 'the obscure decades' of early Christianity, and then fills in some parts of the picture by considering 'in turn each region in which there is evidence that the gospel was preached and churches founded'. Naturally he cannot detail all the data available. Despite lack of explicit documentary proof we can reasonably infer that at least by the middle of the second century Christian communities already existed in some places not mentioned in our sources. This we can do by using evidence from a generation or so later, showing a state of development at that time which implies that church activity must have originated in those places several years earlier. Can you give any examples of localities about which such an inference can be made?

✠ ✠

16.5 *My answer:* My first example is from the Latin-speaking seaboard of North Africa. We have no record of the planting of Christianity in the important Roman province of **proconsular Africa,** the capital of which was Carthage (close to the modern Tunis). We know that there was a large Jewish community in Carthage, and this makes it likely that the Christian message was preached there at an early date, as in other chief cities of the Jewish Diaspora. Yet the first mention we have of Christianity in that province dates from the year 180. It shows that the church must already have been well rooted there by that date. *The Acts of the Martyrs of Scilli* (the first known Christian document written in Latin) refers to a persecution of the church in the province, and describes the heroic fortitude of six simple believers from an out-of-the-way inland township, who were interrogated by the governor at Carthage and then sentenced to death. (Text in Lewis and Reinhold, pp. 593–5.) They had with them a copy of Paul's letters.

16.6 A few years later the fiery Christian controversialist, the Carthage lawyer Tertullian, was writing his brilliant and perfervid works in proconsular Africa. His hyperbolical boast in his *Apology* (*c.* AD 200) about the spread of Christianity, is famous: 'We are but of yesterday, but we have filled every place you have—cities, islands, fortresses, towns, council chambers, even the camps, tribes, courts, palace, senate, the forum. We have left you only your temples.' What Tertullian wrote about Christian conduct and church discipline certainly implied the existence of a well-established community. He referred also to severe measures taken by the proconsul Scapula against the Christians in 211–12. In 220 a Bishop Agrippinus of Carthage assembled a synod of 70 bishops, the leaders of Christian congregations throughout the province. All these indications point to an origin for the church in Roman Africa going back well before the last part of the second century.

Figure 47 An early Christian fresco from the catacombs. It is thought to represent the story of the Samaritan woman at the well, and the seated figure is taken to be Christ the Teacher. (John 4:8–30.) (*Benedictine Sisters of the Catacomb of Priscilla, Rome.*)

16.7 The same kind of inference can be drawn about the founding of churches in several other places: for instance, in Lyons and Vienne, where the sudden savage persecution in 177 claimed the lives of forty-eight Christians, including slaves and well-to-do burgesses, as well as the aged Bishop Pothinus. This is the first evidence we have of the existence of Christian communities in **Gaul.**

·But the most notable instance of all is **Alexandria** in Egypt, the greatest trading centre of the ancient world, where a flourishing church is found at the end of the second century. Alexandria was the chief centre of Diaspora Judaism, and it was to become one of the most influential centres of Christian thought; yet again we have no reliable record of the origins of the church there, or of its progress during the greater part of the second century. There are legends to fill the gap. We do, however, get a hint that Christians were already numerous in Egypt in the reign of Hadrian from some sarcastic remarks about them in a letter of the emperor himself.

16.8 Of great interest, too, are the shadowy border-lands on the eastern confines of the Roman Empire. I mentioned earlier (§ 3.11) that Christianity was planted in **east Syria** at an early date by Aramaic-speaking missionaries. The story of the conversion of Abgar, king of Edessa (Osrhoëne), in the lifetime of Jesus, is evidently a legendary embroidering of traditions from a later date. Eusebius preserves a document, probably of the third century, which purports to be an autograph letter from Jesus to Abgar. However, there is no doubt that there was a flourishing Christian church in that region at least in the second half of the second century. From that base missionaries spread the faith still farther into **Mesopotamia** and eventually into Persia. You will remember that Trajan extended the frontiers of the Roman world eastwards, adding Arabia, Armenia and Mesopotamia to the empire as provinces. Although the next emperor, Hadrian, relinquished the territories that had been annexed by Trajan, the drive to the east was resumed in the Parthian War at the beginning of the reign of Marcus Aurelius, and Mesopotamia became once more a Roman province. Thus there were lines of communication through which the missionary Christian communities to the east could retain links with their fellow-believers in the rest of the Roman world.

Figure 48 Christian sarcophagus (i.e. stone coffin) of the third century, in the church of S. Maria Antiqua, Rome. It contains themes often found in early Christian art. On the left is Jonah, cast up by the whale, and taking his ease in the shade—a familiar symbol of the resurrection of the dead. On the right are Christ the Good Shepherd, shown as a youth carrying a sheep, and the interrupted sacrifice of Isaac by his father Abraham. The praying figure in the centre is often found, representing either the soul of the deceased or the Church, and the man seated and reading a scroll is also a figure of a Christian sage. Possibly these two figures were meant to depict husband and wife buried in this grave; the faces were purposely left unsculpted by the craftsman who sold the sarcophagus, in order that the likeness of the deceased could be put in later according to the buyer's requirements. (Alinari.)

16.9 Unfortunately, we have only tantalizing scraps of information about the appearance of Christianity in those regions. Bardesan of Edessa, writing about the beginning of the third century, refers to 'the new race of us Christians, planted by Christ in every nation', and he mentions the presence of believers in the **Parthian empire.** Other sources speak of early conversions in Armenia and even earlier in **Adiabene,** around the town of Arbela, where a sixth-century chronicle records Christian activity in the reign of Trajan. Can you locate Arbela on any of the maps in your set books?

✠ ✠

Answer: It was a well-known place in the ancient world, and you would expect to find it on the map on page 251 of Salmon's book—but it isn't marked there. If it were, it would be just under the word ADIABENE on that map, east of the Tigris. Arbela still exists in northern Iraq. It is a fantastic mound of piled masonry and rubble rising out of the semi-desert plain beneath the mountains of Kurdistan. (The local inhabitants assured me there that it is the oldest inhabited town in the world—but there are other claimants to that distinction.)

16.10 On an earlier page (§ 11.16) I mentioned traditions of an apostolic mission to **India** in the first century, and of another missionary visit in the second. There were trade links between the Roman world and India, and such visits may well have occurred. As far as firm historical evidence goes, there are indications that there were Christians in India at least by the second half of the third century, probably as a result of missionary activity from Persia.

16.11 Case-studies in church development

Since we cannot here discuss the history of every place included on the map of early Christianity, I suggest that we take just two of them as prominent examples. I will propose an exercise which may help you to realize how the history of the early Church has to be pieced together from many separate items of evidence, and how many gaps remain. From the particulars given by Filson, from your reading of the New Testament, and from other references you may have time to look up in the works listed by Filson or in the appendix to these units, write down as many points as you can in answer to the following question:

> Indicate items of evidence relating to the foundation and development of the churches at (a) **Ephesus,** (b) **Rome,** up to the close of the reign of Marcus Aurelius. Try to mention documentary sources which refer to Christian activity in those cities during that period.

Following up the references to Ephesus and Rome in the index of Filson's book will get you going.

A LONG PAUSE HERE
Do not read on until you have worked on the exercise

Specimen answers and discussion

16.12 (a) **Ephesus**

This important trading port had a privileged status in the Roman empire as a 'free city', with its own senate and assembly (cf. § 8.12 above). It was famous for the cult of its great mother-goddess, who was identified with Artemis and whose shrine was one of the seven wonders of the world. The city was to become a focal point of early Christianity. The province of Asia, of which it was the metropolis, was before long the region in which Christians were most numerous, and so it remained for several centuries.

16.13   We saw in §8.15 that Paul paid a first brief visit to Ephesus after leaving Corinth in about AD 52. When, soon afterwards, the eloquent Alexandrian Jew Apollos arrived at Ephesus, there was a group of Christian believers there. Apollos, a follower of the teaching of John the Baptist, knew and preached the facts about Jesus, but in an evidently incomplete form. Paul's friends Priscilla and Aquila 'took him in hand and expounded the new way to him in greater detail' (*Acts* 18:24–8).

16.14   It was about a year later that Paul returned to Ephesus for the period of intense and successful missionary activity that we have described in §§ 8.16–17. However, there was opposition as well as success; there is a reference to it in Paul's remark that he 'fought wild beasts at Ephesus' (*1 Cor.* 15:32). Soon after the riot of the silversmiths (*Acts* 19), Paul left Ephesus, and we have no explicit evidence that he ever returned. But as I noted in §§ 8.18, 24 it is possible that he did so. John Ferguson argues that there was a distinctive 'Ephesus tradition of the Christian gospel', influenced by Alexandrian thought through Apollos, which is reflected both in *Philippians* and later in *John*. On this view, Paul not only taught but also learned from the Ephesians.

16.15   In the following decades Ephesus was clearly an important centre of Christian thought and activity. The Pauline letter called *Ephesians* was probably not addressed originally to that congregation, but to the churches of Asia in general (cf. Filson pp. 280–3). The Pastoral Epistles allude to authority exercised at Ephesus by Timothy, at Paul's behest (*1 Tim.* 1:3; cf. *2 Tim.* 4:19). Eusebius records the tradition that several 'great luminaries' of the original Palestinian church migrated to the province of Asia. This would probably have occurred after the slaying of James the brother of Jesus, in AD 62, and during the troubled years of the Jewish War. John, 'the disciple of the Lord', was named as chief of these 'luminaries'. Tradition has always affirmed that the *Gospel according to John* was written at Ephesus, and indeed associates all the five Johannine

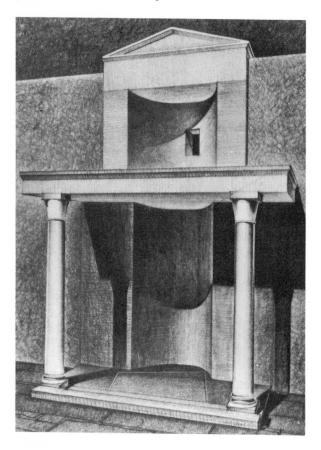

Figure 49 Conjectural reconstruction of the mid-second-century aedicula, *erected by the Christians of Rome in the reign of Antoninus Pius to honour the place in which, according to a very ancient tradition, the body of the Apostle Peter was buried after his martyrdom in the persecution of Nero. The closure slab below, between the two little columns, is thought to have covered a space which was originally a grave. The oblique angle of this slab may preserve the original alignment of the grave. This memorial structure, later the focal point of the whole great basilica of St Peter's, is evidently the* tropaion *of Peter mentioned by the presbyter Gaius about the year 200. (Societäts-Verlag, Frankfurt-am-Main.)*

writings with the same locality. Several sources dating from the end of the second century onwards repeat the assertion that John the Apostle, son of Zebedee, was active at Ephesus. Clement of Alexandria, for example, describes him as the highest church authority in Ephesus and all the surrounding territory. The tomb of John at Ephesus was pointed out and venerated from a very early period.

16.16 However, there was more than one John, and which was which is not altogether easy to decide. Papias distinguishes a 'John the Elder' from the Apostle John. There is good reason to argue that John the prophet who wrote *Revelation* is not the same person as the author of the Johannine letters, who describes himself as 'The Elder'. Was this latter 'John' also the evangelist who wrote the *Gospel of John*? There are stylistic and theological concords between the letters and the Gospel. *John* 21:20–4 asserts that the witness whose testimony underlay the Fourth Gospel was 'the disciple whom Jesus loved', and it seems reasonable to accept the traditional identification of this disciple with John, son of Zebedee. *John* 21:24 suggests, however, that others had a hand in the actual compilation of the Gospel. In *Revelation*, which purports to be written by a John from the Aegean island of Patmos, the first of the letters to 'the seven churches of Asia' is addressed to Ephesus. The church there is praised for its endurance but blamed for falling away from its first fervour (*Rev.* 1:11; 2:1–7).

16.17 At least by the early part of the second century 'monepiscopacy' was well established in the Ephesian church, as we learn from the letter Ignatius of Antioch sent to that church while he was at Smyrna on his journey to Rome. The bishop of Ephesus, Onesimus, and some of his clergy and flock had gone to meet the captive bishop of Antioch and conversed with him in warm mutual affection. They took back with them his letter of praise and exhortation to the church of Ephesus. The opening greeting in this letter of Ignatius is more solemn and respectful than his form of address to any of the other churches he wrote to, with the sole exception of the church of Rome: 'To the deservedly happy church at Ephesus in Asia; notably blessed with greatness by God the Father out of his own fullness; marked out since the beginning of time for glory unfading and unchanging; and owing its unity and its election to the true and undoubted Passion, by the will of the Father and Jesus Christ our God.'

16.18 For the greater part of the second century we are left with no reliable data about the further progress of the Ephesian church. We know that Justin was in Ephesus for a time. He refers to his stay there in his *Dialogue with Trypho*. From the closing decade of the century comes record, preserved by Eusebius, of a dispute in which Victor, bishop of Rome, and Polycrates, bishop of Ephesus, were the protagonists. It concerned two rival reckonings of the date of Easter, and Polycrates appears as the metropolitan bishop of Asia, defending the usage observed in all the churches of his province, which, however, differed from the usage of the Roman church and of most other churches. Victor called for synods of bishops to be held everywhere to discuss the question, and when the Asian bishops under Polycrates persisted in their minority view, Victor was minded to excommunicate them. Replying to Victor, Polycrates appealed to the apostolic origins and prestige of the church of Ephesus, tracing the local Easter usage back to the Apostle John himself. He mentioned other church leaders, including seven bishops from his own family, who had followed that usage. Schism was somehow averted. The episode throws light on the way that ecclesiastical organization in Ephesus and its province had been consolidated during the second century. With such apostolic origins and traditions it is not surprising that the church of Ephesus aspired to a leading place in the Christian world; but in later times its prestige did not keep pace with that of Antioch, Alexandria and Rome.

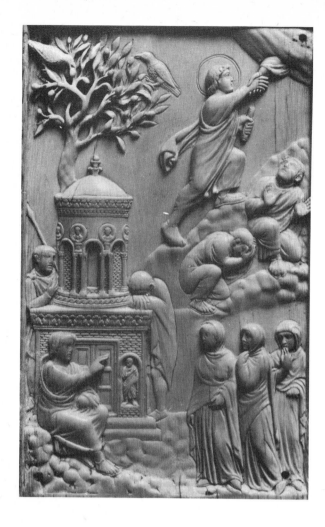

Figure 50 Early mediaeval ivory carving showing the Resurrection of Christ (Bayerisches National-museum, Munich.)

Now let us turn to the second of our two examples.

16.19 (b) **Rome**

We are less well informed about the origins of Christianity in Rome than in Ephesus, but the second-century developments there are far better documented. There was a large Jewish colony in Rome at the time of Christ—estimates of their numbers vary between 20,000 and 60,000 out of a population of about a million. Inscriptions reveal the existence of at least eleven synagogues in the city during the first century. There were 'visitors from Rome, both Jews and proselytes' in Jerusalem on the day of Pentecost (*Acts* 2:10), and perhaps on their return home some of them brought news of the movement in Judaea to the synagogues of Rome. At any rate the Christian message must have reached Rome at a fairly early date. It is not unlikely that the riots among the Jews which Suetonius said were brought about 'at the instigation of Chrestus', and which led to the decree of Claudius expelling the Jews from Rome (cf. § 2.8), were connected with the introduction of Christianity into the Jewish community there. Aquila and Priscilla, who were involved in this expulsion and went via Corinth to Ephesus, may already have been Christians when they were expelled (*Acts* 18:2; 18:26; *Rom.* 16:3).

16.20 Paul's *Epistle to the Romans*, written about the year 57, is the earliest Christian document referring to believers in Rome. To judge from his opening greetings, there was by that date a considerable body of them in the city: 'I send greet-ings to all of you in Rome whom God loves and has called to be his dedicated people. . . . Let me begin by thanking my God, through Jesus Christ, for you all, because all over the world they are telling the story of your faith.'

The theological argument of the letter assumes that the recipients were by no means novices in the faith. If the last chapter of *Romans* really belongs there (and was not originally addressed to the Ephesian congregation, as many scholars think), it gives us the names of many of the Christian community in Rome—almost all (on this hypothesis) expatriates from Asia Minor.

Figure 51 An inscription from the Crypt of Lucina, in the catacombs near the Appian Way, Rome, probably dating from the second half of the second century. It gives the name of a woman, Rufina, in Greek spelling, followed by the Greek word eirene *(peace) and a cross. (Pontifical Archaeological Commission.)*

16.21   We have seen (in §§ 8.19–21) how Paul eventually achieved his long-standing ambition to preach the gospel in Rome personally, when he arrived there as a prisoner bound to appear at Caesar's tribunal. *Acts* 28:17–28 are at first sight puzzling verses, for they indicate that Paul's fellow-Jews in Rome had not even heard of him, and knew of the Christian sect only by disrepute. What about Paul's letter to the Romans, written only a few years before, and what it purports to tell us of flourishing Christianity in Rome? Look at that passage in *Acts* and say if you think it can be reconciled with the data of *Romans*.

✠ ✠

My answer: There is no necessary inconsistency here. Previously, in *Acts* 28:15, Luke related how the Christians of Rome had heard in advance of Paul's approach, and went out down the Appian Way to meet him, as far as Appii Forum and Tres Tabernae. There evidently was an active Christian community in the city at that time, but the Jews whom Paul invited to hear him in Rome had no contact with it. It is not astonishing that there could be a body of Jews so uninformed about Paul, and knowing the Christian sect only by hostile report, when we realize that the Jews in Rome numbered so many thousands. Moreover, this last confrontation of Paul with unbelieving Jewry is evidently intended by Luke to point a moral.

16.22   It was during Nero's reign that the first imperial persecution of Christians occurred, recorded in the famous passage of Tacitus and alluded to by Suetonius (cf. § 2.8). 'Great numbers' of Christians were cruelly done to death in Rome in the summer of 64. Among those martyred in Rome about this time, according to a strong early tradition, were both Paul and Peter. I have already referred to the martyrdom of Paul in § 8.25; the tradition about Peter's presence and martyrdom in Rome is no less emphatic. The early testimonies of Clement of Rome and Ignatius of Antioch to this effect are supported by several other similar references in second-century sources (references in § 18.2 below). Dionysius of Corinth, writing about AD 168, expressly affirms that Peter and Paul 'witnessed', that is, suffered martyrdom in Rome at the same time. *1 Peter*, which may well have been written in the sixties of the first century, ends with greetings from 'Babylon', a cryptic name for Rome. Tradition also associates the *Gospel of Mark*, probably written in the sixties, with Rome.

Papias says that Mark was 'the spokesman for Peter', writing down his recollections. The iconography of the Roman catacombs, and popular devotion at least from the third century, confirms that there was a very firm local tradition about the connection of Peter and Paul with Rome and their martyrdom there.

16.23 As in the case of Paul, the Roman tradition about the death and tomb of Peter too is unchallenged by any rival tradition. (This is quite a relevant consideration when it comes to distinguishing reputable traditions from spurious ones. I have visited four places where it is claimed that the head of St John the Baptist is preserved!) A Roman presbyter Gaius, writing about the year 200, mentioned as a matter of common knowledge that Peter's memorial was to be seen on the Vatican Hill, as was Paul's on the road to Ostia. Recent archaeological excavations under St Peter's Basilica in the Vatican have shown that about the year 160 a memorial structure was built over the place where it was believed that he was buried. In the last television programme of this course we shall be saying more about these excavations, which are also significant for the tangible evidence they provide of Christian activity in Rome at that time. Refer also to the Appendix at the end of these units (§§ 18.0–8), where more particulars will be found.

16.24 The letter of Clement of Rome at the end of the first century is about disciplinary problems in the Corinthian church, but it also reflects the concerns of the Christians of Rome. The Roman spokesman is inclined to moralism, and exhorts his erring brethren in Corinth to humility, unity, discipline and fervour. The letter opens with a reference to 'our recent series of unexpected misfortunes and set-backs' which has preoccupied the Roman church—probably the persecution of Christians in Rome under Domitian about AD 93.

16.25 There is a strong probability that Domitian's own niece, Flavia Domitilla, and her husband, the consul T. Flavius Clemens, embraced Christianity in Rome about this time. Dio Cassius records that they were accused of 'atheism' (i.e. refusal to acknowledge the gods—a common accusation against the Christians) and 'aberration after the manner of the Jews', and that the consul was put to death in 95 and his wife exiled. They were the two most illustrious subjects of Domitian, and he had even designated their two sons as his heirs. Eusebius says that Flavia Domitilla was exiled for confessing Christ. One of the oldest Christian catacombs in Rome is called 'the Cemetery of Domitilla', and inscriptions confirm that it was tunnelled under land owned by Flavia Domitilla and her family. They also show that there was a burial chamber there for members of the Flavian family. Another possible Christian convert from the Roman aristocracy was Pomponia Graecina, wife of Aulus Plautius, the conqueror of southern Britain. Tacitus tells us that she was accused of 'foreign superstition'. There are also inscriptions from the catacombs of Rome commemorating the *gens Pomponia*, including one male member of the family called Pomponius Graecinus.

16.26 The letter written by Ignatius of Antioch to the Roman church about 109 begins with solemn respect: 'To her who has found mercy in the greatness of the all-highest Father, and Jesus Christ his only Son; to the church beloved and enlightened in her love of our God Jesus Christ by the will of him who wills all things; to the church holding chief place in the territories of the district of Rome—worthy of God, worthy of honour, blessing, praise and success; worthy too in holiness, foremost in love, observing the law of Christ, and bearing the Father's name.' Ignatius pleads with the Christians of Rome not to use influence to deprive him of a martyr's death—an indication that some of them must have been in responsible positions in the state. He adds, 'However, I am not issuing orders to you, as though I were a Peter or a Paul'. He does not refer to a bishop of Rome, as he does to bishops of the eastern churches. Filson, as you have no doubt remarked, favours the view that there was no single bishop of Rome at that time. Does the omission by Ignatius of any reference to a leader of the Roman church confirm Filson's theory on this point?

✠ ✠

My answer: The argument is inconclusive. The silence of Ignatius could be explained in other ways. For example, there could have been a vacancy or a recent change in the leadership of the Roman church, so that Ignatius did not know who the leader of that church was at the time he was writing.

16.27　At the end of the second century the church in Rome listed the names of its bishops, going back to Peter, whose first successors are named as Linus and Cletus, and then Clement. Other churches had similar lists going back to an apostolic founder. It is difficult to assess the authenticity of these ecclesiastical pedigrees where other documentary confirmation is lacking. At any rate it is reasonably certain, despite Filson's doubts, that there was a prominent individual leader of the Roman church at a date even earlier than that of Ignatius's letters—namely Clement of Rome. That he was a personage of considerable repute is shown by the amount of pseudepigraphical literature later attributed to him. The *Shepherd of Hermas* declared that it was Clement's office to write to the churches abroad. It has been conjectured, from his aristocratic name, that Clement was a freedman of T. Flavius Clemens.

16.28　The traditional list of the bishops of Rome in the second century gives the following names in succession to Clement: Evaristus, Alexander, Xystus, Telesphorus, Hyginus, Pius, Anicetus, Soter, Eleutherus. The existence of seven of these individuals is confirmed by mention in other contemporary documents, and the dates in which the later ones occupied the Roman bishopric are known fairly accurately. A later document records that Xystus made an agreement on the Easter question with certain Asians, about the year 125. Telesphorus was probably martyred under Hadrian, about 136. Anicetus was bishop from about 155 to 166, Soter from about 166 to 174, Eleutherus from about 174 to 189. The immediate successors of Eleutherus were Victor (189–198) and Zephyrinus (198–217).

Figure 52　The 'Graffiti Wall' on the north side of the aedicula *beneath the high altar of St Peter's, Rome. This wall was added, probably in the early third century, to buttress the memorial structure. Pious pilgrims scratched invocations on the plaster. (Societäts-Verlag, Frankfurt-am-Main.)*

16.29 We learn of many visitors to the church in Rome during the second century. Naturally it enjoyed a special geographical importance as the church of the chief city of the Roman empire, but it is also clear that because of its apostolic connections it had a special religious prestige throughout the whole Church. The Judaeo-Christian community in Jerusalem, which had been the 'mother church' in the earliest days of Christianity, lost its pre-eminence after the destruction of Jerusalem in AD 70. The final ruthless measures of Hadrian in Judaea following the revolt of 132–5 ended any lingering hopes of a restoration of the Jewish holy city (cf. Lewis and Reinhold, pp. 413–4). Rome succeeded to the place which Jerusalem had held in the age of the Apostles, as chief centre of the Christian Church.

16.30 Among visitors from the east to Rome in the mid-second century was Polycarp, the venerable bishop of Smyrna, who was received in fraternal communion by Anicetus, the Roman bishop. Another was the Jewish Christian Hegesippus, who is considered to be a pioneer of the theology of tradition. He came to Rome seeking such apostolic traditions, also during the episcopate of Anicetus, and settled down there. Justin, the philosopher and Christian apologist from Samaria also came to Rome to stay, and set up a school there to teach his 'true philosophy'. Others who journeyed to Rome included Tatian, the Assyrian disciple of Justin; a disputatious follower of Tatian called Rhodo; and Irenaeus, who was also a disciple of Justin in Rome, and later returned there as emissary from the church of Lyons. By the beginning of the third century a visit to Rome was beginning to take on the character of a pilgrimage. Like Origen of Alexandria, men went there because they 'desired to see the ancient church of the Romans'. One such was Abercius, bishop of Hieropolis in Phrygia. About the year 190 he recorded his travels on the tombstone he prepared for himself, which was rediscovered in 1883. His epitaph refers in symbolic language to the dignity of the Roman church. 'Abercius by name, I am a disciple of the pure Shepherd, who feeds his flocks of sheep on mountains and plains. . . . He taught me faithful writings. He also sent me to royal Rome to behold and to see the golden-robed, golden-slippered queen. And there I saw a people bearing the splendid seal.'

16.31 It was not only those reputed for right belief who went to make contact with the Christian community of Rome. Others who were to become notorious as leaders of schism, heresy and Gnostic sects also appeared there, seeking supporters for their systems of thought. They included Valentinus, a learned Gnostic from Alexandria, who taught in Rome for nearly thirty years, from about 140; Cerdon from Syria, followers of Basilides from Alexandria, and other Gnostics called Synerus and Ptolemy; Marcion from Sinope on the Black Sea coast and Apelles his virulently anti-Jewish pupil; Lucan, a later leader of the Marcionite sect in Rome; and Theodotus of Byzantium, preacher of a 'Monarchian' doctrine which so stressed monotheism that it abandoned belief in the divinity of Christ. There was also in Rome a sect of Simonians, said to be followers of the Simon Magus who figures in *Acts* 8:9–24, and who was often regarded as the first founder of Gnosticism. These rival sectarian groups were a thorn in the flesh of the main Church. The most formidable heresiarch was Marcion. His movement originated within the Church, and his doctrinal system, though basically dualist and docetic, was free from the more fantastic extravagances of the other Gnostic sects. It made a one-sided use of Pauline ideas and had a considerable appeal. The rupture between Marcion and the Roman church came in 144; the rival Marcionite church continued to spread and for a long time presented a most serious challenge to orthodoxy.

16.32 The Roman church felt a special responsibility for sending relief and charitable assistance to needy Christians elsewhere. Justin described the system of collections for the needy, taken at the eucharistic service. In a letter to the church of Rome during the reign of Marcus Aurelius, Dionysius, bishop of Corinth, expressed grateful appreciation for such support sent to his church and to many other congregations likewise:

16.33   From the beginning this has been your custom, to do good to all Christians in many ways, and to send contributions to the many churches in every city. You have in various places relieved the poverty of the needy and ministered to the Christians in the mines, by the contributions which you have always sent, preserving the ancient custom of the Romans, true Romans as you are. Your blessed bishop Soter has not only continued this custom but has even increased it, administering the bounty provided for the saints and devoutly exhorting the brethren who come to Rome, as a loving father would exhort his children. (Eusebius, *Ecclesiastical History*, IV, 23. 10.)

16.34   The church of Rome evidently had very considerable resources at its disposal. When Marcion first came to Rome from Pontus, about the year 140, he made himself very much *persona grata* by a gift to the church there of 200,000 sesterces. Tertullian relates that when the Roman church later excommunicated Marcion it was able to return this large sum to him from its available funds.

16.35   Some light on the internal life of the Roman church about the middle of the second century, and on its everyday problems of ecclesiastical discipline, is gained from the *Shepherd of Hermas*. There is a sharper focus on the peril in which the Roman Christians lived in the appendix to Justin's *Apology*. He describes the martyrdom of a Christian teacher named Ptolemaeus who was condemned by the prefect of Rome, Lollius Urbicus, and of two other Christians who protested at the unjust sentence. This occurred shortly before 161. There is also a contemporary account of the martyrdom of Justin himself and a number of other Christians, between the years 163 and 167. They were brought for trial before the new prefect of Rome, Junius Rusticus (a former tutor of Marcus Aurelius), who jeered at their beliefs. Justin answered resolutely and was condemned to death for being a Christian. Others with him also confessed their faith bravely and died for it. Some of them were born of Christian parents, some were converts, catechized by Justin himself. One was a slave from Phrygia.

16.36   The *Muratorian Canon*, giving a list of books of the New Testament accepted as authentic, was probably drawn up in Rome about 180. *1 Clement* was translated from the original Greek into Latin in the same period; it seems that a Latin translation of the Scriptures was by then available. Hitherto the language of the Roman church had been Greek. The gradual swing-over to Latin was beginning, but it was to take many decades to complete. The first great theologian of the Roman church, Hippolytus, was still writing in Greek in the first quarter of the third century. Almost all the early inscriptions in the Christian catacombs of Rome are in Greek.

16.37   It is probable that the Christians were already using catacombs for interment of their dead early in the second century. The Jewish catacomb cemeteries of Rome go back to the first century, and it seems clear that in using such underground galleries and chambers for inhumation the Christians were following the example of the Jews. With their vivid hope of bodily resurrection, the Christians could not accept the ordinary custom of cremation. We shall see in our television programme on the Vatican necropolis that during the second and third centuries devotees of pagan religions too were beginning to prefer inhumation to cremation. Some scholars date the earliest Christian catacomb paintings to the second century, but I think that none of the surviving designs can be dated with certainty before the first quarter of the third century. (I can recommend catacomb-exploring as a fascinating hobby. I pursued it over some seven years, but even then had visited only a relatively small part of that vast subterranean network.)

16.38　Lastly, we may note that, as well as the esteem in which the church of Rome was held by Christians generally for its apostolic origins and charitable activities, and for its important position at the centre of the Roman world, there were also signs that the Roman church and its bishops laid some claim to an authority which gave them a right to teach and correct others. The *Letter of Clement* was widely read and known as an expression of Roman concern for good order in a sister church. Ignatius may well have been referring to it when he wrote to the Roman church: 'You have been a source of instruction to others'. With his generous donation to the church of Corinth (§ 16.32–3 above), Bishop Soter of Rome also sent a letter of admonition. When the Gnostic threat to Christianity was greatest, the faith of the Roman church was appealed to by Irenaeus and others as a touchstone of orthodoxy.

16.39　From the end of the second century we find an assertion of an overriding authority in the actions of the Roman bishop Victor (AD 189–198). His energetic measures in the controversy about the date of Easter, when he called for synods to be held everywhere to establish a uniform usage and then prepared to excommunicate the nonconforming bishops of the province of Asia, have already been mentioned. In Rome itself he excommunicated Theodotus of Byzantium for unsound doctrine. It seems that both Victor and his predecessor Eleutherus, who died in 189, condemned the new ecstatic and eschatological movement called Montanism, which had arisen in Phrygia some time after 156 (cf. R. M. Grant, *Augustus to Constantine: the Thrust of the Christian Movement into the Roman World*, Collins 1971, p. 162). These examples of disciplinary action were to be followed by other bishops of Rome in the following decades. It is significant that from the third century onwards even the eastern churches attributed the drawing up of the 'apostolic constitutions' governing ecclesiastical discipline to two men reputed as Roman bishops, Clement and Hippolytus. Callixtus, bishop of Rome about 217–222, described himself as the occupant of Peter's episcopal chair. In the middle of the third century Pope Stephen (254–257) explicitly claimed primacy over all other bishops as Peter's successor.

(G)　STRUCTURES, TRADITION AND SCRIPTURES

17.0　Threats to the Church's survival

Throughout the period we have been studying, the forms of ecclesiastical order, ministry, worship and organization were developing, often in different ways in different localities, but according to a broad common pattern. For all their variation of usage and their autonomy of action, the local churches were conscious of forming a wider Church embracing them all. Ignatius was the first to call this 'the Catholic Church'. The word meant 'universal' or 'comprehensive'. It is also found in the *Martyrdom of Polycarp*, and it was to become a usual term to describe what may also be called 'mainstream Christianity' or 'the Great Church'. To understand these developments one must bear in mind the constant pressure of external opposition, which forced this Church to develop structures and defences in order to survive attacks and to assert its uniqueness against all rivals.

17.1　In the New Testament writings the opponents envisaged by the Christians were almost always the Jews (cf. C. F. D. Moule, *The Birth of the New Testament*, A. and C. Black, 1971 reprint, Chapter VII). The main body of Jews in Palestine and throughout the Diaspora saw the 'sect of the Nazarenes' as a splinter group of apostates, preaching blasphemous claims about Jesus, and bringing dissension to the people of Israel. Later the opposition widened. There was intermittent persecution, sometimes by the action of the imperial or provincial authorities, sometimes whipped up by popular prejudice. Some reasons for the persecution of Christianity in the Roman world were suggested in Units 10–11, § 5.11. There is record of martyrdoms in Rome, Palestine, Bithynia, the province of Asia, North Africa and the Rhône Valley. We have many details about the heroes of conscience who held firm under persecution, but few about the many who capitulated or compromised. (In persecutions throughout history the former class have usually been the remembered minority, the latter the anonymous majority.)

17.2   There were disputes and divisions within the Church. The Judaeo-Christian groups, at first so influential, declined in numbers and importance. They were under attack from their fellow-Jews; often they were also out of sympathy with and cold-shouldered by their Gentile fellow-Christians. Some of them formed schismatic sects. From the educated class in the Graeco-Roman world Christianity usually met with incomprehension and disdain. It must be admitted that the Christians' own disdain for 'the world', their conviction of its imminent doom, their opting out of public life, and their consciousness of being a people apart as God's chosen ones, would not endear them to their non-believing and less scrupulous neighbours.

17.3   But the greatest challenge that the Church had to face in the realm of ideas, during the second century of its existence, was that of Gnostic syncretism (cf. §§ 4.25–32 above). Both in the minds of Christians themselves and of their pagan neighbours to whom their mission was directed, Gnosticism threatened to dissolve what was distinctive and essential in Christian belief in a morass of bizarre theosophy and moral anarchy. The charges of immorality commonly brought against the Christians were no doubt based on hostile misunderstanding of their 'love-feasts' and of their fraternal affection; but we must also remember that devotees of the dualist Gnostic sects, whom public opinion would include indiscriminately among 'the Christians', *did* hold views that encouraged indifference to mere 'bodily' morality.

17.4   The Church meets the challenge

The reaction of mainstream Christianity against these threats to its survival resulted in the strengthening of ecclesiastical structures and of means for defending the faith. For a final exercise, I want to ask you to reflect on this process. I do not mean to say that the developments within the Church during this period were *only* a reflex action against threats to its survival. Rather, they can be seen as a positive assertion of the values of Christianity and a further unfolding of its potentialities. But in this exercise I want to draw attention to the dialectic by which the post-apostolic Church reacted to the needs and the challenges of a new age. Here is the question for your answer:

17.5   In the first 150 years of its existence the Church of mainstream Christianity, reacting against external opposition and threats of internal disruption, developed features and institutions which strengthened its own organization and cohesion, which enabled it to counteract the activities of rival sects, and which provided it with criteria for determining what was or was not compatible with the doctrines and practices considered essential to authentic Christianity. **List and briefly describe the most important of those features and institutions.** You will find material for your answer in Part Five of Filson's book.

A LONG PAUSE HERE
Do not read on until you have worked on the exercise

Specimen answers and discussion

17.6   (a)   Structures of ministry and ecclesiastical government

The organization of the first Christian congregations, reflected in Paul's letters and in *Acts*, was not juridically structured. The local church appears as a community of mutual love and service, rather than a hierarchical institution. Paul had authority as Apostle-founder of a congregation and appointed ministers to provide pastoral supervision within it, but he was careful to respect the Spirit-given freedom of the community. In the New Testament the pastors are often called either *episkopoi* or *presbyteroi*, that is, 'overseers' or 'elders'. These two words, apparently used interchangeably, were later to give rise to two ecclesiastical terms with different meanings: 'bishops' and 'presbyters' ('priests'). We hear also of 'teachers' and 'evangelists', of 'deacons' and 'ministers', of 'prophets' and possessors of other charismatic gifts.

17.7   Some authors, perhaps unconsciously influenced by their dislike of prelatical pretensions in more recent times, represent the primitive Church as a religious democracy, in which all members were of equal rank, and elder members of the congregations would see to administrative arrangements as necesary. But this is an unreal picture, and does not correspond either to the generally accepted ideas of the time or to the actual organization of the first Jerusalem church. Fluid though the New Testament terminology about the ministry is, it is clear that there was at least a primary and a secondary ministry—that of the Apostles and that of subordinate ministers acting under their authority. In second-generation Christianity, as reflected in the Pastoral Epistles, it is assumed that a quasi-apostolic regional authority is possessed by higher church officers, like Titus and Timothy, who institute the *episkopoi-presbyteroi* in local churches. From this it is not a long step to a system in which one of the local *episkopoi-presbyteroi* is constituted in authority over the others, nor indeed to a hierarchical conception of the Christian ministry.

17.8   *1 Clement* asserts that the Apostles, by virtue of their divine mission, appointed the first overseers for the local congregations, and ordered that on their death 'other accredited persons should succeed them in their office'. In the church situation reflected in the Ignatian letters (at least in Antioch and parts of Asia Minor), we do in fact find **the monarchical bishop** as chief pastor over the local church. He has a kind of apostolic authority, with presbyters and deacons as his subordinates and loyal helpers, and the faithful congregation united around him. 'Make sure that no step affecting the church is ever taken by any-one without the bishop's sanction', Ignatius admonished the Smyrnaeans: 'Only that Eucharist is to be held valid which is celebrated by the bishop himself, or by some person appointed by him.' For Ignatius, the 'church' is not simply the gathering of the Christians in a place, but is an institutional term, distinguishing those who are within the fold, who are living and worshipping under the watchful care of their bishop, from those who reject such unity and obedience. Evidence from later in the second century shows this system of church organization as virtually universal. Bishops of neighbouring churches in a region—for instance the bishops of the province of Asia under the presidency of Polycrates of Ephesus—joined together in concerted action and met in **synods** to discuss questions of general concern. It became the custom for a new bishop to be ordained by the bishops of neighbouring churches.

17.9   A century after the time of Ignatius the church order reflected in writings such as those of Hippolytus of Rome is still more markedly clerical and hierarchical. The ordained clergy, although still chosen by the people, are more clearly a class apart from the laity. No doubt these firm structures of local church government made it easier to maintain internal discipline and unity, easier to resist doctrinal deviations, and easier to identify the like-minded congregations in other regions with whom the local church should maintain communion. But there was loss as well as gain. The freedom of the Spirit, in which the first Christian congregations had gloried, was less apparent under an authoritative ecclesiastical system, especially where legalism and clericalism entered in.

17.10 (b) Apostolic succession and tradition

Concurrently with these developments, great stress was placed upon **the apostolic succession** of bishops, as a guarantee of the **apostolic tradition** of true belief and piety against sectarian aberrations. We have seen that churches in centres like Rome, Antioch and Ephesus traced their pedigrees back through an unbroken succession of bishops to their foundation by Apostles, thus demonstrating their orthodoxy and authority. Champions of the Church, notably Hegesippus, Irenaeus and Tertullian, saw here the sure means of refuting the heretics. They taxed them with inability to prove their apostolic origins; since they could not authenticate their teaching by showing an apostolic succession of bishops, it was without foundation.

17.11 (c) The 'rule of faith' in the baptismal creed

The 'rule of faith' was also provided for each Christian by his **baptismal profession** of the chief articles of Christian belief, later developed into the creeds. The baptismal formula given in *Matt.* 28:19 naturally led to a threefold expression of belief: first in God the almighty Father; secondly in Jesus Christ his Son, truly born of the Virgin Mary, truly crucified, dead, buried and risen to heaven, the future Judge of the living and the dead; and thirdly in the Holy Spirit. To these were added professions of faith about the Church, about the forgiveness of sins, and about the resurrection of the body. The so-called Apostles' Creed, in its simplest form, can be traced back to the last decades of the second century. It took its origin from the baptismal creed of the church of Rome, which we know was used by Irenaeus in Gaul, by Origen in Egypt and by Tertullian in Africa.

17.12 (d) The New Testament canon

As apocryphal writings proliferated, purporting to be written by Apostles or to give apostolic teaching, and as Gnostic teachers arose, claiming to possess the key to salvation in a true and secret *gnosis* or knowledge of Christ and Christianity, it became imperative to define which religious books were to be received and read in the Church, and which were to be rejected as unauthentic or harmful. This was done by establishing **the canon** of the New Testament, a process which, as we can see from the Muratorian fragment, was well advanced in Rome by the end of the period we have been studying. Can you suggest a factor which would have made it especially urgent in Rome in the second half of the second century to lay down clearly what books belonged to the scriptural canon?

✠ ✠

An answer: Probably it was the attempt of Marcion to establish his own canon of Scripture, excluding not only the Old Testament books but also many of the New, that stimulated the mainstream Church, especially in Rome, to draw up its own official canon. Marcion accepted only Luke's Gospel and ten letters of Paul, which he cut and edited in accordance with his own presuppositions.

17.13 The Church's theology and its assertion of its faith against heretical inventions required a firm scriptural base. This it found in the authentication of its own collection of the Christian Scriptures, as well as in the Scriptures of the Old Testament. Christian theology was still in its infancy. Even within the Catholic Church there were many strange variants of doctrinal expression which would not have passed muster in the light of later orthodoxy. The process of working out a consistent dogmatic system was to be slow and lengthy. But in its holy writ the Church saw its title deeds and the source documents of its creeds. Armed with what it revered as the word of God, it was confident that it could refute any false words of men.

17.14 (e) Inter-church communication

Chief factors in the Church's survival and its chief means of asserting its distinctive character were, then, the bonds of a common system of ministry and ecclesiastical organization, of shared loyalty to the apostolic tradition and rule of faith, and of fidelity to the Scriptures as the word of God. These objective aids to unity of faith and purpose were not simply in the theoretical sphere, but were put into practical force in everyday life. Brotherly love was the distinctive Christian virtue. Conscious of forming one greater Church, the local churches kept up frequent communication with other churches, even quite far afield, by interchange of visits and letters, and by charitable and missionary work. Irenaeus, for instance, went from Asia via Rome to the Rhône Valley, where he ministered mainly to Greek-speaking Christians, but also attempted missionary work among the native Gauls.

17.15 (f) Unity in worship

In that practical sphere of Christian life the most important factor of all, for maintaining the sense of community in the Spirit among Christians everywhere, was their unity in prayer and their regular practice of a common pattern of worship. The primary rite, accepted as the foundation of Christian living everywhere, was baptism (cf. §§ 9. 31–34 above). It was the solemn act of admission to the Church and the decisive moment in the life of each Christian, to which he would always look back with awe and thankfulness.

17.16 Sunday, the Christian sacred day (since it marked the resurrection of Jesus) was everywhere observed as the day for communal worship. The ordinary Sunday service had two parts. The first borrowed features from the Jewish synagogue worship, and included prayers, Scripture readings, blessings and a homily. Justin gave a brief account of both parts of the service in his *Apology* addressed to the emperor Antoninus Pius. (Extracts are given by Lewis and Reinhold, pp. 589–90.) The first part he describes as follows: 'On the day which is called the day of the sun there is a gathering in one place of all who live in the towns or in the country places, and the memoirs of the apostles or the writings of the prophets are read, as long as time permits. Then, when the reader has finished, he who presides gives a sermon, admonishing us and exhorting us to imitate these excellent examples.'

17.17 Then followed the celebration of the Lord's Supper, which was evidently at the centre of Christian worship. It was already regarded as not only a sacred meal uniting the worshippers with Christ and with one another, but also as a mysterious cultic act, directed to God. Both the *Didache* and Justin identify it with the 'pure oblation' which the prophet Malachi had predicted would be offered everywhere among the Gentiles (*Mal.* 1:11). The Eucharistic liturgy, based on the narrative of Christ's Last Supper in the Synoptic Gospels and in *1 Corinthians*, was in other respects not standardized in a fixed form everywhere.

Yet though the liturgy was flexible and permitted free forms of prayer, it had certain basic features everywhere recognizable as the same. Justin gives a simple summary of it, and what it meant to the believers, in his *Apology* to the emperor. Since his words take us beneath the surface of the historical events with which we have been concerned in this course, and since we want to realize something of that deeper motivation which enabled the early Church to make its astonishing and eventually victorious penetration into the Roman empire, Justin's description of the Christian mysteries may aptly conclude our study of the rise of Christianity:

17.18   When we have ended the prayers we salute one another with a kiss. Then bread and a cup of wine mixed with water are brought to the one who presides over the brethren. He takes them and offers up praise and glory to the Father of the universe, through the name of his Son and of the Holy Ghost; and he gives thanks at length that we are deemed worthy of these things at his hand. When he has completed the prayers and thanksgiving all the people present assent by saying 'Amen'. Amen in the Hebrew tongue signifies 'So be it'. When he who presides has celebrated the Eucharist [thanksgiving], and all the people have expressed their assent, those who are called among us deacons give to those present a portion of the Eucharistic bread and wine mixed with water, and carry some away to those who are absent. Of this food, called among us 'Eucharist', none is allowed to partake but he that believes that our teachings are true, and has been washed with the baptism for the remission of sins and unto regeneration, and who lives according to the precepts of Christ. For we do not receive them as ordinary food or ordinary drink; but just as the Word of God, Jesus Christ our Saviour, took flesh and blood for our salvation, so also, according to our doctrine, the food which is blessed by the prayer of the word that we have received from him—the food by which, through its transformation, our blood and flesh is nourished—this food is the flesh and blood of Jesus who was made flesh. For the Apostles in the memoirs made by them, which are called Gospels, have thus narrated that the command was given: that Jesus took bread, gave thanks, and said, 'Do this in commemoration of me. This is my body'; and he took the cup likewise and said, 'This is my blood', and gave it to them alone.

APPENDIX

The excavations under St Peter's, Rome, and the television programme on 'The Shrine of St Peter'

18.0 The last television programme of this course is entitled 'The Shrine of St Peter'. It relates to the excavations carried out under the great church of St Peter in Rome, during the forties and fifties of this century. There is abundant literature on this subject, in several languages. For students who would like to study the matter in greater detail I recommend especially two books in English: *The Shrine of St Peter*, by J. Toynbee and J. B. Ward Perkins (Longman 1956), and E. Kirschbaum, *The Tombs of St Peter and St Paul* (English translation, Secker and Warburg 1959).

18.1 Only a small part of the ancient Roman necropolis (i.e. 'city of the dead'), which sprawled over the slopes of the Vatican hill, has been excavated. Other tombs found on another part of the hill show that the area was already in use for burials in the first century, as early as the reign of Nero. (On Roman burial customs, see Units 10–11, § 2.16, and Lewis and Reinhold, pp. 282–6.) It is with the small part of the necropolis which lies under the crypt of St Peter's that our television programme is concerned. Figure 54 shows the plan of this part of the necropolis, with the letters by which the individual mausolea, or tombs, were designated by the archaeologists. Most of the tombs here were erected in the second and third centuries. As you will see, the excavations have no little interest for our course. They illustrate the burial customs and religious beliefs of ordinary people in that period. They also provide some few but significant indications of the gradual penetration of Christianity into the Roman world. And set in the midst of that jumble of ancient tombs and later masonry is the fascinating archaeological riddle of 'the shrine of St Peter'.

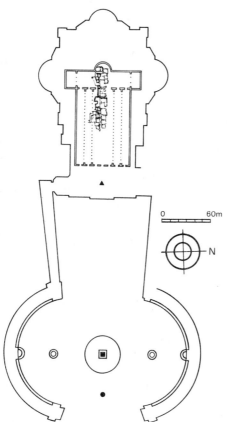

Figure 53 The upper part of this sketch shows the outline of the Renaissance basilica of St Peter's, with the ground plan of Constantine's basilica set within it. Inside the latter is shown the area of the mausolea and tombs uncovered in the recent excavations under St Peter's. The lower half of the sketch shows the outline of Bernini's colonnade enclosing the Piazza of St Peter's. The square surrounded by a circle marks the position of the central obelisk. The black and the triangular dots show the position of other tombs which have been uncovered at various times. They are in the same general alignment as the street of tombs in the Vatican necropolis now excavated. (Rev. Fabbrica di S. Pietro in Vaticano, Rome.)

18.2 We have seen in §§ 16.22–23 that according to early tradition Peter, chief of Christ's Apostles, died a martyr in Rome during the persecution of Nero. Some writers have challenged this tradition, objecting that there is no firm historical evidence to prove that Peter died in Rome, or that he even visited the city. This view, which was perhaps influenced by controversial reaction against the papal claims, is now usually held—by Protestant as well as by Catholic scholars—to be too negative. The link between Peter and the church in Rome is indicated by a number of early sources beginning with the *Letter of Clement*, which dates from the closing years of the first century. After recalling the martyrdom of Peter and of Paul, Clement adds that a great multitude of the faithful suffered with them, giving a noble example 'among us'. Some were women, who suffered terrible indignities and mockery. This seems to point to the Neronian persecution described by Tacitus. Ignatius's reference to the authority of both Peter and Paul over the Roman Christians has been mentioned in § 16.26. Peter's martyrdom in Rome is alluded to in two early second-century apocrypha, the *Ascension of Isaiah* and the *Revelation of Peter*. It is also mentioned by Dionysius of Corinth, by Irenaeus and by Tertullian. (References to these and several other early testimonies, and to the disputes of scholars on this subject, are given in Hennecke-Schneemelcher, *op. cit.*, vol. II, pp. 46–50.) There are further arguments based on Christian iconography, inscriptions and archaeology from the following centuries. The converging force of the arguments generates a strong historical probability in favour of the ancient tradition. This has been reinforced by the results of the Vatican excavations.

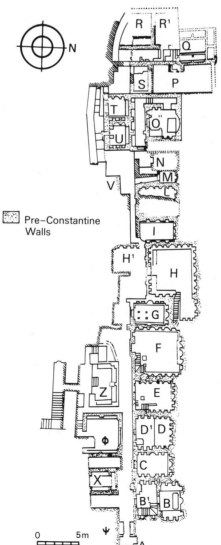

Figure 54 Plan of the excavated mausolea in the Vatican necropolis, which are described in our television programme. The capital letters are those used by the excavators to refer to the individual tombs (Rev. Fabbrica di S. Pietro in Vaticano, Rome.)

147

18.3 The archaeologists have shown that the focal point around which, in the fourth century, the emperor Constantine built the first great basilica in honour of St Peter was a certain small structure which had been erected in the Vatican necropolis about the middle of the second century. This dating can be fixed with reasonable certainty from the maker's stamp on tiles used by the contemporary builders. Figure 49 shows a hypothetical reconstruction of what that structure, or *aedicula*, looked like when it was first erected. It marked a space in what the archaeologists called Graveyard P, which had originally been an open site for the burial of poor persons, and which in the second century was enclosed by the mausolea of more affluent families. (See Figure 55.)

18.4 Without considerable study of the topology and history of the intricate architectural complex which lies beneath the great dome of St Peter's basilica, it is difficult to make an informed judgement about the significance of the Vatican excavations. Figure 53 shows how the mausolea in the ancient Roman necropolis lay in relation to the great church which Constantine later erected. He set his church on a vast platform, half cut into the side of the Vatican hill and half built out on an embankment, which was revetted by huge walls some forty feet high at the outside edge. The sketch in Figure 57 indicates how Constantine enclosed the remains of the *aedicula* in a box-like shrine of precious marble, rising into the apse of his new basilica. The later Renaissance basilica of St Peter's was built over an even greater area than that of Constantine's basilica, but still with the same focal point on which everything was aligned—the encased remains of that modest memorial structure of the second century.

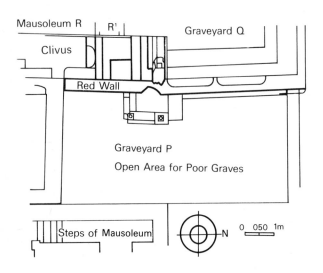

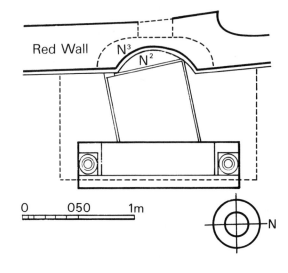

Figure 55 Ground plan of the open cemetery space called 'P' (see its position at the top of the sketch in Figure 54). The aedicula, or memorial of Peter, was the structure shown as built into and abutting on the Red Wall, which formed the upper side of Graveyard P. (Rev. Fabbrica di S. Pietro in Vaticano, Rome.)

Figure 56 Ground plan of the Petrine aedicula (see Figure 55). The two circles represent the two small columns shown in Figure 49. (Rev. Fabbrica di S. Pietro in Vaticano, Rome.)

18.5 In § 16.23 I referred to a celebrated text of the presbyter Gaius preserved by the Church historian Eusebius. About the end of the second century a leader of the Montanist sect, Proclus, was arguing that his sect could claim authority going back to apostolic times because in its homeland, Phrygia, the tombs of Philip and his prophetess daughters (cf. *Acts* 21:8–9) were to be seen. Gaius, writing in Rome about the year 200, retorted: 'But I can show you the tombs of the Apostles; for if you will go to the Vatican district or along the road to Ostia, you will there discover the *tropaia* of those who founded this community.' The word *tropaia* has the rather general significance of 'trophies' or 'triumphant monuments'; but in the context, if Gaius's retort to Proclus's boast about the possession of tombs from apostolic times was to have any edge, it must mean that the Roman community in his day claimed to be able to point out the tombs of Peter and Paul. It is a commonsense conclusion that the second-century *aedicula*, the memorial structure now detected by the Vatican archaeologists in the midst of an ancient cemetery, was the *tropaion* of Peter mentioned by Gaius.

18.6 There is evidence enough from the end of the second century onwards that the little shrine-monument was tended with religious respect. Whether or not it actually was the burial place of the Apostle Peter, it is clear that the Christians of Rome were convinced that it was. And it was because of that conviction that Constantine erected his huge basilica, with ruthless energy and lavish expenditure, to honour St Peter's tomb. But does the historical and archaeological evidence *prove* that the shrine-monument erected by the Christian community about the middle of the second century did in fact mark the grave in which the remains of Peter were laid?

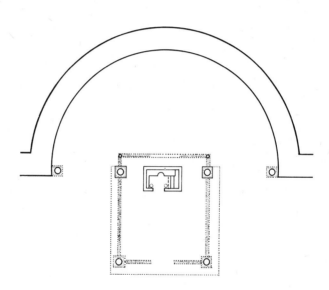

Figure 57 Plan showing how the original second-century aedicula *was enclosed by the Emperor Constantine in the fourth century by a marble rectangle with a space left open in front. This structure was framed in the centre of the apse of the basilica, and further enclosed in a larger railed-off area. It is still the hidden focal point of the whole of the huge basilica which rises above it today. (Rev. Fabbrica di S. Pietro in Vaticano, Rome.)*

18.7 It is possible to push the line of reasoning somewhat further back than the date (about AD 160) which can be established for the building of the *aedicula*. There are indications that the space immediately beneath the structure was originally a grave. There is the oblique alignment of the closure slab of the *aedicula*, and the strictly parallel alignment of earlier adjacent graves on either side—in a remarkable and quite unique arrangement. There is the strange arching up of the foundation of the 'Red Wall' in which the Christian shrine-monument was constructed, a feature which suggests that the second-century builders were avoiding an underlying 'obstacle' which it was considered important not to cut into—and in the setting of that cemetery it is reasonable to suppose that this was a pre-existing trench grave. Naturally there would have already been some external mark to show where such a grave was. In fact the remains of a small protecting wall, dating from the first half of the second century, have been discovered in the earth at the side of the central space, in exact alignment with the oblique angle at which the builders of the *aedicula* later placed their covering slab. (I should add that the space immediately underlying the *aedicula* was found empty. Some bones were found by the archaeologists nearby, but it does not seem possible to draw any firm historical conclusions about them. We know that marauding Saracens broke into the shrine of St Peter in the ninth century and pillaged it.)

18.8 The men who inserted that small protecting wall, and those who dug the even earlier adjacent graves, which are set closely around the central space in the same alignment as the closure slab, were men who would have heard the reminiscences of elders who had lived in the time of Nero. If Peter's remains were recovered by the Roman Christians after his martyrdom during Nero's persecution, and buried in a poor man's grave on the Vatican hill, it would be natural for the place to be reverently remembered and marked by the members of the Roman church. Thus there is a probability that the Christians who erected the *aedicula* in the reign of Antoninus Pius, scarcely a hundred years after the death of Peter, possessed trustworthy information that the cemeterial space which they honoured was in fact the grave of Peter. But scholarly caution requires that we should observe the gaps in the historical and archaeological evidence relating to those hundred years, and to distinguish between what may be reasonably conjectured and what is strictly proven. I leave you to reflect on the judicious comments which Dr Ward Perkins makes on these points towards the end of our television programme.

Figure 58   Nazareth today. (J. Allan Cash.)

19.0 BIBLIOGRAPHY

A useful bibliography will be found in Filson's footnotes and there is a list of British editions at the end of this book. I also recommend the following works for further reference:

D. Ayerst and A. S. T. Fisher (eds.). *Records of Christianity*, Volume I, Basil Blackwell 1971.

C. K. Barrett, *The New Testament Background: Selected Documents*, S.P.C.K. 1957.

C. K. Barrett, *Jesus and the Gospel Tradition*, S.P.C.K. 1967.

H. W. Bartsch (ed.), *Kerygma and Myth: by Rudolf Bultmann and Five Critics*, Harper Torchbooks 1961.

K. Baus, *From the Apostolic Community to Constantine* (vol. 1 of *Handbook of Church History*, edited by H. Jedin), English trans., Herder and Burns Oates 1965.

H. Bettenson (ed.), *Documents of the Christian Church*, Oxford University Press 1967.

M. Black, *The Scrolls and Christian Origins*, Thomas Nelson 1961.

J. Bonsirven, *Palestinian Judaism in the Time of Jesus Christ*, English trans., Holt Rinehart and Winston, N.Y. 1963.

G. Bornkamm, *Jesus of Nazareth*, English trans., Hodder and Stoughton 1969.

G. Bornkamm, *Paul*, English trans., Hodder and Stoughton 1971.

J. Bowker, *Jesus and the Pharisees*, Cambridge University Press 1973.

F. F. Bruce, *New Testament History*, Oliphants 1971.

N. J. Bull, *The Rise of the Church*, Heinemann 1967.

R. Bultmann, *Primitive Christianity in its Contemporary Setting*, English trans., Thames and Hudson 1956.

H. J. Cadbury, *The Book of Acts in History*, Adam and Charles Black 1955.

G. B. Caird, *The Apostolic Age*, Duckworth 1966.

P. Carrington, *The Early Church*, 2 vols., Cambridge University Press 1957.

L. Cerfaux, *The Church in the Theology of St Paul*, Thomas Nelson 1959.

H. Chadwick, *The Early Church*, Pelican History of the Church, Vol. I, Penguin and Hodder and Stoughton 1968.

R. H. Charles, *The Apocrypha and Pseudepigrapha of the Old Testament*, 2 vols., Oxford University Press 1913.

R. H. Charles, *Religious Development between the Old and New Testaments*, Williams and Norgate 1914.

O. Cullmann, *The Christology of the New Testament*, English trans., S.C.M. Press 1963.

J. Danielou, *Gospel Message and Hellenistic Culture*, English trans., Darton, Longman and Todd 1972.

J. G. Davies, *The Early Christian Church*, Weidenfeld and Nicolson 1965.

C. H. Dodd, *Historical Tradition in the Fourth Gospel*, Cambridge Universitty Press 1963.

C. H. Dodd, *The Founder of Christianity*, Collins 1971.

L. Duchesne, *Early History of the Christian Church*, English trans., Volume 1, J. Murray 1909.

M. S. Enslin, *Christian Beginnings*, 2 vols., Harper Torchbooks 1956.

John Ferguson, *The Religions of the Roman Empire*, Thames and Hudson 1970.

J. Finegan, *The Archeology of the New Testament*, Princeton University Press 1969.

R. H. Fuller, *The Foundations of New Testament Christology*, Fontana 1969.

T. R. Glover, *Paul of Tarsus*, S.C.M. Press 1925.

M. Goguel, *The Primitive Church*, English trans., Allen and Unwin 1964.

R. M. Grant, *A Historical Introduction to the New Testament*, Collins 1963.

R. M. Grant, *Gnosticism and Early Christianity*, Harper Torchbooks 1966.

R. M. Grant, *Gnosticism: an Anthology*, Collins 1961

A. von Harnack, *Expansion of Christianity in the First Three Centuries*, 2 vols., English trans., Williams and Norgate 1904–5 (reprint, Books for Libraries 1972).

E. Hennecke—W. Schneemelcher, *New Testament Apocrypha*, 2 vols., Lutterworth Press 1965.

E. W. Hunt, *Portrait of Paul*, Mowbray 1968.

F. J. Foakes Jackson and K. Lake, (eds.), *The Beginnings of Christianity*, 5 vols., Macmillan 1920–33.

M. R. James (ed.), *The Apocryphal New Testament*, Oxford University Press, 2nd edit. 1955.

W. L. Knox, *St Paul and the Church of the Gentiles*, Cambridge University Press 1939.

J. Lebreton and J. Zeiller, *The History of the Primitive Church*, 4 vols., Burns Oates 1942–8.

H. Lietzmann, *A History of the Early Church*, English trans., Lutterworth Press 1967 reprint.

T. W. Manson, *Jesus the Messiah*, Hodder and Stoughton 1943.

B. M. Metzger, *The New Testament: its Background, Growth and Content*, Abingdon Press, U.S.A., 1965.

G. F. Moore, *Judaism in the First Centuries of the Christian Era*, 3 vols., Harvard University Press 1970.

C. F. D. Moule, *The Birth of the New Testament*, Adam and Charles Black 1971.

S. Mowinckel, *He that Cometh*, English trans., Blackwell 1956.

D. E. Nineham (ed.), *Studies in the Gospels*, Blackwell 1955.

A. D. Nock, *Early Gentile Christianity and its Hellenistic Background*, Harper Torchbooks 1964.

W. O. E. Oesterley, *The Jewish Background of the Christian Liturgy*, Peter Smith 1925.

R. H. Pfeiffer, *History of New Testament Times, with an Introduction to the Apocrypha*, Greenwood Press, U.S.A. 1949.

W. M. Ramsay, *St Paul the Traveller and Roman Citizen*, reprint, Baker Book House, Michigan 1960.

A. Richardson, *An Introduction to the Theology of the New Testament*, S.C.M. Press 1958.

A. Schweitzer, *The Quest of the Historical Jesus* (1910), English trans. reprint, Macmillan 1968.

A. N. Sherwin-White, *Roman Society and Roman Law in the New Testament*, Oxford University Press 1963.

K. O. Stendahl (ed.), *The Scrolls and the New Testament*, S.C.M. Press 1958.

J. Stevenson, *A New Eusebius*, S.P.C.K. 1957.

J. S. Stewart, *A Man in Christ: the Vital Elements of St Paul's Religion*, Hodder and Stoughton 1964.

V. Taylor, *The Person of Christ in New Testament Teaching*, St Martin Press 1958.

F. Van der Meer and C. Mohrmann, *Atlas of the Early Christian World*, Nelson 1966.

G. Vermes, *The Dead Sea Scrolls in English*, Penguin 1962.

M. Wiles, *Divine Apostle. The Interpretation of St Paul's Epistles in the Early Church*, Cambridge University Press 1967.

G. A. Williamson, *The World of Josephus*, Secker and Warburg 1964.

INDEX TO UNITS 13-16

(References are to marginal section numbers)

Abercius	16.30	*Apology*, Justin	16.35; 17.16
Abgar	16.8	*Apology*, Tertullian	15.14; 16.6
'Abomination of		Apostles' Creed	17.11
desolation'	3.3	Apostles, The	5.21; 5.35; 5.38; 6.1; 6.4;
Abraham	13.50		6.6 (a); 6.7; 8.7; 9.15; 9.31;
Achaia	2.13; 8.13f; 11.10		10.0–10.3; 11.3; 11.16; 13.9;
Acrostic palindrome	2.30		15.0; 15.5; 15.18; 15.20; 16.29;
Acts of Paul and Thecla	7.1		17.7f; 17.10; 17.12; 17.15–17.18;
Acts of the Apostles	1.2f; 2.11f; 2.19; 3.9; 5.6; 5.9;		18.2; 18.5
	5.23; 6.0–8.25; 9.23; 9.33; 11.0;	Apostolic Fathers	2.23; 15.0–15.24
	11.2; 11.11; 11.16; 12.1; 13.4;	*See also* Church Fathers	
	13.12–13.17; 13.21; 13.56;	Apostolic preaching *See*	
	15.0; 16.2; 17.6	Preaching in early Church	
Acts, historical value	6.0–6.3	Apostolic succession	16.27; 17.10
Acts of the Martyrs of Scilli	16.5	Apostolic tradition	17.10; 17.14
Acts of Thomas	11.16	Appearances of Risen	
Adam	9.10	Christ	6.6 (i); 6.7
Address to the Greeks, by		Appian Way *See* Roman	
Tatian	15.13	roads	
Adiabene	16.9	Appii Forum	16.21; Fig. 33
Adonai	13.38	Aquae Salviae	8.25; Fig. 35
Adriatic	7.5; 8.12	Aquila	16.13; 16.19
Aedicula	18.3; 18.5–18.8; Figs. 49, 52	Arabia	8.5f; 16.8
Aeons	4.28; 13.49	Arabs	11.3
Aegean Islands	11.14; 16.1; 16.16	Aramaic	3.11; 4.3; 5.2; 5.5; 5.23; 8.2;
Aegean Sea	8.12		13.12; 13.17; 13.21; 13.26;
Africa, Proconsular	16.5f		13.40; 16.8
Against all heresies, Justin	15.13	Aratus	4.22
Against heresies, Irenaeus	15.18	Arbela	16.9
Agrapha	2.26	Archaeology and	
Agrippinus	16.6	Christianity	2.28; 4.11 (n); 8.25; 11.13;
Ain Feshka	4.11; Fig. 8		16.23; 18.0–18.8
Alexander of Rome	16.28	Archelaus	3.17; 3.19
Alexandria	2.21; 3.7; 4.9; 4.32; 8.2; 11.10;	Arianism	13.44
	13.53; 16.7f; 16.30	Aristides	15.12
Alexandrians	11.4	Ariston	15.12
Allegory	15.10	Armenia	16.8f
Amanuenses	7.2	Artemis	4.21; 8.17; 16.12
Amen	9.6; 17.18	Arthur, King	2.5
Ananias	8.5; 11.6; 13.16	Ascension of Christ *See*	
Anatolia	8.15	Jesus Christ	
'Ancient of Days'	13.22; 13.55	*Ascension of Isaiah*	18.2
Andrew	11.16	Asia	11.3f
Angels	4.6; 9.12	Asia Minor	2.9; 2.12; 3.6; 3.9; 3.11; 4.15;
Anglo-Saxons	2.5		4.19; 8.0; 8.5–8.10; 8.13; 8.24;
Anicetus	16.28; 16.30		11.14f; 12.2; 15.8; 16.1; 16.20;
Annals of Tacitus	2.7		16.39; 17.8
Annas	3.21	Asia, Proconsular	8.0; 8.12; 8.15–8.18; 15.7;
Antichrist	15.20		16.12; 16.5; 16.17f; 17.1; 17.8;
Antinomianism	9.23; 9.38–9.42; 10.5		17.14
Antioch	8.0; 8.5; 8.15; 9.21; 11.8; 12.0;	Asiarchs	2.13
	14.0; 15.9; 16.17f	Astrology	4.26f; 9.7; 9.13
Antioch Christians	11.11; 15.7; 17.8; 17.10	Atheism	16.25
Antiochus Epiphanes	3.3; 13.22	Athenagoras	15.14
Antipas *See* Herod		Athens	4.22; 8.2; 8.13; Figs. 29, 30
Antipas		Attis	4.23
Antoninus Pius	15.13; 15.15; 17.16; 18.18	Augustine	5.23 (n)
Apelles	16.31	Augustus Caesar	2.0; 3.9; 3.13; 3.17
Aphrodite	8.13	Aulus Plautius	16.25
Apocalyptic	4.29; 9.12; 9.35–9.37; 13.19;	Autolycus	15.4
	13.22–13.27; 13.56; 15.15		
Apocrypha	2.21; 2.24; 13.26; 15.2		
Apocryphal gospels	12.1	Babylon	3.9; 16.22
other writings	7.1; 11.16; 15.2; 15.18; 17.12;	Babylonia	4.26; 13.22
	18.2	*Babylonian Talmud*	2.17
Apollos	11.10f; 13.53; 16.13f	Balkans	7.5
Apologists	15.11–15.14	Balsdon, J. P. V. D.	2.11

W. M. Ramsay, *St Paul the Traveller and Roman Citizen*, reprint, Baker Book House, Michigan 1960.

A. Richardson, *An Introduction to the Theology of the New Testament*, S.C.M. Press 1958.

A. Schweitzer, *The Quest of the Historical Jesus* (1910), English trans. reprint, Macmillan 1968.

A. N. Sherwin-White, *Roman Society and Roman Law in the New Testament*, Oxford University Press 1963.

K. O. Stendahl (ed.), *The Scrolls and the New Testament*, S.C.M. Press 1958.

J. Stevenson, *A New Eusebius*, S.P.C.K. 1957.

J. S. Stewart, *A Man in Christ: the Vital Elements of St Paul's Religion*, Hodder and Stoughton 1964.

V. Taylor, *The Person of Christ in New Testament Teaching*, St Martin Press 1958.

F. Van der Meer and C. Mohrmann, *Atlas of the Early Christian World*, Nelson 1966.

G. Vermes, *The Dead Sea Scrolls in English*, Penguin 1962.

M. Wiles, *Divine Apostle. The Interpretation of St Paul's Epistles in the Early Church*, Cambridge University Press 1967.

G. A. Williamson, *The World of Josephus*, Secker and Warburg 1964.

INDEX TO UNITS 13-16

(References are to marginal section numbers)

Abercius · 16.30

Abgar · 16.8

'Abomination of desolation' · 3.3

Abraham · 13.50

Achaia · 2.13; 8.13f; 11.10

Acrostic palindrome · 2.30

Acts of Paul and Thecla · 7.1

Acts of the Apostles · 1.2f; 2.11f; 2.19; 3.9; 5.6; 5.9; 5.23; 6.0–8.25; 9.23; 9.33; 11.0; 11.2; 11.11; 11.16; 12.1; 13.4; 13.12–13.17; 13.21; 13.56; 15.0; 16.2; 17.6

Acts, historical value · 6.0–6.3

Acts of the Martyrs of Scilli · 16.5

Acts of Thomas · 11.16

Adam · 9.10

Address to the Greeks, by Tatian · 15.13

Adiabene · 16.9

Adonai · 13.38

Adriatic · 7.5; 8.12

Aedicula · 18.3; 18.5–18.8; Figs. 49, 52

Aeons · 4.28; 13.49

Aegean Islands · 11.14; 16.1; 16.16

Aegean Sea · 8.12

Africa, Proconsular · 16.5f

Against all heresies, Justin · 15.13

Against heresies, Irenaeus · 15.18

Agrapha · 2.26

Agrippinus · 16.6

Ain Feshka · 4.11; Fig. 8

Alexander of Rome · 16.28

Alexandria · 2.21; 3.7; 4.9; 4.32; 8.2; 11.10; 13.53; 16.7f; 16.30

Alexandrians · 11.4

Allegory · 15.10

Amanuenses · 7.2

Amen · 9.6; 17.18

Ananias · 8.5; 11.6; 13.16

Anatolia · 8.15

'Ancient of Days' · 13.22; 13.55

Andrew · 11.16

Angels · 4.6; 9.12

Anglo-Saxons · 2.5

Anicetus · 16.28; 16.30

Annals of Tacitus · 2.7

Annas · 3.21

Antichrist · 15.20

Antinomianism · 9.23; 9.38–9.42; 10.5

Antioch · 8.0; 8.5; 8.15; 9.21; 11.8; 12.0; 14.0; 15.9; 16.17f

Antioch Christians · 11.11; 15.7; 17.8; 17.10

Antiochus Epiphanes · 3.3; 13.22

Antipas *See* Herod Antipas

Antoninus Pius · 15.13; 15.15; 17.16; 18.18

Apelles · 16.31

Aphrodite · 8.13

Apocalyptic · 4.29; 9.12; 9.35–9.37; 13.19; 13.22–13.27; 13.56; 15.15

Apocrypha · 2.21; 2.24; 13.26; 15.2

Apocryphal gospels other writings · 12.1 · 7.1; 11.16; 15.2; 15.18; 17.12; 18.2

Apollos · 11.10f; 13.53; 16.13f

Apologists · 15.11–15.14

Apology, Justin · 16.35; 17.16

Apology, Tertullian · 15.14; 16.6

Apostles' Creed · 17.11

Apostles, The · 5.21; 5.35; 5.38; 6.1; 6.4; 6.6 (a); 6.7; 8.7; 9.15; 9.31; 10.0–10.3; 11.3; 11.16; 13.9; 15.0; 15.5; 15.18; 15.20; 16.29; 17.7f; 17.10; 17.12; 17.15–17.18; 18.2; 18.5

Apostolic Fathers *See also* Church Fathers · 2.23; 15.0–15.24

Apostolic preaching *See* Preaching in early Church

Apostolic succession · 16.27; 17.10

Apostolic tradition · 17.10; 17.14

Appearances of Risen Christ · 6.6 (i); 6.7

Appian Way *See* Roman roads

Appii Forum · 16.21; Fig. 33

Aquae Salviae · 8.25; Fig. 35

Aquila · 16.13; 16.19

Arabia · 8.5f; 16.8

Arabs · 11.3

Aramaic · 3.11; 4.3; 5.2; 5.5; 5.23; 8.2; 13.12; 13.17; 13.21; 13.26; 13.40; 16.8

Aratus · 4.22

Arbela · 16.9

Archaeology and Christianity · 2.28; 4.11 (n); 8.25; 11.13; 16.23; 18.0–18.8

Archelaus · 3.17; 3.19

Arianism · 13.44

Aristides · 15.12

Ariston · 15.12

Armenia · 16.8f

Artemis · 4.21; 8.17; 16.12

Arthur, King · 2.5

Ascension of Christ *See* Jesus Christ

Ascension of Isaiah · 18.2

Asia · 11.3f

Asia Minor · 2.9; 2.12; 3.6; 3.9; 3.11; 4.15; 4.19; 8.0; 8.5–8.10; 8.13; 8.24; 11.14f; 12.2; 15.8; 16.1; 16.20; 16.39; 17.8

Asia, Proconsular · 8.0; 8.12; 8.15–8.18; 15.7; 16.12; 16.5; 16.17f; 17.1; 17.8; 17.14

Asiarchs · 2.13

Astrology · 4.26f; 9.7; 9.13

Atheism · 16.25

Athenagoras · 15.14

Athens · 4.22; 8.2; 8.13; Figs. 29, 30

Attis · 4.23

Augustine · 5.23 (n)

Augustus Caesar · 2.0; 3.9; 3.13; 3.17

Aulus Plautius · 16.25

Autolycus · 15.4

Babylon · 3.9; 16.22

Babylonia · 4.26; 13.22

Babylonian Talmud · 2.17

Balkans · 7.5

Balsdon, J. P. V. D. · 2.11

Baptism	3.9 (d); 4.15; 5.23; 5.38; 9.3; 9.31–9.34; 11.5; 13.42; 14.1f; 15.6; 15.15; 17.11; 17.15; 17.18
Bardesan	16.9
Bar-Kochba	13.2
Barnabas	4.21; 8.7–8.12; 11.8f
Barnabas, Epistle of	2.24; 15.10
Bar-nasha	13.26
Bartholomew	11.16
Baruch, Apocalypse of	13.23
Basilica of St Peter	1.6; 16.23; 18.3–18.8
Basilides	16.31
Battle of Britain	5.12
Beatitudes	5.29
Benjamin	8.2
Beroea	8.13
Bettenson, H.	2.9
Bible-reading by early Christians	12.3
Bishops	5.37 (n); 11.12; 15.2; 15.7–15.9; 15.14; 15.16–15.18; 16.6f; 16.17f; 16.26; 16.30; 17.6; 17.8; 17.10
Bishops of Rome *See* Roman Bishops	
Bithynia	2.9; 8.12; 11.15; 15.23; 16.2; 17.1
Black Sea	11.14; 11.16; 16.31
Body of Christ	9.24; 9.26; 9.31; 9.35f
Bonsirven, J.	4.3
Bornkamm, G.	5.23
Britain, Roman	16.0f; 16.25
Bruce, F. F.	1.4
Bultmann, R.	4.29f
Byzantium	16.31
Caesar	3.9; 8.20; 16.21
Caesarea (Palestinae)	6.6 (i); 8.0; 8.14; 8.19f; 11.7
Caesarea Philippi	3.18; 13.30
Caligula	3.19f
Callixtus	16.39
Canon, New Testament	2.19; 5.9; 12.2f; 15.2; 15.17; 16.36; 17.12
Canon, Old Testament	2.20f
Cappadocia	11 3; 11.14f
Carrington, P.	1.4
Carthage	16.5f
Catacombs	16.22; 16.25; 16.36f; Fig. 44
Catholic Church	15.17; 17.0; 17.13
Celtic tribes	16.1
Cemetery of Domitilla	16.25
Cenchreae	8.13
Census	4.14
Cephas	6.7; 8.7; 11.11
Cerdon	16.31
Chalcedon, Council of	13.17
Charismatic gifts	17.6
Charles, R. H.	2.22
Chrestos	2.8; 16.19
Christian creed	15.22; 17.11; 17.15
Christians, Life-style of	15.21f; 17.22
Christology:	
in early Church	13.0–13.62
in Palestinian Church	13.12–13.17
in Synoptic Gospels	13.18–13.33
in Paul	13.34–13.44
in Fourth Gospel	13.45–13.52
in *Epistle of Hebrews*	13.53f
and monotheism	13.56–13.62
Church and synagogue	2.17; 17.16
Church Fathers	5.17
See also Apostolic Fathers	
Church of England	2.21
Churchill, Winston	5.12
Cicero	7.3
Cilicia	8.2; 8.8; 8.12; 11.4
Cirencester	2.30
Circumcision	9.21
Claudius	2.8; 3.20f; 16.0f; 16.19
Clement, Letters of	8.23; 9.27; 14.2; 15.5; 16.36; 16.38; 17.8
Clement of Alexandria	15.18; 16.18
Clement of Rome	2.23; 12.0; 16.22; 16.24; 16.27; 16.39; 18.2
Cleopatra of Jerusalem	3.18
Cletus	16.27
Collections	8.8; 9.44; 10.1; 16.32
Colossae	8.16
Colossian Christians	9.13
Commodus	15.14
Communal life of early Church	8.7
Constantine	18.3f; 18.6; Fig. 53
Constantinople, Council of	13.7
Corinium	2.30
Corinth	2.13; 8.12–8.14; 8.19f; 8.23; 11.10–11.12; 16.19
Corinthian Christians	8.13f; 9.22; 9.30; 15.5; 16.24
Corinthian Jews	8.13
Corinthians, Letters to	1.5; 7.3; 8.16; 9.35; 11.11f; 17.17; Fig. 36
Cornelius	3.9; 6.6 (i); 11.7; 13.15
Cosmic powers	9.11–9.13
Council, Jewish *See* Sanhedrin	
Council of Jerusalem	8.11; 11.11
Covenant, New	4.19; 5.23; 9.25; 13.53
Covenant, Old	4.2; 5.32; 5.37; 9.43–9.46; 13.53
Creed, Nicene *See* Nicene Creed	
Creed, Apostles *See* Apostles Creed	
Creed of early Church	8.7
Cretans	11.3
Crete	11.14
Cullmann, O.	13.11
Cybele	4.23
Cyprus	2.13; 8.9; 11.8f; 11.14
Cyrenaica	11.14
Cyrene	11.3; 11.8
Cyrenians	11.4
Dalmatia	7.5; 11.14
Damascus	7.0; 8.4–8.6; 9.26; 11.6
Daniel, Book of	3.5; 13.22–13.27; 13.55
Date of Gospels	5.2; 12.1
David	3.22; 9.45
Day of Judgement	5.21
'Day of the Lord'	4.16; 9.29; 9.35–9.37
Deacons	15.8; 17.6; 17.8; 17.18
Dead Sea Scrolls	2.25; 4.11; Figs. 5, 9
Demigod	13.49
Demonology	9.1; 9.11–9.16
Demythologizing	4.30; 13.62
Derbe	8.9
Deutero-Canonical Books	2.21; 13.47
Deutero–Isaiah	13.26
Devils *See* Evil Spirits	
Dialogue concerning Christ	15.12
Dialogue with Trypho	15.13
Diana	4.21

Diaspora, Jewish	3.7; 4.9; 6.3; 8.1f; 8.10; 9.22; 9.44; 11.3; 11.8; 11.11f; 11.14; 16.2; 16.5; 16.7; 16.19; 16.21; 17.1
Diatessaron	15.13
Didache in early Church	13.13 (n)
Didache, The	2.24; 13.17; 15.6; 17.17
Dio Cassius	16.0; 16.25
Diognetus, Epistle to	15.1; 15.12; 15.21–15.24
Dionysius of Corinth	11.12; 15.18; 16.22; 16.32; 18.2
Dionysus, Cult of	4.23
Disciples, The	5.5; 5.35; 5.40; 8.8
Dispersion, Jewish *See* Diaspora, Jewish	
Ditheism	13.58
Divinity of Emperor	13.12; 13.46
Divinity of Christ *See* Jesus Christ	
Docetists	4.28; 13.61; 15.8f; 15.23
Dodd, C. H.	5.10 (n); 5.12; 5.18 (n)
Dominus et Deus	13.46
Domitian	2.9f; 2.16; 3.9; 12.2; 13.46; 16.24f
Doxology	13.41
Dualism	4.26; 10.5; 17.3
Early Christian congregations, location of	8.1; map A on page 11
Easter	16.18; 16.28; 16.39
Edessa	16.8f
'Edhah	5.36
Ego eimi	13.50
Egypt	2.21; 3.6; 4.31; 11.3; 11.10; 11.14; 11.16; 16.7; 17.11
Ekklesia	5.36
Elders	8.10; 8.18; 17.6; 18.8
Elemental spirits *See* Evil spirits	
Eleusis	4.23
Eleutheros	16.28; 16.39
Enoch, Similitudes of	13.23
Epaphrus	8.16
Ephesian Christians	13.3; 16.11–16.18; 16.20; 17.10
Ephesus	2.13; 4.21; 8.0; 8.12; 8.15–8.18; 11.14; 16.11–16.18; 17.8
Ephesus, Council of	13.7
Epicurean philosophers	4.22
Epimenldes	4.22
Episkopoi	17.6
Eschatology	1.5; 5.21f; 9.3; 9.35–9.37; 9.41; 13.52; 13.60; 16.39
Essenes	4.10; 4.13–4.15
Ethiopia	6.6 (g); 11.15
Euangelion	5.1
Eucharist	4.23 (f); 9.27; 9.33f; 16.32; 17.17f; Fig. 42
See also Lord's Supper; Holy Communion	
Eunuch of Ethiopia	6.6 (g); 11.5
Euphrates	3.10
Europe	8.12
Eusebius	15.2; 15.7; 15.12; 15.17f; 16.8; 16.15; 16.18; 16.25; 18.4
Evaristus	16.28
Evil spirits	9.1; 9.11–9.13; 9.35
Excavations under St Peter's	1.11; 16.23; 18.0–18.8
Excommunication	16.18; 16.34; 16.39
Exorcism	8.17
Exposition of the Sayings of the Lord	15.17
Ezekiel	13.21
Ezra, Fourth Book of	13.23
Fall of Jerusalem	11.2
Family in Jewish religion	4.3
Famine relief *See* Collections	
Ferguson, J.	1.6; 4.19f; 4.24; 8.22; 16.14
Festus *See* Porcius Festus	
Finegan, J.	2.28
Filson, F. V.	1.2f; 1.5; 2.5; 2.6–2.10; 2.18; 2.21; 2.25; 3.0–3.2; 3.10; 3.14f; 4.3; 4.27; 5.4; 5.18; 5.20; 6.0 (n); 6.5; 7.2; 7.4f; 8.0f; 8.11f; 8.22; 9.3f; 9.23; 11.2; 12.2; 13.10; 13.13 (n); 15.3f; 16.4; 16.11; 16.15; 16.26f; 17.5
'First, The'	2.13
Flavia Domitilla	16.25
Forgiveness	5.26; 15.15; 17.11
Form Criticism	5.3–5.7; 13.9; 13.48
Founding of the Church	5.36; 9.43
Fourth Gospel *See* John, Gospel of	
Fuller, R. H.	13.11
Gaius Minucius Fundanus	2.9
Gaius the Presbyter	16.23; 18.5; Fig. 49
Galatia	8.9; 8.12; 8.15; 11.15
Galatian Christians	9.22
Galatians, Letter to	7.3; 9.20; 9.42
Galilee	3.17; 3.19; 3.21; 11.7
Gallio	2.13; 8.13
Gamaliel	8.3
Gaul	3.19; 15.16; 16.7; 17.11
Genesis	9.10; 13.47
Gentile Christians	2.24; 4.18f; 5.5; 8.11; 9.4; 9.7; 9.13; 9.26; 9.40; 9.45; 13.21; 13.38f; 15.2; 17.0; 17.2
Gentile cults	4.21f; 8.17; 9.16; 13.2; 16.12
Gentiles	3.7; 4.1; 5.5; 6.4; 7.0; 8.8; 8.10f; 8.13; 9.4; 9.10; 9.13; 9.14–9.16; 9.26; 9.40; 9.43–9.45; 10.0; 11.2; 11.7; 17.7
Glory	5.40; 9.36; 13.51; 15.20
Glossolalia	9.30
Gnosis	4.27; 15.18; 17.12
Gnosticism	2.24; 4.27–4.32; 10.5; 13.49; 13.61; 15.2; 15.17f; 16.31; 16.38; 17.3; 17.12
'God-fearers'	3.7; 9.44; 11.7
Gortyna	15.18
Grant, R. M.	16.39
Grammateus	2.13
'The Great Church'	17.0
Greece	2.12; 3.9; 4.19; 8.0; 8.11; 8.13f; 8.18; 11.14; 12.2; 16.1
Greek	2.31; 5.2; 5.5; 8.2; 15.4; 16.36
Greek Christians	4.19
Greek-speaking Christians *See* Hellenistic Christians	
Hadrian	2.6; 2.9; 15.12; 15.17; 16.7f; 16.28f
Hanukkah	3.4
Hasidim	4.6; 4.10
Hasmonean rule *See* Maccabean revolt and rule	
Healing of crippled boy	6.6 (c)

Hebrew language   4.9; 13.21; 17.18

Hebrews, Letter to   7.2; 9.12; 12.2; 13.53; 13.56; 13.59; 15.1

Hegesippus   16.30; 17.10

Hellenism   2.16; 3.10; 4.1; 4.19–4.32; 8.2; 9.4; 9.7; 13.9; 15.11

Hellenistic Christians   5.5; 5.36; 9.44; 11.4f; 13.17; 13.28; 17.14

Hellenistic Jews   4.9; 8.7; 13.28

Hellenists   4.9; 5.5; 11.4f

Hellespont   8.12

Hennecke, E.-Schneemelcher, W.   2.24; 7.1; 10.4; 18.2

Herculaneum   11.13

Heresiarch   16.31

Heresy   16.31

Heretics   15.21; 17.10

Hermes   4.21

Herod Agrippa I   3.20; 11.1

Herod Agrippa II   3.21

Herod Antipas   3.19f; 4.9; 4.15

Herod the Great   3.12–3.22

Herodians   4.9

Hierapolis   8.16; 11.16; 12.2; 15.17

Hieropolis   16.30

High Priests   3.2; 3.13; 3.21 (vi); 4.1; 4.8; 9.27; 13.15; 13.24f; 13.30

Hippolytus   16.36; 16.39; 17.9

Hitler, Adolf   5.12

Holy Communion   9.27
   See also Eucharist Lord's Supper

Holy Ghost   *See* Holy Spirit

Holy Spirit   6.2; 8.12; 9.21; 9.28–9.31; 9.38–9.41; 10.1; 11.15; 12.3; 13.13; 13.15; 13.30; 13.59; 14.0f; 17.9; 17.11; 17.15; 17.18

Horeb   13.50

Hyginus   16.28

Iconium   2.13; 8.9

Idol worship   13.2

Idumaea   3.17

Ignatius, Letters of   2.23; 4.28; 12.0; 13.3; 14.2; 15.7–15.8; 15.16; 16.17; 16.22; 16.26f; 16.38; 17.0; 17.8f; 18.2

Illyricum   7.5; 8.14

Immortality   4.6; 4.23; 4.26; 9.37

India   4.26; 11.16; 16.10

Indian Christians   11.16

Inter-testamentary books   2.22; 9.10; 13.23

Iran   4.26
   See also Persia

Iraq   16.9

Irenaeus   15.9; 15.18; 16.30; 16.38; 17.10f; 17.14; 18.2

Israel, New   4.19; 9.24f; 9.27

Israel, People of God   4.2f; 4.6; 4.16; 5.32; 5.35; 9.25f; 9.43–9.46; 10.2; 13.28; 17.1

Israel, Religion of   2.17; 3.2–3.5; 4.0–4.18; 5.31f; 9.7f; 9.10; 9.26; 11.7; 13.2; 13.19; 13.22–13.24; 13.26–13.28

Italy   11.13; 11.32; 12.2; 16.1

Ituraea   3.18

James, Brother of Jesus   2.10; 3.21; 6.1; 6.7; 8.7; 8.11; 9.45; 11.11; 12.2; 16.15

James, Brother of John   3.20; 6.1; 10.0

James, Epistle of   9.23; 12.2

James, M. R.   2.24

Jehovah   3.3 (n)

Jeremias, J.   2.26

Jerusalem   3.2; 3.9 (b); 3.12f; 3.17; 5.6; 6.2; 6.5; 6.6; 7.0; 7.5; 8.0; 8.3f; 8.7; 8.14; 8.18–8.20; 9.44f; 11.3; 13.13; 13.17; 15.6; 16.19; 16.29

Jerusalem Christians   2.17; 9.4; 9.10; 9.23; 9.44–9.46; 10.3f; 11.0; 11.8; 15.12

Jerusalem Conference (Council)   *See* Council of Jerusalem

Jesus Christ:

   ascension   6.6 (a)

   atoning death   5.40; 6.7; 9.14–9.16; 9.32; 13.35; 13.53

   authority   13.19

   birth   2.0; 3.9 ;13.8

   baptism   5.23; 9.33; 13.30

   character   5.1

   commission to apostles   5.38; 14.1

   controversies   3.9; 4.17

   crucifixion   2.10; 2.16; 3.9; 5.5f; 5.35; 5.39f; 6.6–7.0; 8.4; 9.32; 13.13; 13.16; 13.35; 13.52; 13.55; 13.61f; 15.20; 17.11

   divinity   13.0–14.2

   earthly ministry   13.17; 13.19; 13.60

   emanation from God   13.44

   eschatology   5.21f; 13.21–13.27; 13.61

   exaltation   5.40; 6.6; 9.14f; 9.17; 13.13–13.17; 13.37–13.40; 13.44; 13.53; 13.55; 13.57; 13.60; 14.2

   extra-Gospel sayings   2.26

   family   3.21; 6.1; 8.7; 8.11; 9.45; 16.15

   fulfilment of prophecy   5.5; 13.54

   glory   13.17; 13.24; 13.52; 13.56; 13.58

   Jewish background   4.4–4.18; 5.1; 13.2

   Judge   5.21; 6.6; 13.15; 13.19f; 13.24; 13.57; 15.20; 17.11

   language   3.11; 5.2; 5.5

   Last Supper   5.37; 17.17

   Lord   5.0; 5.9; 8.5; 8.17f; 8.20f; 9.14; 9.17; 9.20; 9.38; 13.13; 13.16f; 13.35; 13.38–13.40; 13.45f; 13.57; 14.1

   Messiah   4.16; 6.4; 8.5; 9.14; 9.45; 13.2; 13.13f; 13.21; 13.30f

   miracles   5.2–5.7; 13.13; 13.15; 13.19; 13.33

   non-biblical allusions   12.2; 13.1; 13.3; 13.17

   obedience to God   9.16

   oral tradition   5.5–5.10; 12.2

   passion   5.5f; 5.39f; 8.19; 13.52; 16.17

   pre-existence   9.17; 13.13; 13.16; 13.21; 13.35f; 13.44; 13.46; 13.50f; 13.53; 13.56; 13.59f

   Redeemer   9.14

   resurrection   5.0f; 5.5f; 5.35; 5.40; 6.4–7.0; 8.4; 8.10; 9.14; 9.16; 9.32f; 10.0; 10.2f; 13.0; 13.14; 13.35; 13.37f; 13.44–13.46; 13.52; 13.57; 13.61; 17.11; 17.16

   Saviour   9.14; 9.43; 13.14f; 13.19; 13.26f; 13.55; 17.18

   Second Adam   9.10

   Second Coming   9.35–9.37; 9.41; 13.14; 13.17; 13.19f; 13.24; 13.61; 15.6

Sermon on the Mount	5.31	John, Apostle	3.20; 6.1; 10.0; 11.5; 11.14;
Son of David	9.45		12.2; 15.9; 15.17; 16.15f;
Son of God	13.28–13.31; 13.36; 13.43f;		16.18
	13.41–13.63; 16.17; 16.26;	John, Gospel of	2.19; 2.28; 4.24; 5.10; 5.14;
	17.11		9.34; 12.1; 13.4; 13.21; 13.31;
Son of Man	13.16; 13.21–13.27; 13.52;		13.33; 13.45–13.52; 13.56f;
	13.55		16.14–16.16
status	5.19; 5.40; 10.3; 13.0–13.62	John the Baptist	3.19; 4.15; 13.20; 16.13
subordination to the		John the Elder	16.16
Father	13.44; 13.57	John, Letters of	13.54f; 16.16
'Suffering Servant'	4.16; 13.12	John Mark See Mark	
titles	13.0–13.63	John the prophet	16.16
unity with God	13.49; 13.51	Joppa	9.21; 11.7
'world-picture'	9.7	Jordan	13.20; 15.6; Fig. 4
worship of	13.1; 13.41	Joseph	3.17
Jesus Christ and:		Josephus	2.10; 2.25; 3.20f; 4.6; 4.10;
The Apostles	7.0; 10.2; 13.20; 13.29; 15.5		4.15
Caesarea Philippi	13.30	Judaea	2.7; 3.6f; 3.9f; 3.12; 3.16f; 3.21;
the Church	9.26f; 9.31; 9.35; 10.0; 13.37;		4.0; 4.14; 6.1; 6.7; 8.3; 8.7f;
	13.40; 13.49		9.10; 9.15; 11.0; 11.3; 11.5;
Church Councils	13.7		11.11; 16.19; 16.29
creation	13.36; 13.47; 13.53; 13.59f	Judaean Christians	6.1; 8.7f; 10.1; 11.7; 11.11;
Docetism and Gnosticism	4.28		13.2; 13.17; 15.2; 16.29; 17.2
Herod Antipas	3.19	Judaism	2.17; 3.3; 4.6; 4.12; 4.26; 6.2;
the Herodians	4.9		13.21; 13.47; 15.12
the Holy Spirit	5.0; 9.28; 10.1; 12.2f; 13.13;	Judaizers	8.11; 9.22; 9.42; 15.10
	13.15; 13.30; 13.59; 14.0–14.2	Judas Maccabeus	3.6
the Jews	2.15; 2.17; 3.9	Jude	12.2
John the Baptist	4.15; 5.23; 13.30	Judgement	5.26; 9.9; 15.20
the Lord's Supper	9.27; 9.32; 17.18	Junius Rusticus	16.35
Mary	4.28; 13.3; 13.19; 13.57; 17.11	Jupiter	4.21
Paul	8.3; 8.17; 9.7; 9.14–9.19; 9.23;	Justification	9.19–9.23; 9.31; 9.40–9.42;
	9.26–9.43; 11.1		13.42
the Pharisees	4.7; 13.19	Justin Martyr	15.3; 15.11; 15.13; 16.18;
Roman rule	3.9 (b)		16.30; 16.35; 17.16f
the Sabbath	13.19; 13.50		
the Trinity	14.0–14.2	Kepha	5.36
the Zealots	4.14	Kerygma	13.13
Jesus Christ: Teaching		Khirbet Qumran	4.13; Fig. 10
general	5.0; 5.5; 5.19–5.40; 10.3	Kingdom of God	5.20; 5.22f; 7.0; 8.21; 9.33;
the Beatitudes	5.29		13.19
the Church	5.36f	Kirschbaum, E.	18.0
eschatology	5.21; 5.34	Knox, R.	2.32
God as Father	5.24	Koine Greek	8.2
judgement	5.26	Kosher laws	11.11
Kingdom of God	5.26f; 5.32–5.35; 5.40	Kurdistan	16.9
love of God	5.25	Kyrios	13.17; 13.38–13.40; 13.54
love of neighbour	5.25		
moral standards	5.31	Lake of Galilee	15.6
New Covenant	5.32; 5.37	Lake, Kirsopp	15.3
outcasts and sinners	5.30	Language of Jesus	3.11
parables	5.3; 5.5; 5.34; 13.29	Laodicea	8.16
prayer	5.28	Last Days	5.21; 13.19f; 15.6
repentance	5.23	Last Supper	5.6; 5.9; 5.23; 17.17
Sermon on the Mount	5.31	Law of Moses See Jewish	
service	5.35	Law	
taking up of cross	5.29	Lawyers	4.6f
worldly wealth	5.29	Legalism of Pharisees	4.6f; 9.7
Jewish Christians	2.17; 9.4; 9.10; 9.23; 9.44–9.46;	Legends	2.5; 5.11–5.15; 7.1; 16.7
	10.3f; 11.0; 11.8; 15.12	Letters of Ignatius	13.3; 16.17; 16.26f
Jewish Christian		Levant	3.1; 3.10
Hellenists	5.5	Levites	9.27
Jewish Law	3.7; 3.20; 4.0–4.18; 8.2f; 8.5;	Lewis, N. and	
	8.11; 9.19–9.23; 10.1; 12.3;	Reinhold, M.	2.6; 2.7; 2.9; 13.1; 15.14; 15.16
	13.2; 13.9; 15.10	Libya	11.3
Jewish Scriptures	2.18; 2.20f; 2.43; 4.3; 4.6;	Life in Christ	5.0; 9.28–9.30
	5.5; 6.7; 8.2; 9.21; 9.29; 10.4;	Lietzmann, H.	1.4; 3.6 (n)
	12.3	Linus	16.27
Jewish sects	2.19; 4.6–4.18	Liturgy	5.8; 17.17
Jewish War See War of		Logia	15.17
AD 66–73		Logos	13.46–13.49; 13.55; 13.61
Job, Book of	13.47	Lollius Urbicus	16.35

Lord's Supper 5.9; 9.3; 9.27; 9.31–9.34; 17.17
   See also Eucharist;
      Holy Communion
'Love-feasts' 17.3
Lucan 16.31
Luke, Evangelist 6.0; 7.6; 8.7; 8.21; 9.23; 11.11; 12.1; 13.12; 16.21
Luke, Gospel of 1.2; 2.19; 3.9; 4.0; 5.2; 5.8; 5.17; 6.0; 7.0; 13.12; 13.18; 13.21; 13.33; 17.12
Luther, Martin 5.36 (n)
Lycaonia 2.13; 4.21
Lydda 11.7
Lyons 15.16; 16.7; 16.30
Lystra 2.13; 4.21; 8.9; 8.12

Maccabean revolt and rule 3.1–3.6; 3.20; 4.0; 4.6; 4.14
Macedonia 8.0; 8.11; 8.13f; 8.18; 15.9; 16.1
Madras 11.16
Magic 4.26; 8.17
Magistrates 2.13
Magnesians 14.2
Malachi 17.17
Malta 2.13
Malthace of Samaria 3.17; 3.19
Manuscripts, New
   Testament 12.2f
Maranatha 13.17; 13.40
Marcion 15.18; 16.31; 16.34; 17.12
Marcus Aurelius 15.4; 15.13f; 15.18; 16.8; 16.11; 16.32; 16.35
Mariners 16.2
Mark, Gospel of 1.2; 2.19; 5.2; 5.8; 5.17; 13.21; 13.33; 13.54; 16.22
Martyrdom of Polycarp, The 15.16; 17.0
Martyrdom of Stephen 6.6f; 13.16
Mary 4.28; 13.3; 13.19; 13.57; 17.11
Matthew, Gospel of 1.2; 2.19; 5.2; 5.8; 5.17; 11.9; 13.18; 13.21; 13.33; 13.54; 15.9
Medes 11.3
Mediterranean 3.7; 3.9; 16.2
Melito of Sardis 15.18
Merchants 16.2
Mercury 4.21
Mesopotamia 3.10; 11.3; 11.16; 16.8
Message of early Church 6.4
Messiah 4.16; 5.32; 6.6 (e); 8.5; 9.14; 9.45f; 10.2; 13.2; 13.13f; 13.17; 13.21; 13.23; 13.25; 13.30; 13.32
Michael the Archangel 9.12
Miletus 8.18
Ministers 17.6
Ministers, authority of 15.15; 16.15; 16.38; 17.7
Minucius Felix 15.14
Miracles 5.2; 5.7; 6.6 (c)
   See also Jesus Christ
'Miracle stories' 5.3
Mishnah 2.17
Missionary expansion,
   non-Pauline 11.1–11.16
Missionary journeys of
   St Paul *See* Paul
Mithras 4.23
Monarchical bishops 17.8
Monepiscopacy 15.8; 16.17
Monotheism 9.8; 13.2f; 13.56; 13.58
Montanism 9.8; 13.2f; 13.56; 13.58
Moore, G. F. 4.3
Mosaic Law *See* Jewish
   Law

Moses 5.23; 13.50
Moule, C. F. D. 17.1
Mount Sinai 13.19
Muratorian Canon 15.17; 16.36; 17.12
Mylapore 11.16
Mysterion 4.23f; 9.33
Mystery religions 4.23f; 9.34
Myth 4.26; 4.29f; 5.2; 5.11–5.15; 13.9

Nabatea 3.1
Nag Hammadi 4.31
Naples 11.13
Natural theology 9.8
Nazarenes 4.18f; 11.0; 17.1
Nazareth 3.19; 8.5; 13.1; 13.57; Fig. 58
Neo-Pythagoreans 4.26
Nero 2.7f; 2.16; 3.21; 8.25; 16.1; 16.21f; 18.1f; 18.8
New Adam 9.14
New Covenant *See*
   Covenant, New
New English Bible 1.2; 13.43
New Israel 9.24–9.27
New Testament 1.2; 1.5; 2.3; 2.6; 2.11f; 2.19; 2.27; 3.0; 4.28; 5.9; 12.2; 13.0; 13.3f; 13.7–13.55; 15.0; 15.2; 15.15; 15.17; 16.11; 17.7; 17.12f
Nicaea, Council of 13.7
Nicene Creed 13.44
Nineham, D. 1.6; 5.15
Nirvana 4.26
Nock, A. D. 4.24
North Africa 17.1

Old Covenant *See*
   Covenant, Old
Old Testament 4.4; 4.28; 5.5; 10.4; 13.19; 13.28f; 13.47; 13.54; 14.0; 15.10; 17.12f
Olympus 4.21; 4.26
Onesimus 16.17
Oral tradition 5.5–5.10; 12.2; 15.17
Origen 11.16; 16.30; 17.11
Original sin 9.10
Orontes 8.8
Orthodoxy 16.31; 16.38; 17.10; 17.13
Osborne, H. 2.1 (n)
Osrhoëne 16.8
Ostia, Road to *See*
   Roman roads
Overseers 17.6; 17.8

Pagan world and religion 3.3; 4.19–4.32; 6.0; 6.3; 8.1f; 9.4; 9.7; 9.10; 9.13; 9.16; 9.34; 11.8; 11.14f; 13.28; 13.39; 15.11f; 16.37
Palestine 2.12; 3.7; 3.11–4.4; 5.5; 8.19; 13.28; 17.1
Palestinian Christians 10.0; 11.14; 13.12; 16.15
Pamphylia 8.9; 11.3
Pantaenus 11.16
Papias 12.2; 15.17; 16.16; 16.22
Papyri 2.26
Parables 5.3; 5.5; 5.34
Parousia *See* Second
   Coming
Parthia 3.1; 3.10; 11.16; 16.8f
Parthians 11.3
Parties in early Church 11.0–11.16; 13.0; 17.2
'Passion narrative' 5.3; 5.6; 5.39

Passover	1.6; 4.24; 8.14
Pastoral Epistles	7.2; 8.24; 16.15; 17.7
Pater Noster	2.30f
Patmos	16.16
Paul	
appeal to Caesar	8.20
appearance	7.1
apostleship	9.44; 11.12; 17.6
authority	7.0; 10.0; 10.2; 11.12; 13.41; 17.6; 18.2
belief in evil spirits	9.1
biographical data	7.3; 8.2f
Christology	13.12; 13.33–13.44; 13.58
chosen by God	7.0; 8.5; 10.0–10.2
civic pride	8.2
confronts Jews	8.6; 8.10; 16.21
conversion	6.6 (h); 7.0; 8.4; 9.26; 11.6
culture	8.2
dangers	8.0; 8.6f; 8.19; 8.21
disability	8.8
discourses	9.23
early life	8.2f
ecstasy	8.8
education	8.3
enters Europe	8.2
escapes	8.6f
eschatalogical ideas	9.3; 9.35–9.37
evangelical tactics	8.12f
house arrest at Rome	8.21–8.24
journeys	7.5f; 8.0–8.24
journey to Rome	8.19–8.21; 11.3
key ideas	9.6–9.46
letters	1.6; 6.3; 7.0–10.4; 11.0; 11.2; 12.0; 12.2; 13.4; 13.34–13.44; 15.9; 15.24; 16.5; 17.6; 17.12
martyrdom	8.23; 8.25; 16.21f; 18.2
message for today	9.0f
method of preaching	8.10; 9.44
miracles	8.17
mission	7.0; 8.0–8.24; 11.0–11.2
pastoral concern	9.2
'party'	11.10f
persecution of the Church	8.4; 9.20; 10.2
place in early Church	10.0–10.5
prayer	13.41
preaching	5.8
relatives	8.3
Roman citizenship	8.2
sacramental ideas	9.3; 9.31–9.34
soteriology	9.14–9.16; 13.45
studies	8.3
supernatural guidance	8.12
teaching	5.9; 6.7; 9.0–9.46; 13.34–13.44; 16.31
'thorn in the flesh'	8.8
tomb	8.25; 18.15
trade	8.2
vocabulary	13.43
'world-picture'	9.7
Paul and:	
Antioch	8.8–8.10
Athens	8.13
Arabia	8.5f
Asia Minor	8.9; 8.12f; 8.15f
Barnabas	8.7–8.12; 15.10
Corinth	8.13f
Damascus	8.5f; 11.6
Ephesus	8.15–8.18; 16.13–16.15
Galatia	8.12; 8.14
Gamaliel	8.3
Greece	8.13f
Jerusalem	8.7f; 8.19f; 11.11
Jerusalem Council	11.11
Jewish Law	8.3; 8.5; 8.11; 10.1
Macedonia	8.13; 8.18
Peter	8.7; 8.25; 10.0; 10.4; 11.11f; 16.22f; 16.26; 18.2
Rome	8.21f; 16.20; 16.23; 16.26; 18.2
Spain	7.5; 8.23
Stephen	8.4
Pauline churches	8.1; 10.3; 11.0
Pella	15.6
Penance	15.15
Pentecost, Day of	6.6 (b); 9.23; 9.29; 11.2f; 12.3; 13.13; 16.19
Peraea	3.19; 3.21
Perkins, J. B. Ward	18.0; 18.8
Persecution of Christians	2.7–2.10; 3.20 (v); 8.4; 11.5; 12.2; 15.9; 15.13; 15.16f; 15.21f; 16.5–16.7; 16.22; 16.24f; 16.28; 16.35; 17.1; 18.2; 18.8
Persia	9.12; 11.16; 13.22; 16.8; 16.10
Persian mythology	3.6 (n)
Peter	3.9; 3.20; 5.36; 6.1; 6.6 (b) (c); 8.7; 8.11; 8.25; 9.15; 9.21; 9.33; 10.0; 10.4; 11.5; 11.7; 11.11f; 12.2; 13.12–13.15; 13.30; 16.22f; 16.26f; 16.39; 18.0–18.8
Peter, Letters of	10.4f; 11.15; 15.9; 16.22
Pharisees	4.6; 4.14; 4.18; 5.30; 8.2f; 9.7; 9.12; 9.37; 9.42; 13.28
Philip of Gortyna	15.18
Philip, son of Herod	3.18
Philip, Apostle	11.16
Philip the evangelist	6.1; 6.6 (g); 11.5; 11.16; 18.5
Philippi	2.13; 15.9
Philippian Christians	8.13f; 15.9
Philippians, Letter to	7.3; 8.14; 15.5; 16.14
Philo	2.25; 4.10; 14.37
Phoenicia	11.8
Phrygia	8.12; 8.15; 11.3; 11.16; 16.30; 16.35; 16.39; 18.5
Pisidian Antioch	8.9f
Pius of Rome	15.15; 16.28
Platonism	4.26; 4.28; 9.26; 9.37; 15.13
Pliny	2.9; 4.10; 4.13; 13.1; 13.3; 15.23
Politarchs	2.13
Polycarp, Letter of	15.9–15.24
Polycarp of Smyrna	12.0; 15.7; 15.9; 15.16f; 15.23; 16.30
Polycrates	16.18; 17.8
Polytheism	9.7; 9.13; 13.28
Pompeii	2.30f; 11.13
Pompey	3.6
Pomponia Graecina	16.25
Pontius Pilate	2.7; 2.10; 2.16; 3.9; 3.19
Pope Stephen	16.39
Porcius Festus	8.20
Post-apostolic Church	13.34
Pothinus	16.7
Prayer	5.28; 13.41; 17.15–17.18
Preaching of early Church	5.5; 6.6 (i) 6.7; 8.10; 9.15; 13.12–13.17; 13.21
Predestination	8.10
Prefect	3.9 (b); 16.35
Preparatio evangelica	13.27
Presbyteroi	17.6
Presbyters	15.8; 17.8
Priests	17.6
Priscilla	16.13; 16.19
Proclus	18.5

Proconsul | 2.13; 8.13; 16.6
Procurator | 3.9 (b); 3.21 (vi)
'Pronouncement stories' | 5.3
Prophets, Christian | 17.6; 17.16
Proselytes: | 3.7; 16.2; 16.19
Protestant churches | 12.3
Protestant scholars | 18.2
Proverbs, Book of | 13.47
Providence of God | 9.7
Psalms, Book of | 9.10; 13.54
Pseudepigrapha, New Testament | 2.24; 15.2; 15.8; 16.27
Pseudepigrapha, Old Testament | 2.22
Ptolemaeus | 16.35
Ptolemies | 3.2
Ptolemy | 16.31
Punishment, eternal | 5.26; 9.37
Puteoli | 2.31; 11.13

Qahal | 5.36f
Quadratus | 15.12
Queen of Ethiopia | 11.5
Quirinius | 3.9
Qumran | 2.25; 4.11–4.13

Radio programmes | 1.6; 2.11; 4.24; 9.34
Ramsey, Sir W. | 2.14; 4.21
Redaction Criticism | 5.3
Redeemer | 9.14
'The Red Wall' | 18.7
Reinhold, M. See Lewis, N and Reinhold, M.
Relief, famine See Collections
Renaissance basilica of St Peter's | 18.4; Fig 53
Repentance | 5.23
Resurrection of Jesus See Jesus Christ
Resurrection of the body | 4.6; 9.3; 15.20; 16.37; 17.11
Resurrection of the dead | 9.35–9.37
Return of Christ See Second Coming
Revelation | 3.9; 9.12; 12.2; 13.21; 13.55; 16.16
Revelation of Peter | 15.18; 18.2
Rhodo | 16.30
Rhône valley | 17.1; 17.14
Righteousness | 9.20; 15.20
Rock | 5.36
Roman Africa | 16.6
Roman bishops | 15.5; 16.26–16.28; 16.38f
Roman Britain | 16.0f
Roman Catholic scholars | 18.2
Roman Christians | 4.19; 7.6; 8.20; 9.22; 11.13; 15.5; 15.7; 16.17–16.37; 18.2–18.8
Roman empire | 1.6; 2.0–2.17; 3.6–3.22; 4.1f; 8.12; 9.8; 16.0f; 16.8; 16.12; 17.17
Roman religion | 4.19
Roman roads | 8.12
    Appian Way | 11.13; Figs. 33, 51
    Via Laurentina | 8.25
    Road to Ostia | 8.25; 16.23; 18.5
Roman rule | 3.9; 3.17–3.22; 16.0
Romans, Letter to | 7.3; 9.2; 9.20; 11.13; 16.20f
Russell, Bertrand | 2.1 (n)
Rylands Library | 2.28; Fig. 18

Sabbath | 13.19; 13.50

Sacramentalism | 9.31–9.34
Sacramentum | 9.33
Sadducees | 4.8
St Peter's, Rome | 1.6; 2.29; 16.23; 18.0f
Salmon, E. T. | 2.6f; 2.25; 16.9
Salvation through name of Jesus | 6.6 (d); 13.14; 13.41
Samaria | 3.17; 3.20; 6.2; 11.5
Samaritans | 4.1; 11.5; Fig. 6
Sanhedrin | 4.8; 6.6 (e) (f); 13.15; 13.24
Saracens | 18.7
Satan | 9.1; 9.11; 15.20
Saul | 6.6 (h); 8.2
Saviour | 9.14
Scapula | 16.6
Schism | 16.18; 16.31; 17.2
Scribes | 4.7
Schneemelcher, W. See Hennecke, E.-Schneemelcher, W.
Schweitzer, A. | 5.21 (n)
Sea of Galilee | 3.18; Figs. 16, 22
Second Adam | 9.10
Second Apology of Justin | 15.13
Second Coming | 5.21f; 9.35–9.37; 9.41; 13.14; 13.17; 13.19–13.27; 15.6
Seleucia | 13.2
Seneca | 2.13
Septuagint | 2.21; 4.24; 5.23; 8.2; 13.38
Serapis | 4.23
Sermon on the Mount | 5.31
'Servant of Yahweh' | 13.12; 13.27
'Servant Songs' | 4.16
Shepherd of Hermas, The | 15.15; 16.27; 16.35
Sherwin-White, A. N. | 2.11
Shrine of St Peter | 18.0–18.8
Silas | 8.12
Simeon | 4.0
Similitudes of Enoch See Enoch, Similitudes of
Simon Magus | 16.31
Simon Peter See Peter
Simon the Zealot | 4.14
Simonians | 16.31
Sinope | 16.31
Sitz im Leben | 5.3
Slaves | 16.7; 16.35; Fig. 40
Smyrna | 12.0; 15.7; 15.9; 15.13; 15.16; 16.17; 17.8
Social customs | 2.13; 15.21
Son of David | 9.45
Son of God | 13.21; 13.28f; 13.30; 13.36
Son of Man | 4.29; 13.16; 13.21–13.25; 13.52
Soter | 16.28; 16.33; 16.38
Sovereignty of God | 9.6f
Soviet encyclopaedia | 2.1 (n)
Spain | 7.5; 8.23
Spirit of God See Holy Spirit
Staniforth, M. | 15.3; 15.20 (n); 15.21 (n)
Stephen | 6.1; 6.6f; 8.4; 11.4f; 13.12; 13.16; 13.21
Stoic philosophers | 4.22; 4.26; 9.7; 9.26; 13.47; 15.13
Strategoi | 2.13
Sub-apostolic age | 2.23; 15.0–15.22
Suetonius | 2.8; 2.16; 16.19; 16.22
'Suffering Servant' | 13.12; 13.26f
Sunday | 17.16
Synagogue | 4.3; 8.10; 8.13; 8.15; 9.44; 16.19; 17.16
Syncretism | 4.25–4.32; 17.3

Synerus	16.31	Wiles, M.	1.6; 10.5
Synods	16.8; 16.39; 17.8	Wilson, R. McL.	2.24
Synoptic Gospels	2.19; 5.2–5.10; 5.17–5.40;	*Wisdom, Book of*	13.36; 13.47
	9.37; 12.0; 13.4; 13.18–13.21;	Wisdom literature	9.29; 9.37
	13.60; 17.17	Women in the Church	8.13
Synoptic problem	5.7; 5.17	Word of God	13.46f; 13.55; 17.13f; 17.18
Syria	2.12; 3.2; 3.6; 3.9; 3.11;	World War I	5.12
	3.17; 4.19; 4.31; 8.8; 11.6;	Worship in early Church	12.3; 17.15–17.17
	12.2; 15.6–15.8		
		Xystus	16.28
Tacitus	2.7; 2.16; 16.0; 16.22; 16.25;		
	18.2	Yahweh	3.3; 4.17; 5.35; 13.22; 13.38
Ta eschata	5.21 (n)	Yarmuk Gorge	15.6
Talmud	2.17; 2.25	Yugo-Slavia	7.6
Tarsus	3.9f; 8.2f; 8.8		
Tatian	15.13; 16.30	Zebedee	16.15f
Tax collectors	3.9 (b)	Zephyrinus	16.28
Taylor, V.	13.33	Zeus	3.3; 4.21
'Teacher of righteousness'	4.12		
Telesphorus	16.28		
Television programmes	1.6; 16.37; 18.0–18.8		
Temple, Jewish	3.2f; 3.9 (b); 3.13; 4.1; 4.3;		
	4.9; 4.12; 5.28; 6.6 (c) (d) (e);		
	8.14; Fig.39		
Temples, pagan	2.9; 4.26; 16.6		
Tertullian	15.14; 16.6; 16.34; 17.10f; 18.2		
Tetrarch	3.19 (iv)		
Theodotus	16.31; 16.39		
Theophilus	8.22; 12.1		
Theos	13.43		
Theophilus of Antioch	14.0; 15.14		
Thessalonians, Letters to	9.35		
Thessalonica	2.13; 8.13		
Thomas, Apostle	11.16; 13.46		
Thomas, D. A. T.	1.6		
Thomas, Gospel of	11.16		
Tiberius	2.6f; 3.19; 3.19		
Timothy	8.12; 16.15; 17.7		
Timothy, Letters to	7.2; 8.24; 11.14		
T. Flavius Clemens	16.25; 16.27		
Titus	17.7; Fig. 38		
Titus, Letter to	7.2; 8.24; 11.14; 13.54		
Titus, Roman commander	3.9 (b)		
Torah	4.2f; 9.7; 13.19		
Toynbee, J.	18.0		
Trajan	2.9; 13.1; 13.3; 15.7; 16.8f		
Travel diary of Luke	7.6		
Tres Tabernae	16.21		
Trinity	13.6; 14.0–14.2		
Troas	8.12		
Tropaia	18.5		
Trypho	15.13		
Tunis	16.5		
The Twelve	6.7; 10.0; 10.2		
Tyrannius Rufinus	2.9		
Universal sinfulness	9.9–9.10		
Valentinus	16.31		
Vatican Hill	16.23; 18.0; 18.4; 18.8		
Vatican necropolis	16.37; 18.1–18.18; Fig. 54		
Vespasian	3.21; 16.1; Fig. 37		
Vesuvius	11.13		
Via Laurentina *See* Roman Roads			
Victor of Rome	16.18; 16.28; 16.39		
Vienne	15.16; 16.7		
War of AD 66–73	3.9 (b); 4.2; 4.7; 4.12; 4.14;		
	4.18; 9.46; 11.2; 16.15; 16.29		
'The Way'	11.6		
'We-passages'	8.12		

SCRIPTURE REFERENCES

(The numbers at the left of each column give the scriptural chapter and verse references)

Old Testament

Genesis

1:2	14.0
4:26	13.41
6:2	13.28
12:8	13.41

Exodus

3:14–5	13.50
4:22	13.28

Deuteronomy

6:4–8	13.2
14:1	13.28

1 Samuel

10:10	14.0

2 Samuel

7:14	13.28

1 Chronicles

16:8	13.41
17:13	13.28
22:10	13.28
28:6	13.28

Nehemiah

13:1	5.36

Job

1:6	13.28

Psalms

2:7	13.28
29:1	13.28
30:5	13.16
74:2	5.36
89:19–37	4.16
102:25–27	13.54

Proverbs

8:1–36	13.36

Isaiah

1:2	13.28
7:10	13.54
8:12–13	13.54
9:2–7	4.16
30:1	13.28
45:23	13.37
52:13–53:12	4.16; 13.12

Jeremiah

31:20	13.28
33:14–16	4.16

Ezekiel

1:17	2.30
1:27–28	13.22
37:8	14.0

Daniel

2:47	4.24
7:9, 13	13.55
7:13–14	13.22
9:25–27	4.16

Hosea

1:10	13.28
11:1	13.28

Joel

2:32	13.41
3:1–2	14.0

Malachi

1:11	17.17

Apocrypha or Deutero-canonical Books

Wisdom

3:1–9	9.37
7:22–27	13.36
7:26	13.59

Ecclesiasticus

24:1–34	13.36

New Testament

Matthew

1:16	5.23
1:21	13.19
2:1–18	3.16
2:22	3.17
3	5.22
4:17	5.22
4:19	5.23
5:3–10	5.22
5:5	5.22
5:11–12	13.20
5:14	5.23
5:27–28, 31–32	13.19
5:27–30	5.22
5:33–34, 38–39	13.19
5–6	5.22
6:9–13	5.22
6:10	5.23
6:12	5.24
6:13	15.24
6:16–18	5.22
6:19–21	5.22
6:25–34	5.22
6:32	13.29
7:11	5.22
7:21	13.29
9:28–30	13.19

9:36	4.17
10:1–11:1	5.23
10:29, 32–33	13.29
10:32–33	13.20
10:37–39	13.20
11:27	13.31
11:28–29	13.20
12:6, 8	13.19
12:28	5.23
13	5.23
13:25–27	13.19
13:39–42	13.19
15:17–20	5.22
16:13–17	13.30
16:13–20	3.18
16:18	5.23
16:19	5.23
16:20	13.21
16:21	5.26
16:24–26	5.22
16:27	13.24
17:12, 22–23	5.26
17:24–27	13.20
18:17	5.23
18:18	5.23
19:21	13.20
19:21–34	5.22
19:27–28	13.20
19:29	13.20
20:1–16	5.23
20:17–19	5.26
20:25–28	5.23
21:1–19	5.23
21:33–42	13.29
22:1–14	5.23
22:17	3.9 (b)
22:34–40	5.22
23:1–36	4.7
24:1–2	3.9 (b)
24:9–31	13.20
24:30	13.24
24:30–31	13.19
24:36	13.32
25:31–46	13.19; 13.20
26:2, 28–29	5.26
26:28	5.23
26:41	15.24
26:63–66	13.25
27–28	5.25
28:18	13.19
28:18–19	5.38
28:18–20	9.33
28:19	14.1; 17.11
28:20	13.20

Mark

1	5.22
1:15	5.22
1:41	13.19
2:5–12	13.19
3:6	4.9
4:41	13.33
6:14–29	3.19 (iv)

7:1–5	4.17
8:15	3.19 (iv)
8:29–30	5.23; 13.21
9:41–42	13.20
10:9–12	5.10
12:13	4.9
13:31	13.19
14:24	5.23

Luke

1:15, 35, 41, 67	14.0
1:68–79	5.23
2:25–26	14.0
2:49	13.29
3:4	5.22
3:1	3.18 (iii)
4:14	14.0
4:18	5.22
6:15	4.14
7:34, 39–47	5.22
9:20–21	5.23
10:22	13.31
11:2–4	5.22
12:12	14.0
12:32	5.23
13:1	3.9 (b)
13:31–32	3.19 (iv)
14:12–14, 21	5.22
15:8–32	5.22
17:20–21	5.22
17:22–25	5.26
17:22–30	13.24
18:9–14	5.22
18:10–14	5.22
18:16–17	5.22
19:1–10	5.22
20:23	13.29
22:20	5.23
22:24–27	5.23
22:28–30	13.20
23:46	13.16

John

1	13.52; 13.58
1:1–18	13.46
1:14	4.28; 13.52
2:11	13.52
4:6	4.28
5:18	13.50
6:29–47	13.50
8:58	13.50
10:29	13.51
11:26	13.50
12:41	13.52; 13.54
13:21	5.25
13:31	13.52
14:1	13.50
14:9, 11	13.51
14:13–14	13.50
14:16, 25–26	14.1
14:21, 28	13.50
15:1–10	9.27
15:5–7	13.50

163

Ref	Loc
16:7–15	14.1
16:14	13.52
17:2–5	13.52
17:5	13.51
19:28	4.28
20:28–29, 31	13.46
21:20–24	16.16
21:24	16.16

Acts

Ref	Loc
1	13.12
1:8	14.0
1:17–26	5.23
1:22	6.6 (a)
2	6.2; 11.3
2:1–39	9.29
2:2–47	14.0
2:10	16.19
2:22–36	13.13
2:24–36	6.6 (b)
2:36	13.17
2:41	9.33
3:12–26	13.14
3:15	13.15
3:15, 21	6.6 (c)
4:2	6.6 (d)
4:9–12	6.6 (d)
4:9–13	13.14
4:20	6.6 (d)
5:3–4	14.0
5:29–30	6.6 (e)
5:29–32	13.15
5:37	4.14
5:42	6.6 (e)
6	11.4
6:1	4.9
7	13.16
7:55–60	6.6 (f)
7:56–57	13.25
7:58–8:1	8.4
7:60	13.16
8	11.5
8:9–24	16.31
8:29, 39	14.0
8:30–35	6.6 (g)
8:30–38	13.12
9	11.6
9:1–19	8.4
9:3–29	6.6 (h)
9:4–5	9.26
9:5–16	13.16
9:10–19	8.5
9:14, 21	13.41
9:15–16	7.0
9:23–25	8.6
9:26–30	8.7
9:30	8.8
10	11.7
10:1–18	9.21
10:4, 35	9.23
10:19–20	14.0
10:36–43	6.6 (i)
10:42	13.15
11:25–31	8.8
12:1–19	3.20
12:17	11.11
12:22–23	3.20
13:14	8.9; 15.10
13:2, 4	14.0
13:46–47	8.10
13:49	8.9
14	4.20
14:11–18	4.21
14:27	8.10
15:7–11	11.11
15:14–18	9.45
15:28	14.0
15:36–39	11.9
16:6	8.12; 14.0
16:37–39	3.9 (f)
17	4.20
17:16–34	4.22
17:24–28	9.6
17:31	13.15
18:2	2.8; 13.53; 16.19
18:12–17	2.13
18:18–22	8.14
18:19–21	8.15
18:23	8.15
18:24–26	4.15
18:24–28	11.0; 16.13
18:26	16.19
19	4.20; 16.14
19:1–7	4.15
19:10	8.16
19:21	8.20
19:23–41	4.21; 8.17
20	8.14
20:15–38	8.18
20:28	14.0
21:18	11.11
21:18–25	10.1
21:21–26	8.19
21:39	8.2
21:40	8.2
22:3	4.7; 8.3
22:4–11	8.4
22:25–29	3.9 (f)
23:6–9	4.7
23:11	8.20
23:16	8.3
24:5	4.18
25:11–12	8.20
25:13–26, 32	3.21
26:2	3.21
26:12–18	8.4
28	11.13
28:14	2.31
28:15	16.21
28:17–28	16.21
28:30–31	3.9 (f)

Romans

Ref	Loc
1:4	13.37
1:7–14	11.13
1:8	13.41
1:11–15	8.20
1:16	9.43
1:18–25	9.6
1:18–3:20	9.9
1:19–21	9.8
2:5, 16	9.36
3:1–4	9.43
3:20–8:39	9.19
3:23	9.10
4:16–25	9.25
5:12–14	9.9
5:12–19	9.10
6:3–11	9.32
7:5–6	9.28
7:7–25	9.9
7:21–25	9.40
7:25	13.41
8:1	9.38
8:3	13.36
8:9	14.1
8:9–28	9.28
8:13	15.24
8:18–25	9.36
8:32	13.36
8:38	9.11
9:1–11:36	9.43
9:2–3	9.46
9:5	13.43
9:24–29	9.25
9:30–33	9.19
10:9	13.40
10:12–13	13.41
11:25–32	9.46
11:32	9.9
11:36	9.6
12:15	9.42
12:14	15.24
13:11–12	9.36
14:8–9	9.36
15:19	7.5; 8.14
15:20	11.14
15:23, 28	8.23
15:24, 28	7.5
15:27	9.44
16:1	8.13
16:3	16.19
16:20	9.11

1 Corinthians

Ref	Loc
1:2	13.41
1:3	13.41
1:7–8	9.36
1:10	9.39
1:12	11.10
1:13–17	9.32
1:23	15.24
2:6–7	9.6
2:9–16	9.28
3:4–5, 22	11.10
3:12–15	9.36
3:16	9.28
4:5	9.36
4:6–7, 15	9.39
4:11–13	15.24
5:1–7:40	9.39
5:5	9.11; 9.36
6:2–3	9.36
6:11	9.32
6:19–20	9.28
7:5	9.11
7:10, 11	5.10
8:4–6	9.16
8:5	13.39
8:6	13.36
9:1	8.4
9:19	9.28; 10.0
9:21	9.38
10:1–4	9.32
10:14–22	9.32
10:14–11:34	9.39
10:17, 23	9.25
10:19–21	9.16
10:20–21	9.11
11	9.33
11:18–32	9.25
11:23–32	9.32
11:32	9.36
12:3	13.40
12:3–13	9.28
12:12–13	9.32
12:12–27	9.25
13:1–13	9.39; 9.42
14:1	9.30
14:1–39	9.39
14:1–40	6.7
15:3–8	5.23
15:5	8.4; 10.2
15:8–10	8.4; 9.25
15:9	13.44
15:27–28	13.36
15:28	16.14
15:32	8.16
16:9	13.17
16:22	

2 Corinthians

Ref	Loc
1:3–4	9.6
1:14	9.36
1:19	13.36
1:20	13.41
2:9–10	9.39
2:11	9.11
3:1–6	9.39
3:3–18	9.19
3:17–18	9.28
4:1	10.2
4:4	9.11; 13.36; 13.58
4:5	13.40
4:8–11	15.24
4:14	9.36
5:10	9.36; 15.24
6:4–9	15.24
6:10	15.24
6:14	9.39
10:8	9.39
10:14–16	8.23
10:16	8.20
11:5	10.0
11:14	9.11
11:22	9.43
11:26	8.0
11:32–33	8.6
12:1–10	8.8
12:7	9.11
12:8	13.41
13:5–10	9.39
13:13	14.1
13:14	9.28; 13.41

Galatians

Ref	Loc
1:1	7.0; 13.41
1:3	13.41
1:8	11.12
1:11–12	8.4
1:13	8.4; 9.25
1:13–14	4.7
1:13–17	8.4
1:14	8.3
1:17	8.5; 8.6
1:18	5.36
1:18–24	8.7
1:21	8.8
1:23	8.8
2	8.11
2:2	10.0
2:9	10.0
2:10	9.44
2:11–14	9.21; 11.11
2:15–3:25	9.19
2:20	9.28; 9.29; 13.36
3:14	9.43
3:21	9.9

3:29	9.52	*1 Thessalonians*	
4:3	9.11	2:18	9.11
4:4	13.36	2:19	9.36
4:6–7	9.28	3:5	9.11
4:21–5:6	9.19	3:12	13.41
4:24–31	9.25	3:13	9.36
5:13–14, 25	9.39	4:2–12	9.39
5:13–6:10	9.39	4:8	9.28
5:16–25	9.28	4:15–18	9.36
5:19–21	9.9	5:12–22	9.39
6:1, 8	9.28	5:23	9.36

Ephesians		*2 Thessalonians*	
1:20–23	13.38	1:6–10	9.36
1:22–23	9.25	2:1–12	9.36
2:1–10	9.19	2:9	9.11
2:2	9.11	2:16	13.41
2:3	9.9	3:6–15	9.39
2:18	9.28		
2:19	15.24	*1 Timothy*	
3:6	9.25	1:3	16.15
4:4, 30	9.28		
4:5	9.32	*2 Timothy*	
4:16	9.25	2:9	8.24
5:6	9.9; 9.36	4:6–8	8.24
5:23–32	9.25	4:18	13.41
5:25–27	9.32	4:19	16.15
6:11–12	9.11		
		Titus	
Philippians		2:13	13.43
1:6, 10–11, 23	9.36	3:4–6	9.32; 14.1
1:12–13	3.9 (f)		
1:23	9.36	*Hebrews*	
1:27	9.28; 9.38	1:1–4	13.53
1:27–2:18	9.39	1:3	13.59
2:1	13.40	1:8–9	13.54
2:1–2	9.28	1:10–11	13.54
2:6	13.36		
2:10–11	13.37	*James*	
2:12	15.24	2:10–26	9.23
3:1–10	9.19		
3:5–6	8.2	*1 Peter*	
3:6	8.4	1:12	11.15
3:9–10	9.25	2:9–10	11.15
3:9–14, 20–21	9.36	2:21, 22, 24	15.24
3:12	8.4	3:14–15	13.54
3:17–4:9	9.39	3:22	13.55
4:3	15.5	4:7	15.24
4:5	9.36	4:12–19	3.9 (g)
4:22	3.9 (f)		
5:20	15.24	*2 Peter*	
		1:1, 3	13.55
		3:15–17	10.5
Colossians			
1:7	8.16	*1 John*	
1:8–24	9.25	1:2–3	13.55
1:9–12	9.6	4:2–3	4.28; 15.24
1:13	13.36	5:20	13.55
1:13–16	9.11		
1:15	13.58	*2 John*	
1:15–17	13.36	7	4.28; 15.24
1:26–27	9.36		
2:9	13.36	*Revelation*	
2:12–13	9.32	1:11	16.16
2:15	9.11	2:1–7	16.16
2:19	9.25	5:12–14	13.55
3:3–4	9.28	7:10, 17	13.55
3:4	9.36	12	9.12
4:12–14	8.16		
4:14	6.0		

13–16	13.55
17	3.9 (g)
17:14	13.55
18	3.9 (g)
19:12–13, 16	13.55
21:22	13.55
22:1, 3	13.55
22:13	2.30; 13.55

ACKNOWLEDGEMENTS

Grateful acknowledgement is made to the following sources for material used in these units:

Text

Penguin Books Ltd. for Maxwell Staniforth (trans.) *Early Christian Writings: The Apostolic Father* (Penguin Classics 1968), Copyright © Maxwell Staniforth, 1968

Illustrations

Palestine in the time of Jesus: Verlag Herder for *Atlas zur Kirchengeschichte,* © Verlag Herder K.G. Freiburg im Breisgau, 1970; *Maps A, B and C:* from Van der Meer and Mohrmann, *Atlas of the Early Christian World* (trans. M. F. Hedland and H. H. Rowley) Nelson, London; *Figures 1, 4, 11, 12, 32 and 41:* Matson Photo Service, California; *Figure 2:* Radio Times Hulton Picture Library; *Figures 3, 5, 9 and 14:* Israel Department of Antiquities and Museums; *Figures 6, 7, 8, 10 and 22:* Israel Government Tourist Office; *Figures 13, 15, 17, 19, 21 and 23:* Victoria and Albert Museum; *Figures 16, 33, 39, 41, 46 and 58:* J. Allan Cash; *Figure 18:* John Rylands Library, Manchester; *Figures 20, 44 and 51:* Pontifical Archaeological Commission, Rome; *Figures 24 and 25:* National Gallery; *Figures 26–31, 34, 35* and *38:* Mansell Collection; *Figure 36:* Chester Beatty Library, Dublin; *Figure 37:* Ashmolean Museum, Oxford; *Figures 40, 49 and 52-7:* Societäts-Verlag, Frankfurt-am-Main; *Figure 42:* The Hamlyn Group. Photo: John R. Freeman and Co; *Figures 43 and 47:* Benedictine Sisters of the Catacomb of Priscilla, Rome; *Figure 45:* The Hamlyn Group. Photo: Alinari; *Figure 48:* Alinari; *Figure 50:* Bayerisches Nationalmuseum, Munich; *Figures 53–57:* from *Esplorazioni sotto la Confessione di S. Pietro in Vaticano*—copyright Rev. Fabbrica di S. Pietro in Vaticano, Rome.

3:29	9.52
4:3	9.11
4:4	13.36
4:6–7	9.28
4:21–5:6	9.19
4:24–31	9.25
5:13–14, 25	9.39
5:13–6:10	9.39
5:16–25	9.28
5:19–21	9.9
6:1, 8	9.28

Ephesians

1:20–23	13.38
1:22–23	9.25
2:1–10	9.19
2:2	9.11
2:3	9.9
2:18	9.28
2:19	15.24
3:6	9.25
4:4, 30	9.28
4:5	9.32
4:16	9.25
5:6	9.9; 9.36
5:23–32	9.25
5:25–27	9.32
6:11–12	9.11

Philippians

1:6, 10–11, 23	9.36
1:12–13	3.9 (f)
1:23	9.36
1:27	9.28; 9.38
1:27–2:18	9.39
2:1	13.40
2:1–2	9.28
2:6	13.36
2:10–11	13.37
2:12	15.24
3:1–10	9.19
3:5–6	8.2
3:6	8.4
3:9–10	9.25
3:9–14, 20–21	9.36
3:12	8.4
3:17–4:9	9.39
4:3	15.5
4:5	9.36
4:22	3.9 (f)
5:20	15.24

Colossians

1:7	8.16
1:8–24	9.25
1:9–12	9.6
1:13	13.36
1:13–16	9.11
1:15	13.58
1:15–17	13.36
1:26–27	9.36
2:9	13.36
2:12–13	9.32
2:15	9.11
2:19	9.25
3:3–4	9.28
3:4	9.36
4:12–14	8.16
4:14	6.0

1 Thessalonians

2:18	9.11
2:19	9.36
3:5	9.11
3:12	13.41
3:13	9.36
4:2–12	9.39
4:8	9.28
4:15–18	9.36
5:12–22	9.39
5:23	9.36

2 Thessalonians

1:6–10	9.36
2:1–12	9.36
2:9	9.11
2:16	13.41
3:6–15	9.39

1 Timothy

1:3	16.15

2 Timothy

2:9	8.24
4:6–8	8.24
4:18	13.41
4:19	16.15

Titus

2:13	13.43
3:4–6	9.32; 14.1

Hebrews

1:1–4	13.53
1:3	13.59
1:8–9	13.54
1:10–11	13.54

James

2:10–26	9.23

1 Peter

1:12	11.15
2:9–10	11.15
2:21, 22, 24	15.24
3:14–15	13.54
3:22	13.55
4:7	15.24
4:12–19	3.9 (g)

2 Peter

1:1, 3	13.55
3:15–17	10.5

1 John

1:2–3	13.55
4:2–3	4.28; 15.24
5:20	13.55

2 John

7	4.28; 15.24

Revelation

1:11	16.16
2:1–7	16.16
5:12–14	13.55
7:10, 17	13.55
12	9.12
13–16	13.55
17	3.9 (g)
17:14	13.55
18	3.9 (g)
19:12–13, 16	13.55
21:22	13.55
22:1, 3	13.55
22:13	2.30; 13.55

ACKNOWLEDGEMENTS

Grateful acknowledgement is made to the following sources for material used in these units:

Text

Penguin Books Ltd. for Maxwell Staniforth (trans.) *Early Christian Writings: The Apostolic Father* (Penguin Classics 1968), Copyright © Maxwell Staniforth, 1968

Illustrations

Palestine in the time of Jesus: Verlag Herder for *Atlas zur Kirchengeschichte*, © Verlag Herder K.G. Freiburg im Breisgau, 1970; *Maps A, B and C:* from Van der Meer and Mohrmann, *Atlas of the Early Christian World* (trans. M. F. Hedland and H. H. Rowley) Nelson, London; *Figures 1, 4, 11, 12, 32 and 41:* Matson Photo Service, California; *Figure 2:* Radio Times Hulton Picture Library; *Figures 3, 5, 9 and 14:* Israel Department of Antiquities and Museums; *Figures 6, 7, 8, 10 and 22:* Israel Government Tourist Office; *Figures 13, 15, 17, 19, 21 and 23:* Victoria and Albert Museum; *Figures 16, 33, 39, 41, 46 and 58:* J. Allan Cash; *Figure 18:* John Rylands Library, Manchester; *Figures 20, 44 and 51:* Pontifical Archaeological Commission, Rome; *Figures 24 and 25:* National Gallery; *Figures 26–31, 34, 35 and 38:* Mansell Collection; *Figure 36:* Chester Beatty Library, Dublin; *Figure 37:* Ashmolean Museum, Oxford; *Figures 40, 49 and 52-7:* Societäts-Verlag, Frankfurt-am-Main; *Figure 42:* The Hamlyn Group. Photo: John R. Freeman and Co; *Figures 43 and 47:* Benedictine Sisters of the Catacomb of Priscilla, Rome; *Figure 45:* The Hamlyn Group. Photo: Alinari; *Figure 48:* Alinari; *Figure 50:* Bayerisches Nationalmuseum, Munich; *Figures 53-57:* from *Esplorazioni sotto la Confessione di S. Pietro in Vaticano*—copyright Rev. Fabbrica di S. Pietro in Vaticano, Rome.

THE EARLY ROMAN EMPIRE AND THE RISE OF CHRISTIANITY

1
2 } The Historical Background
3

4
5 } Philosophy under the Early Empire

6
7 } Petronius and Juvenal

8
9 } Roman Art

10
11 } Social Life in the Early Empire

12   Roman Britain in the Early Empire

13
14
15 } The Rise of Christianity
16